CARBON MARKETS IN A CLIMATE-CHANGING CAPITALISM

The promise of harnessing market forces to combat climate change has been unsettled by low carbon prices, financial losses, and ongoing controversies in global carbon markets. And yet, governments around the world remain committed to market-based solutions to bring down greenhouse gas emissions. This book discusses what went wrong with the marketisation of climate change and what this means for the future of action on climate change. The book explores the co-production of capitalism and climate change by developing new understandings of relationships between the appropriation, commodification, and capitalisation of nature. The book reveals contradictions in carbon markets for addressing climate change as a socio-ecological, economic, and political crisis, and points towards more targeted and democratic policies to combat climate change. This book will appeal to students, researchers, policy makers, and campaigners who are interested in climate change and climate policy, and the political economy of capitalism and the environment.

Gareth Bryant is Lecturer in Political Economy at The University of Sydney. His research explores the marketisation of different areas of socio-ecological life, with a focus on climate and education policy. Gareth's research has been published in *Environment and Planning A*, *Antipode*, *Energy Policy*, *Annals of the American Association of Geographers,* and *New Political Economy*. He was awarded the Global Network for Financial Geography (FINGEO) dissertation prize and the Australian International Political Economy Network (AIPEN) journal article prize. Gareth co-edits the online blog *Progress in Political Economy* (*PPE*).

CARBON MARKETS IN A
CLIMATE-CHANGING CAPITALISM

GARETH BRYANT
The University of Sydney

CAMBRIDGE
UNIVERSITY PRESS

University Printing House, Cambridge CB2 8BS, United Kingdom

One Liberty Plaza, 20th Floor, New York, NY 10006, USA

477 Williamstown Road, Port Melbourne, VIC 3207, Australia

314-321, 3rd Floor, Plot 3, Splendor Forum, Jasola District Centre, New Delhi - 110025, India

79 Anson Road, #06-04/06, Singapore 079906

Cambridge University Press is part of the University of Cambridge.

It furthers the University's mission by disseminating knowledge in the pursuit of education, learning and research at the highest international levels of excellence.

www.cambridge.org
Information on this title: www.cambridge.org/9781108421737
DOI: 10.1017/9781108377591

© Gareth Bryant 2019

This publication is in copyright. Subject to statutory exception and to the provisions of relevant collective licensing agreements, no reproduction of any part may take place without the written permission of Cambridge University Press.

First published 2019

A catalogue record for this publication is available from the British Library

ISBN 978-1-108-42173-7 Hardback

Cambridge University Press has no responsibility for the persistence or accuracy of URLs for external or third-party internet websites referred to in this publication, and does not guarantee that any content on such websites is, or will remain, accurate or appropriate.

For Kara

Contents

Acknowledgements		*page* xi
Introduction		1
	Paradox in Paris	1
	A Short History and Overview of Carbon Markets	4
	Mainstream and Critical Approaches to Carbon Markets	9
	Carbon Markets as Least Cost Emissions Reductions	9
	Carbon Markets as Accumulation Strategy	11
	Carbon Markets as Politics	13
	Chapter Outline	15
1	**Conceptualising Carbon**	18
	Introduction	18
1.1	Climate Change as Market Failure	19
	1.1.1 Pigou: Externalising Carbon Pollution	19
	1.1.2 Coase: Universalising Climate Action	21
	1.1.3 The Economic Ideology of Nature	23
1.2	Climate-Changing Capitalism	25
1.3	Mapping the Appropriation of Carbon in the EU ETS	32
	1.3.1 The Social Organisation of Carbon	33
	1.3.2 The Spatial Organisation of Carbon	36
	1.3.3 States and the Socio-Spatial Organisation of Carbon	39
	Conclusion	41
2	**Internalising Carbon**	43
	Introduction	43
2.1	The Development of the EU ETS	44
	2.1.1 International, EU, and National Contexts	45
	2.1.2 Government, Industry, and NGO Positions	47

vii

viii   *Contents*

		2.1.3	Creating a 'Level Playing Field'	49
	2.2		The Carbon Commodity	52
		2.2.1	Commodifying Nature	52
		2.2.2	The Installation–Emissions Relationship	54
		2.2.3	Equalising (Some) Difference	56
	2.3		Trading Carbon Allowances	60
		2.3.1	RWE's Trading Strategy	60
		2.3.2	RWE's Allowance Trading	64
			Conclusion	71
3			Externalising Carbon	73
			Introduction	73
	3.1		The Development of the CDM and JI	74
		3.1.1	The 'Kyoto Surprise'	74
		3.1.2	The Linking Directive	78
	3.2		The Spatio-Temporal Fix	80
		3.2.1	Capitalist Crisis and the Spatial Fix	80
		3.2.2	Carbon Offsetting as a Spatio-Temporal Fix	82
	3.3		Trading Carbon Credits	86
		3.3.1	E.ON's Offset Strategy	87
		3.3.2	E.ON's Offset Trading	89
			Conclusion	96
4			Valuing Carbon	98
			Introduction	98
	4.1		Trading Carbon	99
		4.1.1	The Financial Infrastructure of Carbon Trading	99
		4.1.2	The Rise and Fall of Carbon Trading Profits	101
	4.2		Finance, Nature, and Value in Carbon Markets	108
		4.2.1	Carbon Markets as Accumulation Strategy	108
		4.2.2	Carbon as Rent	109
		4.2.3	Carbon as Capital	111
	4.3		Capitalising Carbon	113
		4.3.1	Carbon as Credit	114
		4.3.2	Carbon as Collateral	116
		4.3.3	Carbon as Risk	119
			Conclusion	121
5			Contesting Carbon	123
			Introduction	123
	5.1		Reforming the EU ETS	124

5.2	The Techno-Politics and Post-Politics of Carbon Markets		127
	5.2.1	The (Techno-)Politics of Market Design	127
	5.2.2	Post-Politics as De-Politicisation	128
	5.2.3	States, Value, and Nature	129
5.3	Contesting the 'Value' of Carbon		131
	5.3.1	The Reach of Value: Industrial Gas Offset Restrictions	131
	5.3.2	The Force of Value: Managing Allowance Supply	134
	5.3.3	The Priority of Value: 2030 Climate and Energy Package	140
	Conclusion		145

Conclusion   147

References   151
Index   179

Acknowledgements

This project started in 2011 as a fledgling PhD thesis motivated by a fascination with political economy and a concern about the direction of climate change policy. Its current form owes a huge debt to Matt Lloyd, commissioning editor at Cambridge University Press, whose enthusiasm and guidance gave me the confidence and opportunity to realise my research as a thoroughly renovated book, and editorial manager Esther Miguéliz Obanos, whose expertise and organisation got it into shape. In between, Stuart Rosewarne was there every step of the way. Stuart offered critical insights and encouragement as my thesis supervisor and generously read and commented on each of the draft book chapters. I would not have been in a position to write this book without Adam Morton's invaluable advice and support in navigating all aspects of academic life. Many thanks to Bruce Knobloch for compiling the index and Ezhilmaran Sugumaran for managing the book production process. As the product of such a formative research experience, this book has been inspired and nourished by the colleagues, comrades, students, and friends who have shared study spaces, departmental corridors, classrooms, conferences and workshops, critical feedback, examination and referee reports, edited collections, reading groups, picket lines, campaign meetings, café tables, bar stools, and homes with me. They include, but are not limited to: Mike Beggs, Steffen Böhm, Dick Bryan, Damien Cahill, Lynne Chester, Brett Christophers, Joe Collins, Linda Connor, Huon Curtis, Siddhartha Dabhi, Gareth Dale, Jacqueline Dalziell, Bill Dunn, Osman Faruqi, Sujatha Fernandes, Nick Fraser, James Goodman, Beth Green, Natasha Heenan, Elizabeth Hill, Elizabeth Humphrys, Kurt Iveson, Martijn Konings, Bron Lee, Jenny Leong, Geoff Mann, Jonathan Marshall, James McCarthy, Cat Moir, Jason W. Moore, Peter Newell, Claire Parfitt, Matthew Paterson, Joy Paton, Rebecca Pearse, Jamie Peck, Andrew Phelan, Scott Prudham, Lee Rhiannon, Ariel Salleh,

Susan Schroeder, Dave Smith, Ben Spies-Butcher, Frank Stilwell, Dinesh Wadiwel, and Sophie Webber. During the writing of this book we lost John Kaye: MP, engineer, and honorary political economist, whose brilliant policy mind and vision for justice are imprinted in the following pages. Mum and John, Dad and Jo, Julie, Myles, Jem and Darcy, Mark, Des, and the rest of my extended family provided me with all the support and understanding a son and brother could ask for, as they have always done. Most of all my work is sustained by my partner Kara. Her limitless love and care, and our everyday conversations and adventures, made this book, as with everything in our lives, possible. Kara, this is for you, and us.

Some aspects of this book have been developed from research published in the following articles:

- Bryant, G. (2016). Creating a level playing field? The concentration and centralisation of emissions in the European Union Emissions Trading System. Energy Policy, 99, 308–318.
- Bryant, G. (2016). The politics of carbon market design: Rethinking the techno-politics and post-politics of climate change. Antipode, 48(4), 877–898.
- Bryant, G. (2018). Nature as accumulation strategy? Finance, nature, and value in carbon markets. Annals of the American Association of Geographers, 108(3), 605–619.

Thanks to Elsevier, Sage, and Taylor & Francis, and the editors of *Energy Policy, Antipode*, and the *Annals of the American Association of Geographers* for permissions to adapt this work.

Introduction

Paradox in Paris

As climate change emerged as one of the major global challenges of our time, carbon markets were put forward by governments around the world as its defining policy framework. Market-based climate policy was hailed for its unique ability to use price incentives to achieve environmental goals cost effectively. By creating new economic winners and minimising losers from climate action, carbon markets promised to encourage political consensus for decarbonisation. Following the 1997 Kyoto Protocol, which placed emissions trading and carbon offsetting at the heart of the international climate regime, carbon markets were established in a wide range of jurisdictions. In the two decades following Kyoto, carbon markets had been implemented at supranational, national, regional, and city-scales in the European Union, the United States, China, Japan, Canada, Australia, New Zealand, South Korea, and Switzerland. Carbon offset projects had similarly proliferated throughout developing and ex-Soviet Union countries (World Bank 2017 p. 12). When the Paris Agreement once again made market-based measures a key mechanism for achieving national emissions reduction commitments, momentum towards carbon markets appeared to be stronger than ever.

Yet, as negotiations got underway for the Paris Agreement, the place of carbon markets was far from certain. Just a month out from the meeting, business organisations representing many of the world's largest polluting companies and financial institutions were sounding the alarm about the absence of references to market mechanisms in the draft negotiating text (International Emissions Trading Association 2015). The carbon market provisions that eventually emerged will have significant implications for the operation of the new 'bottom-up' Paris model of global climate governance, where governments set their own targets, subject to periodic review. While the Paris Agreement abandoned the Kyoto practice of seeking agreement between countries on targets, like Kyoto, it makes it possible that climate action in one country will count towards the commitments of another country through emissions trading or carbon offsetting (UNFCCC, 2015 Article 6). However, after almost twenty years of experience of carbon markets, the text of the Paris Agreement gave very little indication about how to achieve its market-based vision.

Uncertainty over the proper role of carbon markets reflected troubles in the world's major existing carbon trading schemes, most importantly, the European Union Emissions Trading System (EU ETS). Over ten years of operation, promises that the EU ETS would harness market forces to slow global warming had been unsettled by systemically low carbon prices, heavy financial losses, and ongoing controversy over much needed reforms. These pressures had intensified in the period between the failed Copenhagen climate conference and Paris. European allowance prices headed and remained under €10 after 2012, from earlier highs of over €30 (Intercontinental Exchange 2017). This is well below the levels estimated by carbon market advocates to be necessary to meet the Paris ambition to limit warming to 1.5°C (High-Level Commission on Carbon Prices 2017). Together with the even greater drop in UN carbon offset prices to less than €1, this sparked an 80 per cent collapse in the trading value of global carbon markets between 2011 and 2015 (World Bank 2012 p. 10, 2015 p. 13). In response, major banks and other businesses that had aimed to profit from trading carbon began to lose interest in the market (Straw & Platt 2013; World Bank 2015 p. 35). Just as the world was turning its attention to the next global agreement on climate change, significant political oxygen within Europe was forced to turn inward to long and drawn out debates over the question of whether and how to rescue the EU ETS (Wettestad & Jevnaker 2016).

The Paris Agreement thus reflected a paradox in global climate policy: strong commitment to the superiority of market-based approaches, if not their institutional requirements, persists in the context of crises in existing carbon trading schemes and a rapidly warming climate. In the current conjuncture, how this paradox of carbon markets is understood, and responded to, has become a significant factor in shaping the course of the crisis of climate change. However, dominant narratives in existing research do not sit well with the practical experience of marketised climate policy. Some strands of literature on carbon markets were overly optimistic about their capacity to lower emissions, create new climate-friendly industries, and accommodate improvements in policy design. However, critical perspectives have often been so focused on opposing the market-based policy approach that they have missed opportunities to explore what the experience of carbon markets reveals about the co-production of capitalism and climate change.

This book offers an account of what went wrong with the marketisation of climate change and what it means for the future of global climate action, by placing its analysis of carbon markets in the context of a 'climate-changing capitalism'. This moves research on market-based climate policy forward by foregrounding the capitalist relations, actors, and institutions that are changing the climate, in order to better understand how carbon markets, as a constituent part of the climate crisis, are changing capitalism. A central premise of the book is that climate policy must simultaneously address climate change as a socio-ecological, economic, and political crisis. From this perspective, the efficacy of carbon markets is co-dependent on their impacts on, among many other factors, the burning of fossil fuels, investments in renewable energy, the distribution of income, the operation of financial markets, the regulatory capacity of states, and the strategies of climate activists.

The analysis proceeds by developing concepts of 'appropriation', 'commodification' and 'capitalisation' as a typology of capitalist relations with, and within, nature. Each is explored in relation to different meanings of 'carbon'. Climate change is produced through capital's drive to appropriate carbon by burning fossil fuels. Carbon markets commodify carbon by representing different forms of carbon appropriation as tradeable carbon allowances and credits. States are central to both relations, in delivering fossil fuels for capital and instituting carbon markets. While the appropriation of carbon has traditionally supported accumulation in fossil fuel industries, the commodification of carbon makes processes of appropriation a direct object of capitalisation, as carbon-derived financial assets potentially emerge as new forms of capital. Thus, the book posits commodification as a key mediator of the internal relations between accumulation by appropriation in the sphere of 'reproduction' and accumulation by capitalisation within circuits of capital.

Through a detailed study of the EU ETS and its links with the UN offsetting mechanisms, the book identifies three contradictions of carbon markets in a climate-changing capitalism. First, carbon markets apply principles and tools of formal market equality to address what is a substantively unequal socio-ecological problem. This allows less effective forms of climate action to be substituted for more effective forms of climate action, which are rendered equivalent. Second, the economic viability of carbon markets depends on the maintenance of fossil fuel industries that require phasing out. This creates significant tensions for states seeking to support carbon markets as a new site of accumulation. Third, carbon markets shape climate politics in a way that prioritises the singular logic of price incentives over pluralistic policy

4   *Introduction*

debate. This undermines the political and institutional conditions necessary for a more targeted and multi-pronged framework for climate action. The book argues that the contradictions of carbon markets combine to hinder pathways out of the broader climate crisis despite, and sometimes through, reforms within the marketised policy paradigm. Before outlining the structure of the book, it is necessary to provide some more historical and institutional context on carbon markets and an overview of the key ways they have been understood.

A Short History and Overview of Carbon Markets

The policy predecessor to carbon markets was sulphur dioxide trading in the United States. From the 1970s, under significant influence from the emerging neoclassically oriented environmental economics discipline and its construction of ideas of 'efficiency', the Environmental Protection Authority began to introduce elements of emissions trading in its regulation of pollution (Lane 2012). Growing support for the market-based approach vis-à-vis 'command and control' measures among sections of government, business and non-government environmental organisations resulted in amendments to the Clean Air Act in 1990 that established a nation-wide sulphur dioxide trading scheme. The scheme aimed to address acid rain problems by reducing sulphur dioxide emissions from fossil fuel-powered electricity generators by 50 per cent compared to 1980 levels. Its key innovation was that, within the overall cap, emissions allowances allocated or auctioned to certain power plants could be traded to cover the pollution of other power plants. According to the prevailing economic theory, the ability to trade would enable the marginal price movements of sulphur dioxide allowances, not the decisions of state regulators, to decide how the overall environmental goal would be met.

Dominant interpretations of the environmental success of the sulphur dioxide trading scheme played an important role in international negotiations on climate change. Economic assessments of the scheme highlighted its achievements in lowering abatement costs compared with direct regulation, spurred by greater than anticipated cost reductions in low-sulphur coal and scrubber technologies that remove sulphur dioxide emissions (Schmalensee et al. 1998; Stavins 1998). Economists argued that the omniscience of the price mechanism produced the most efficient combination of fuel changes and new technologies compared to anything that could have been mandated by governments (Burtraw et al. 2005 pp. 268–70). Other studies challenged this interpretation, pointing towards unrelated factors at play, such as changes in the transport industry reducing fuel costs (Ellerman & Montero 1998), and other government policies, such as performance standards and support for research and development, in driving technological innovation (Taylor et al. 2005 p. 370). Indeed, in Europe, more direct regulatory measures achieved greater sulphur dioxide emissions reductions than the United States over the same period (Milieu et al. 2004; Vestreng et al. 2007). Nonetheless, the US government used the purported success of sulphur dioxide trading to push for a market-based approach to achieving greenhouse gas emissions targets under the 1997 Kyoto Protocol.

US negotiators extolled the cost-efficiency of tradeable permits in advancing their goal of 'binding but flexible' commitments in the Kyoto Protocol (Grubb et al. 1999 pp. 88–91). At the time, many European negotiators opposed or were sceptical of market-based measures. The US sought to overcome this opposition by making the inclusion of carbon trading instruments a condition for agreement on key European demands for binding emissions reduction targets. The US also successfully overturned opposition from developing countries that viewed market-based approaches as diluting the responsibility of developed countries with historically high emissions to act. This was achieved through the transformation of a Brazilian idea for a clean development fund for developing countries, financed by a levy on developed countries that did not meet their targets. This proposal was flipped by US negotiators into a mechanism where emissions reductions from clean development projects in developing countries could be sold to developed countries and count towards their targets (Grubb et al. 1999 pp. 94, 101–3). The Clean Development Mechanism (CDM) was thus born as one of three market-based mechanisms in the Kyoto Protocol, alongside its close relative, Joint Implementation (JI), and Emissions Trading between developed countries. All three mechanisms introduced flexibility in how emissions targets could be met (UNFCCC, 1997).

The CDM and JI follow the same carbon market model, known as 'baseline and credit'. Both instruments facilitate the development of individual projects, such as the construction of wind farms, the installation of energy efficient light bulbs, or the destruction of potent industrial gases, which claim to reduce greenhouse gas emissions in different ways. The reduction claim is assessed according to the difference between actual greenhouse gas emissions and a baseline scenario of what would have occurred in the absence of the project. The difference is rewarded with an amount of carbon credits equal to the quantity of emissions reduced by the project. Carbon credits – Certified Emission Reductions (CERs) in the case of the CDM and Emission Reduction Units (ERUs) in the case of JI – can be sold to governments and, with the development of the EU ETS, individual companies. These state and corporate actors can then surrender the credits to meet their respective climate commitments, as an alternative to reducing their own emissions. The CDM and JI both follow this basic framework but are institutionally and geographically distinct, with separate UN governing bodies and different project locations. CDM projects must be located in countries that are not part of Annex I to the 1992 United Nations Framework Convention on Climate Change (UNFCCC). These are countries that didn't have emissions targets under Kyoto and are mostly developing countries. JI projects must be located in Annex I countries that did have Kyoto targets, including European, Anglosphere and ex-Soviet Union countries, and Japan (UNFCCC, 1997).

The period following the Kyoto conference witnessed a dramatic shift in the centre of gravity for global carbon markets. Despite US negotiators achieving almost everything that was on their agenda at the outset of negotiations, the US Senate never ratified the Kyoto Protocol and President George W. Bush withdrew Bill Clinton's executive support for it in 2001 (Grubb et al. 1999 p. 112; Meckling 2011 pp. 134–5). The success of the market-based agenda therefore failed to bring about global intergovernmental climate consensus. Yet, in the aftermath of Kyoto, oil companies BP and Shell instituted internal carbon trading systems and the United Kingdom and Denmark implemented national-level schemes (Betsill & Hoffmann 2011 p. 93). The EU then shifted from an ambivalent position to carbon market leaders by legislating, in 2003, what would become the world's largest international carbon market as the 'cornerstone' of EU climate policy (European Commission 2016 p. 1; Wettestad 2005).

The EU ETS, which started on 1 January 2005, operates differently to the CDM and JI as a 'cap and trade' carbon market. Rather than awarding carbon credits for emissions reductions, a quantity of carbon allowances, known as European Union Allowances (EUAs), each representing one tonne of carbon dioxide-equivalent (CO_2-e), is created that is equal to an overall emissions level. Currently, emissions of CO_2, nitrous oxide (N_2O) and perfluorocarbons (PFCs) in certain sectors are covered and the cap is set at 21 per cent below 2005 levels by 2020. EUAs are distributed to operators of more than 11,000 'installations' – generally power stations or manufacturing facilities – by governments through free allocation or auctioning, depending on specific country and industry circumstances. Installations are situated in all 28 EU member states (including, at the time of writing, the United Kingdom), as well as Iceland, Liechtenstein and Norway. They are responsible for around 45 per cent of EU emissions. Industries including electricity generation and gas supply, oil refining, iron and steel, aluminium, cement, ceramics, paper, chemicals, and aviation are covered. This geographical and sectoral coverage has evolved over three distinct phases: phase one, a 'trial' period from 2005 to 2007, phase two, coinciding with the Kyoto Protocol commitment period from 2008 to 2012, and a post-Kyoto third phase from 2013 to 2020 (European Commission 2016). Once allocated or auctioned, carbon allowances can be traded between operators of installations. This allows operators of individual installations to comply with the emissions cap by purchasing additional allowances from the operators of other installations with excess allowances, rather than reducing their own emissions.

The link established between the EU ETS and the Kyoto mechanisms, agreed to in 2004 and commencing in practice in 2008, gave European installations another source of carbon commodities and underpinned the expansion of the CDM and JI. From phase two of the EU ETS, carbon credits from the CDM and JI, with certain quantitative and qualitative restrictions, could be surrendered by EU ETS installations in lieu of carbon allowances. The link with the CDM and JI therefore allowed the overall EU ETS cap to be exceeded on the basis that an equivalent quantity of emissions was reduced by offset projects outside the cap. With the establishment of this link, over half of global demand for CERs and ERUs came from the EU ETS between 2008 and 2012 (World Bank 2012 p. 68). This supported the rapid growth of the Kyoto markets over this period. The rate of registration for CDM projects peaked at 953 new projects in December 2012, bringing the total number of projects to 7,248. The rate of CER issuance peaked three months later, at 63 million CERs in March 2013, bringing the total number of issued CERs to 1.27 billion. From then, the CDM project pipeline mostly dried up, reaching 7,792 projects at the end of 2017, which had been issued with 1.89 billion CERs (UNEP DTU 2018a). The trajectory of JI followed a similar pattern, though on a smaller scale, and with a more abrupt decline, with no projects having been registered or credits being issued since 2014. In total, 574 projects were issued 863.5 million ERUs (UNEP DTU 2018b).

The implementation and expansion of the EU ETS and Kyoto mechanisms generated economic activity for actors beyond the operators of installations and offset projects. What can be called the carbon trading industry comprises carbon brokers, exchange platforms, emissions auditors, offset project developers, news services and law firms, among many other actors. These businesses developed largely from the EU ETS and the CDM/JI to grow the transaction value of global carbon markets from less than US$1 billion in 2004, the year before the EU ETS commenced, to a high of US$176 billion in 2011. Almost all of this trading was associated with the EU ETS and Kyoto mechanisms: 84 per cent of this came from trading

EUAs and 15 per cent came from trading CERs and ERUs (World Bank 2012 p. 10). A crash in carbon prices saw the rise in the transaction value of the global carbon market come to a halt. In 2014, the transaction value of global carbon trading hit its lowest point since its 2011 high at US\$30 billion, and only marginally recovered in the years that followed (World Bank 2014 p. 15).

Outside of the EU ETS and Kyoto mechanisms, the development of carbon markets has been uneven. The most significant setback for carbon markets globally came with the failure of US legislators in 2009–10 to pass a proposed national cap and trade system, upon which predictions that carbon would be a US\$2 trillion market by 2020 were based (Hoffman & Twining 2009; Meckling 2011 pp. 61–2). The roll-out of carbon markets internationally was also partially reversed with the repeal of Australia's carbon pricing mechanism in 2014, which was set be linked to the EU ETS, although a weaker offsetting mechanism was subsequently developed in its place (Pearse 2017b). Despite these problems, at the beginning of 2018, 36 national level and 25 subnational carbon trading schemes had been implemented or scheduled. This brought the total share of global greenhouse gas emissions covered by carbon pricing (including carbon taxation) to just over 20 per cent (World Bank 2017 pp. 12–13).

This history of carbon markets points towards a disjuncture between the promise and experience of the market-based approach, which helps explain the paradox on display in Paris. The promise of carbon markets is summed up in the way the European Commission, which oversees the EU ETS, introduces the rationale of the scheme. The Commission lauds the socio-ecological efficacy of emissions trading in creating a low carbon economy, the way it enters into the economic calculations of, and creates value for, business, and its capacity to manage difficult climate politics by devolving decision-making to the market:

Emissions trading systems are among the most cost-effective tools for cutting greenhouse gas emissions. In contrast to traditional 'command and control' regulation, trading harnesses market forces to find the cheapest ways to reduce emissions ... By putting a price on carbon and thereby giving a financial value to each tonne of emissions saved, the EU ETS has placed climate change on the agenda of company boards across Europe. Pricing carbon also promotes investment in clean, low-carbon technologies. (European Commission 2016 p. 2)

The brief snapshot presented in this section suggests global carbon markets, centred around the EU ETS and its links with the CDM and JI, have a more chequered history. The socio-ecological results of the 'grand policy experiment' of sulphur dioxide trading, which supported the initial adoption of carbon markets, are disputed (Stavins 1998). The 'new carbon economy' that has been built around carbon markets has faltered (Boyd et al. 2011). Global climate politics remains fractious despite the Kyoto Protocol cementing carbon trading as 'the only game in town' (Jotzo 2005 p. 81). With notable exceptions, aspects of these disconnections have been reproduced in the economics, political economy and post-structuralist literature on carbon markets.

Mainstream and Critical Approaches to Carbon Markets

Carbon Markets as Least Cost Emissions Reductions

Economists have sought to evaluate the socio-ecological efficacy of the EU ETS by quantifying the impact of the instrument on greenhouse gas emission levels. This work is guided by the same economic logic that calls for the adoption of market mechanisms in the first place. The logic starts with the premise that climate change is a case of 'market failure' that can be addressed by putting a price on carbon, which 'internalises' the costs of carbon pollution as an 'externality'. Carbon markets are preferred over carbon taxation because different actors have different marginal abatement costs. In this context, the ability to trade is said to offer the most efficient way to find 'least cost' emissions reductions (Tietenberg 2006). While acknowledging problems in design and implementation, and the need for reform, economists have largely agreed that the EU ETS has reduced emissions in a cost-efficient manner.

Over the first ten years of the scheme, levels of emissions covered by the EU ETS reduced by about 20 per cent (Ellerman et al. 2016 p. 97). The task of economists operating within the dominant economic discourse is to disaggregate the effect of the EU ETS from other factors, most importantly the economic recession beginning in 2008, as well as energy prices, weather patterns and other polices. Various econometric techniques have been deployed to assess this at aggregate, sector and firm levels (e.g. Abrell et al. 2011; Anderson & Maria 2011; Egenhofer et al. 2011; Ellerman et al. 2010; Gronwald & Hintermann 2015). Summarising these studies, Martin et al. (2016 p. 143) state that 'concerning the issue of carbon emissions, the available evidence suggests that the EU ETS has had a robust negative impact on them'. This evidence, to date, is mostly focused on the first two phases of the scheme, and points towards EU ETS-induced emissions reductions of about 3 per cent per year (Martin et al. 2016 p. 143).

In a similar vein to the logic governing the issuance of carbon credits from offset projects, economists measure emissions reductions in relative rather than absolute terms. As Martin et al. (2016 p. 131) note, 'one should consider an emissions trading scheme to be effective only if it leads to emissions that are lower than would have been the case without the policy'. Thus, the socio-ecological effectiveness of climate policy is not measured against the goal of curtailing climate change as such, but against counterfactual emissions scenarios constructed by economists. The shortcoming of this method is that actions that may be relatively less polluting than 'business as usual', and thus evidence of effective policy, may not deliver a pathway to a safe climate. This can be illustrated with the case of emissions reductions achieved through 'fuel switching'.

Most of the emissions reductions found by economists in the first phase of the EU ETS were a result of switching between existing coal and natural gas power generation capacity (Delarue et al. 2008 p. 45; Ellerman et al. 2010 p. 192). At any point in time, the combination of gas and coal prices, the energy efficiency of different plants, consumer demand, load capacity, as well as other regulatory and infrastructure factors, determine what mix of fuel is used to generate and sell electricity into the grid. The introduction of a carbon price adds an additional factor to these determinations, which can bring forward the point in the 'merit order' between fuels at which gas-fired power becomes relatively more profitable than coal-fired power (Ellerman et al. 2010 p. 174). Fuel switching is said to have been the cost-efficient option in phase one of the EU ETS because it 'was the easiest to achieve and required the least lead time' (Ellerman et al. 2010 p. 192).

The central place of fuel switching in these economic accounts of the emissions reductions engendered by the EU ETS calls into question positive assessments of the socio-ecological efficacy of carbon markets. Scientific studies have found that the lower emissions created by burning gas rather than coal to generate electricity may be cancelled out by increased methane leakage in upstream sectors, which are not covered by the EU ETS (Wigley 2011). More importantly for our purposes, fuel switching is an action that works entirely within prior patterns of carbon-intensive investment, and therefore does not contribute to the necessary transformation of energy systems in a low-carbon direction (International Energy Agency 2015). What makes fuel switching the cost-efficient option for reducing emissions – the fact it did not require significant and new long-term investments – also makes it an ineffective way of addressing climate change.

The dominant economic literature is therefore limited by a preoccupation with assessing whether emissions reductions are cost efficient, not whether such actions address the causes of climate change. This leads to a focus on redesigning carbon markets in a way that more closely matches economic theory, avoiding more fundamental questions about the goal of cost efficiency itself. It is necessary to move beyond the marginal abatement cost curve and pay attention to the variegated impacts of particular efforts to reduce emissions in their historical and geographical context. By critically examining the socio-ecological relations embedded in emissions reductions identified by economists and engendered by carbon markets, it becomes possible to link the shortcomings of dominant economic theories and climate policies, paving the way for more critical perspectives.

Carbon Markets as Accumulation Strategy

Existing political economy accounts offer a more critical approach to studying carbon markets that is grounded in the relationship between states and capital. Indeed, dominant arguments in this tradition conceptualise carbon markets as a state-sanctioned accumulation strategy for capital. This perspective is summed up by Bumpus and Liverman (2008 p. 142), who argue that 'given the considerable profits to be made from trading in carbon reductions, offsetting and other profits from emission reduction can be seen as a form of "accumulation by decarbonisation"'. They nominate a number of different ways in which carbon markets create opportunities for profits. Firstly, existing polluters can profit from passing on the costs of allowances allocated for free, selling surplus allowances and avoiding costly methods of reducing their own emissions. Secondly, new carbon trading industries can profit from selling credits produced by offset projects, charging fees for the consulting services required to make the market function and trading carbon derivative instruments in financial markets (Bumpus & Liverman 2008 pp. 141–3). With each, there is a key role for 'state intervention to establish and regulate new markets and stabilise capital investments in nature' (Bumpus & Liverman 2008 p. 145).

Together and separately, Newell and Paterson provide the most sustained political economic account of the role of the state in driving the carbon market accumulation strategy (Newell & Paterson 1998, 2009, 2010; Paterson 2010, 2012; Newell 2012). Their work is in part informed by the Marxist notion that advanced capitalist states face twin, though often contradictory, imperatives of accumulation and legitimation as they seek to reproduce capitalism and through this, state institutions (Hay 1994; O'Connor 1973). By this reckoning, carbon markets offered states the prospect of supporting capital accumulation and securing democratic legitimacy. First, states could respond to democratic pressures for action on climate change in a way that aligned with broader policy tendencies towards marketisation. Second, carbon markets could avoid direct confrontation with existing fossil fuel interests while promoting new sites of accumulation for other actors (Newell & Paterson 2010 pp. 26–8).

The political economic literature on carbon markets is divided, however, on the implications of the accumulation strategy. Newell and Paterson (2009 p. 94) identified carbon markets, alongside other market-based initiatives such as carbon disclosure, as precursors to an emerging regime of '"climate capitalism" where successful accumulation strategies are to be found in decarbonising the economy'. The analysis was aware of the potential for stagnation and failure of this scenario, but held that carbon markets had the potential to lead to climate-friendly accumulation with varying levels and forms of regulation and justice, depending on the balance of political forces (Newell & Paterson 2010 chapter 10). The finance sector was nominated as particularly important here, as 'a powerful constituency that benefits from climate-change policy, which is crucial politically' (Newell & Paterson 2010 p. 10).

Conversely, a large amount of political economic research views the accumulation dynamics created by carbon markets as reinforcing capitalism's dependence on fossil fuels and generating additional socio-ecological damage (Bachram 2004; Böhm et al. 2012; Böhm & Dabhi 2011; Bond 2012; Lohmann 2010, 2011a, 2011b; Pearse 2016; Rosewarne 2010; Vlachou 2014; Vlachou & Konstantinidis 2010). These arguments are supported by scathing case studies and critiques from social movements and activist researchers (Bachram 2004; Böhm & Dabhi 2009; Ghosh & Sahu 2011; Gilbertson & Reyes 2009; Lohmann 2006; Smith 2007). Summarising this research, Pearse and Böhm (2014 p. 10) conclude that rather than charting a climate-friendly accumulation pathway, carbon markets 'bolster existing emissions-intensive accumulation processes rather than disrupt them'.

Existing political economic research on carbon markets as new sites of accumulation better accounts for the initial emergence and expansion of the EU ETS and Kyoto mechanisms than the financial turmoil that has engulfed these schemes. There is evidence, for example, that the UK government in particular sought to foster a carbon trading industry centred on the City of London (Department for Environment, Food, and Rural Affairs 2003; Meckling 2011 p. 109). But, as outlined, opportunities for accumulation have faltered. Major financial institutions based in the City of London, including Deutsche Bank, Barclays, JP Morgan, Morgan Stanley, and UBS closed or scaled back their carbon trading desks (Straw & Platt 2013 p. 25). Value write downs for mostly developing country investors from offset project assets left stranded by the crash in CER prices were estimated at US$66 billion (Philp 2013; World Bank 2014 pp. 98–9).

The persistent economic woes of the EU ETS and the CDM suggest states have been reluctant to support, or faced difficulties in supporting, a new carbon market accumulation strategy. To better understand why, it is necessary to move beyond debates over whether opportunities for accumulation in carbon markets leads to positive or negative outcomes, and examine the contradictions internal to the accumulation strategy itself, and how this manifests for states. Existing work has tended to apply political economic ideas of the capitalist state to climate policy without embedding this analysis in a recognition of the position of the state in regulating capitalist ecologies. This focus has wider importance for understanding broader and unexplored tensions in the commodification of 'nature as accumulation strategy' (Smith 2006), given the faltering of markets in other 'ecosystem services' (Bigger 2017; Dempsey & Suarez 2016).

Carbon Markets as Politics

Post-structuralist research has analysed carbon markets from a very different starting point. The focus is less on states and accumulation and more on the 'technologies, techniques, practices and rules' that create carbon markets (Lovell & Liverman 2010 p. 256). Much of this research draws on governmentality, actor-network and performativity approaches, but there are also important examples of scholarship that addresses or synthesises political economic concerns (Lane & Stephan 2015). Broadly and heterogeneously post-structuralist accounts have sought to locate new forms of politics in carbon markets. Introducing a special issue on this topic, Stephan and Paterson (2012 p. 557) state: 'By drawing on a broader understanding of the political and hence locating politics not just in the policy process leading up to the decision to implement a carbon market, the contributions to this volume show how these markets themselves are fundamentally political.'

A focus on the expansive political life of carbon trading has uncovered politics in a wide range of seemingly idiosyncratic spaces and processes. This work has scrutinised the technical features that allow carbon markets to function, such as the global warming potentials that commensurate different greenhouse gases (Cooper 2015; Lohmann 2009; Lövbrand & Stripple 2011; MacKenzie 2009a), how accountants record carbon credits and allowances in company balance sheets (Lovell 2013; Lovell et al. 2013) and the economic modelling underpinning allowance allocation formulas (MacKenzie 2009b). The regulators and traders that make carbon markets have been studied in terms of the local cultural contexts that have shaped the trajectory of the EU ETS in comparison to other schemes (Knox-Hayes 2016), the emotional and ethical logics and motivations of carbon traders (Descheneau & Paterson 2011; Paterson & Stripple 2012) and the various experts that operate between the regulatory and day-to-day life of carbon markets (Kuch 2015). Various rationalities have been identified as emerging between the interaction of state and non-state actors in the governance of carbon markets, including those of private calculation (Lövbrand & Stripple 2012), depoliticisation (Methmann 2013) and economic theory (Blok 2011; Callon 2009). Lastly, differences between and within carbon markets have been highlighted by focusing on the social and discursive formation of particular carbon currencies (Descheneau 2012; Stephan 2012) and the specific technologies of individual offset projects (Bumpus 2011; Lohmann 2005; Lovell & Liverman 2010).

The political implications of this research tend to hinge on the recognition that meaningful contestation occurs in multiple settings, that a variety of market designs exist, and thus, that the experience and outcomes of carbon markets are subject to considerable levels of contingency. Lovell and Liverman (2010 p. 255) frame their approach as an alternative to literature that is 'polarised, either for or against offsetting, often on principles and values rather than detailed empirical investigation or a careful assessment of different types of offsets'. The details of carbon markets are important, according to MacKenzie (2009a p. 441), because 'whether or not carbon markets are environmentally and economically effective depends on such specifics'. Further, the details of carbon markets, 'as experimental objects' (Callon 2009 p. 538), are in a constant state of flux, and thus amenable to change because they are 'more contingent, recent and modifiable than most of us may think' (Lövbrand & Stripple 2011 p. 198). MacKenzie (2009a p. 452, 2009b) labels this terrain the 'techno-politics' of carbon markets and urges researchers and activists to adopt a 'politics of market design'.

Important reforms to the design of carbon markets have indeed been achieved, but the positive impacts of these reforms have often not been realised. As will be outlined in this book, the EU ETS has been reformed with each phase of the scheme, and through specific policy interventions. MacKenzie (2009b pp. 171–4) focuses on one instance of techno-political reform to address the problem of over-allocation: changing the formula used by the European Commission to assess the allocation plans of national governments to incorporate verified emissions data and more rigorous modelling of future emissions, from phase two. Despite reducing allocation levels, MacKenzie's (2009b p. 175) pre-recession hope that this change could 'prove to have been effective in ending over-allocation' was misplaced; an overall surplus of around 2 billion allowances had accumulated by the end of the second phase (European Commission 2014g p. 8).

The systemic nature of problems such as the allowance surplus in the EU ETS despite a series of reforms indicates the need to better understand both the possibilities and constraints of the techno-politics encouraged by marketised policy frameworks. It is important not to lose sight of how new forms and sites of politics in and around carbon markets are relating to the broader landscape of climate politics. Swyngedouw (2010) takes a dim view of marketised politics as 'depoliticising' climate change, symptomatic of the current 'post-political' condition. Yet, from Kyoto to Paris, via the EU ETS, carbon markets have not successfully ringfenced climate change from politics, as policy responses inside and outside the market paradigm remain heavily contested. What remains unresolved is how the institutionalisation of carbon markets has changed the nature of political contestation over climate change, which will be explored, along with the socio-ecological and economic dimensions of carbon markets, in the following chapters.

Chapter Outline

Chapter 1 presents the conceptual approach and empirical basis of the book. It contrasts understandings of climate change as market failure with the 'climate-changing capitalism' alternative. The chapter argues that the dominant economic discourse tends to externalise the origins of carbon pollution and universalise climate solutions. Building on Marxist ecology, the chapter develops 'climate-changing capitalism' as a concept that illuminates the co-production of capitalism and climate change. This perspective focuses on the capitalist value relations and state institutions that organise the appropriation of carbon by capital, and structure the regulation of, and contestation over, climate change, including through carbon markets. The chapter then maps the organisation of carbon appropriation in the EU ETS by constructing a database that links companies and installations. This exercise reveals a socio-spatially uneven carbon market, in which most greenhouse gases emissions are emitted by a relatively small number of large-scale fossil fuel-intensive power stations and factories, which are owned by an even smaller group of corporations and governments.

Chapters 2 and 3 jointly evaluate the relationship between carbon markets and climate change as a socio-ecological crisis. The chapters, respectively, conceptualise the processes involved in the commodification of carbon that are internal and external to the EU ETS. Chapter 2 examines the political and institutional development of the EU ETS and analyses its regulatory basis in terms of how carbon commodities are defined and delimited. It demonstrates that carbon allowances are commodified representations of

16   *Introduction*

carbon appropriation, which equalise variegated relationships between installations and emissions. Chapter 3 focuses on the CDM and JI, showing that
carbon credits in these schemes are made by extending processes of commodification to relationships between offset projects and emissions reductions,
which provides a spatio-temporal fix to polluters in the EU ETS.

The chapters present case studies of the trading patterns of the two most
polluting companies in the EU ETS between 2005 and 2012: German power
companies RWE and E.ON. Reconstructing and tracing the particular forms
of carbon appropriation traded by these major polluters – an alternative
method to the narrow economic approach of quantifying relative emissions
reductions – shows that carbon markets allow more marginal changes to be
substituted for potentially transformative actions. This reflects the contradiction between the formal equality of carbon markets and the substantive
inequality of climate-changing capitalism, which manifests within the EU
ETS and is intensified by the link to the Kyoto offsetting mechanisms.

Chapter 4 shifts focus from the concrete aspects of carbon commodification to the value relations that are co-imbricated with carbon trading. The
purpose is to analyse the relationship between carbon markets and climate
change as an economic crisis. The chapter explores and reconsiders the rise
and fall of the carbon market accumulation strategy associated with the EU
ETS and the CDM/JI that is discussed in the political economic literature. It
does so with reference to the third part of the book's typology of capitalist
relations with, and within, nature: capitalisation. By moving beyond rent-
based accounts of carbon markets, and analysing whether and how carbon
commodities have become new forms of capital, the chapter advances a conception of value that is actively constituted by finance and nature. An examination of carbon commodities as credit, collateral and risk reveals tensions
between state support for accumulation by appropriation and accumulation
by capitalisation. This engenders a contradiction, the second identified in the
book, whereby carbon market accumulation strategies in a climate-changing
capitalism require the ongoing combustion of fossil fuels.

Chapter 5 places contestation at the centre of the analysis, looking at the
relationship between carbon markets and climate change as a political crisis.
The chapter engages with perspectives on carbon markets as techno-politics
or post-politics by considering how carbon markets have reshaped the institutional and political conditions for climate policy. The empirical focus is on
debates over reforms to the technical design of the EU ETS, its links with
the Kyoto offsetting mechanisms, and its relationship with other policies.
These debates between states, capital and environmental organisations concerned the force, reach and priority of carbon market value determinations

in climate policy. The outcomes showed that real, though uneven and limited, reform within the market paradigm is possible. However, the institutionalisation of the market-based approach, and its subsequent crisis, simultaneously disadvantaged political movements pursuing other important policies promoting renewable energy and energy efficiency. Herein lies the third and final contradiction of carbon markets, which advantage a singular political logic of efficient pricing at the expense pluralistic policy debates and frameworks needed to create pathways to counter climate-changing capitalism.

The Conclusion discusses the implications of the analysis in the book for new carbon markets and the future of climate policy. It points to ways the contradictions of carbon markets are manifesting in novel and heightened ways in the new Chinese emissions trading scheme, which became the world's biggest from the end of 2017. This is contrasted with recent orientations of climate movements towards contesting climate change at grounded and financial spaces of fossil fuels. The Conclusion argues these actions can inform a more democratic, multi-pronged and targeted approach to climate policy that can move the world towards a post-carbon economy.

1

Conceptualising Carbon

Introduction

All evaluations of purported solutions to climate change are shaped by their understanding of the problem. There is scientific consensus that atmospheric concentrations of carbon dioxide are at their highest point in hundreds of thousands of years, that the primary source of the increase has been the burning of fossil fuels, and that the overall effect of this is a warmer and more unstable climate (IPCC, 2014). Yet, this does little to establish the political economic character of climate change. Too often, the partial and contested perspectives on climate change that underpin policy analyses remain implicit. The dominant economic discourse is a prime culprit here, with particularly problematic implications. Economic understandings of climate change as 'market failure' directly inform the adoption of market solutions to climate change, and evaluations of policy efficacy, but this is rarely justified.

This chapter contrasts competing approaches to conceptualising 'carbon' by questioning the diagnosis of climate change offered by dominant economic frameworks and presenting an alternative approach that is grounded in capitalist relations with, and within, nature. The purpose is to lay the foundations to evaluate the socio-ecological, economic, and political aspects of carbon markets in the context of a 'climate-changing capitalism'. The main relation with nature explored in the chapter is the 'appropriation' of carbon, which paves the way for subsequent analysis of the 'commodification' and 'capitalisation' of carbon in the following chapters. The chapter also introduces themes that are critical for understanding the three key contradictions of carbon markets explored in this book: the unequal nature of the climate problem when viewed from outside the market paradigm, the close relationship between fossil fuels, value and accumulation, and the central place of the state in mediating contestation over climate change.

The first section argues that economic notions of market failure tend to displace attention away from the origins of, and disperse responsibility for addressing, climate change. It charts the legacy of Pigou (1932) and Coase (1960) in economic notions of carbon pollution as 'externality' and climate action as 'reciprocal cost', which combine to create an economic ideology of nature. The second section surveys key contributions from Marxist ecology to develop the notion of 'climate-changing capitalism' as an alternative framework for conceptualising the co-production of capitalism and climate change. It outlines how the appropriation of carbon by capital, organised by capitalism's peculiar value relations and regulated by capitalist states, creates climate change, and how climate change, including direct climate impacts and political responses such as carbon markets, shapes capitalism. The final section of the chapter applies this approach to examine patterns of carbon appropriation in the European carbon market. It reveals that responsibility for greenhouse gas emissions is highly unequal, being clustered among a relatively small number of privately and state-owned corporations, and the large-scale power plants and factories they control.

1.1 Climate Change as Market Failure

1.1.1 Pigou: Externalising Carbon Pollution

Environmental economists, operating within the oeuvre of neoclassical economics, conceptualise carbon pollution as an 'externality'. The foundation of this conception is Pigou's (1932) contribution to welfare economics. The study of economic welfare, according to Pigou (1932 pp. 10–14), is concerned with changes in human satisfaction and dissatisfaction that can be measured in monetary terms. Pigou's analysis is methodologically individualist in viewing the operation of the economy through the lens of the rational behaviour of individual agents. This behaviour is analysed by employing a marginalist method that focuses on incremental changes in prices and quantities in order to measure and manage 'private' and 'social' economic welfare. Private welfare is made up of 'physical things or objective services' that directly benefit the owners of resources (Pigou 1932 pp. 134–5). Social welfare extends the consideration of the costs and benefits of goods and services to indirect effects on all actors, including those who are not directly a party to economic transactions yielding private welfare (Pigou 1932 pp. 134–5).

Pigou's work focuses on situations where private welfare and social welfare diverge, creating either positive or negative externalities. The latter, where private welfare is greater than social welfare, is most pertinent for the study of climate change. Negative externalities arise when:

> One person, A, in the course of rendering some service, for which payment is made, to a second person, R, incidentally also renders disservices to other persons (not producers of like services), of such a sort that payment cannot be exacted from the benefited parties or compensation enforced on behalf of the injured parties. (Pigou 1932 p. 183)

In this formulation, negative impacts of economic activity are defined in terms of the relationship of affected parties to economic exchange. 'Uncompensated or uncharged effects' occur when the private benefits accruing to parties involved in an economic exchange impose social costs on others who are external to the exchange relationship (Pigou 1932 p. 191). This divergence in private and social welfare is a problem, according to Pigou (1932 p. 172), because 'self-interest will not, therefore, tend to make the national dividend a maximum'. meaning overall resource allocation will be suboptimal. This inefficient outcome is the crux of the problem of externalities, which cause 'injury to the sum total of economic satisfaction' (Pigou 1932 p. 28).

The Pigouvian framework feeds into environmental economic approaches that diagnose the cause of climate change as unpriced carbon pollution. The result of this negative externality is market failure: private benefits of current levels of carbon pollution are below the social costs of climate change because these costs are not reflected in the price of carbon-intensive goods and services. The most prominent expression of this logic was the UK government's *Stern Review*, which attempted to quantify the loss of economic welfare from carbon emissions in terms of global economic output. The report famously asserted that 'unpriced emissions' of greenhouse gases have created a 'market failure on the greatest scale the world has seen' that will reduce global GDP by 5–10 per cent per year by 2100 (Stern 2007 pp. 25, 35).

The diagnosis of climate change in the *Stern Review* illustrates how the Pigouvian framework displaces enquiry away from the actors, institutions and relations that generate carbon pollution. The focus on unpriced carbon pollution effects a first level of displacement by situating the problem as external to idealised efficient markets. A similar externalisation of carbon pollution is evident in scientific enquiry when climate models consider the 'physical properties of [greenhouse gases] in isolation from the surrounding social relations that produced them and give them meaning' (Demeritt 2001b p. 316). The dominant economic framework gives this external conception a marketised inflection by comprehending the external character of pollution in relation to the price system. This mode of thinking extends beyond the

1.1 Climate Change as Market Failure

origins of carbon pollution to its effects, which are only viewed as a problem if it reduces the efficiency of markets in the aggregate. Thus, the notion of 'externality' effects a secondary analytical displacement away from the uneven, particular and non-monetary impacts of climate change to an undifferentiated, aggregate and formal economy.

When understandings of the causes of environmental challenges are displaced to a malfunctioning price system, policy responses to the problem move in the same direction. If environmental costs are external to the market, it becomes necessary to internalise those costs by adjusting market prices. By adjusting market prices, it is possible to optimise the allocation of resources for economic ends. Pigou is well known for advocating an important role for states in achieving this by instituting what have become known as 'Pigouvian taxes'. He reasoned that:

> For every industry in which the value of the marginal social net product is less than that of the marginal private net product, there will be certain rates of tax, the imposition of which by the State would increase the size of the national dividend and increase economic welfare; and one rate of tax, which would have the optimum effect in this respect. (1932 p. 224)

Some governments around the world have responded to climate change with Pigouvian-style carbon taxes at domestic and sub-domestic levels (World Bank 2017 p. 12). However, the major international climate policies that are the focus of this book depart from Pigou's proposal for states to directly adjust market prices to efficient levels. As discussed in the Introduction, carbon markets, such as the EU ETS and the Kyoto mechanisms, ostensibly allow the market to find least cost abatement options by allowing the formation of carbon prices through the trading of carbon credits and allowances.

1.1.2 Coase: Universalising Climate Action

Environmental policies that use tradeable permits represent an important market-based deviation to taxation that can be traced back to Coase's (1960) influential critique of the Pigouvian tradition. The overall objective of Coase's paper, *The Problem of Social Cost,* for which he was awarded the economics equivalent of the Nobel Prize, is broadly in line with Pigou's goal of managing externalities to achieve an efficient allocation of resources. For example, Coase (1960 p. 15) asserts that 'the economic problem in all cases of harmful effects is how to maximise the value of production'. However, Coase's paper strongly objects firstly to Pigou's method of analysing externalities and secondly to Pigou's proposals for addressing them.

Coase refines the analysis of externalities by dispensing of the Pigouvian concern with distribution of costs and benefits between private and social spheres. Instead, all costs are treated in reciprocal terms. The argument is illustrated with a simple example of two neighbouring farmers, where the cattle owned by one stray onto and damage the crops owned by the other:

It is true that there would be no crop damage without the cattle. It is equally true that there would be no crop damage without the crops ... If we are to discuss the problem in terms of causation, both parties cause the damage. If we are to attain an optimum allocation of resources, it is therefore desirable that both parties should take the harmful effect (the nuisance) into account in deciding on their course of action. (Coase 1960 p. 13)

By making costs reciprocal the analysis of the 'harmful effects' of externalities is extended beyond costs imposed on third parties to the costs incurred by parties in addressing that harm.

The reciprocity of costs transforms the economic reasoning behind efforts to correct market failure to a problem of 'avoid[ing] the more serious harm' (Coase 1960 p. 2). As Coase (1960 p. 27) explains:

The problem which we face in dealing with actions which have harmful effects is not simply one of restraining those responsible for them. What has to be decided is whether the gain from preventing the harm is greater than the loss which would be suffered elsewhere as a result of stopping the action which produces the harm.

Government policy therefore risks imposing costs in addressing a harm that will outweigh the benefits. From this perspective, Pigouvian taxation is potentially inefficient because governments cannot know the price that will generate optimal outcomes.

If Pigou's framework externalises the causes of pollution, Coase's framework universalises responsibility for fixing environmental problems to all parties – polluters and non-polluters alike. Governments no longer have a role in directly adjusting market prices. Instead, impacts that are viewed as external to the market are to be internalised by expanding the sphere of market until everything is covered by property rights, enrolling all actors into the market solution. Popularised as the 'Coase theorem', the argument is that given clearly defined property rights and no transaction costs, trade between private actors will produce an efficient allocation of resources and maximise the total value of production. In the example above, this means finding the combination of crops and cattle that generates the highest value output, regardless of who is causing the damage. The Coase theorem holds that trading will create the optimal outcome independent of the initial distribution of rights (Coase 1960 p. 15).

Universalising responsibility to address climate change by making the costs of carbon pollution reciprocal with the costs of emissions reductions

1.1 Climate Change as Market Failure

serves to limit the scope of climate action. Policy responses are understood to impose costs to the economy that may create greater inefficiencies than the costs of climate change. This is what Coase (1960 p. 34) is referring to when he argues, contra Pigou, that 'from an economic point of view, a situation in which there is "uncompensated damage" ... is not necessarily undesirable'. Here, Coase is introducing an important caveat to acting against externalities, aimed to prevent action that results in a sub-optimally *low* level of pollution. Once again, this economic logic has parallels in scientific constructions of climate change in climate models that 'universalise the objects of their knowledge ontologically. Physical sciences represent [greenhouse gases] in terms of certain objective and immutable physical properties' (Demeritt 2001b p. 313). In the marketised inflection given to this by Coase, carbon pollution becomes part of the idealised perfect market with similarly objective and immutable properties. An effective natural limit is thereby placed on climate action that does not maximise the value of production. The logic underpins the cost-benefit analysis conducted by Stern (2007 p. 299), who dismissed the possibility of reducing global atmospheric concentrations of greenhouse gases to anything below 450 parts per million as 'prohibitively expensive' – levels the IPCC (2014 p. 21) says are likely to be needed to prevent global warming of over 2 degrees Celsius.

1.1.3 The Economic Ideology of Nature

Combined, Pigou, and Coase provide the conceptual basis for an economic version of what Smith (2008) termed the 'ideology of nature', comprised of contradictory yet complementary external and universal conceptions of nature. The external conception of nature views nature as external from society, often as 'pristine, God-given, autonomous' (Smith 2008 p. 11). In the Pigouvian tradition, this translates to the externalisation of carbon pollution from the market via the notion of externalities. Smith (2008 p. 28), along with Harvey (1996 p. 122), links the externalisation of nature with projects aimed at the 'subjugation' or 'domination' of nature. This is also evident in the Pigouvian faith that society can perfect its use of nature (i.e. carbon pollution) with appropriate market-based solutions. The universal conception of nature, in contrast, views society as nature, and therefore, governed by natural laws (Smith 2008 p. 12). Coase's notion of the reciprocity of costs is presented in a similarly universal manner, where the efficiency of markets becomes a ubiquitous natural law. The political implications of the universal conception of nature is not its subjugation or domination, but rather submission to nature (i.e. the market), because 'capitalism is natural; to fight it is to fight human nature' (Smith 2008 p. 29). Coasian market solutions universalise responsibility for climate change by implicating all actors in the pursuit of economic optimality.

In harbouring both external and universal conceptions of nature, the ideology of nature is somewhat contradictory because society is both separate from, and the same as, nature (Smith 2008 pp. 11–12). However, these contradictory positions also complement each other politically because, as Harvey (1996 p. 149) argues, the external and universal conceptions of nature function as two sides of 'a pendulum between cornucopian optimism and triumphalism at one pole and unrelieved pessimism … of our powers to escape from the clutches of naturally imposed limits … at the other pole'. On one side of the coin, Pigou's understanding of the cause of climate change as unpriced emissions displaces attention from the origins of carbon pollution. This encourages market-based policy solutions in the confidence that externalities can be managed separately from the underlying causes of climate change. On the other side of the coin, if no one is responsible for climate change in Pigou's framework, everyone is potentially responsible for climate action in Coase's universalising notion of reciprocal costs. This disperses responsibility for addressing climate change to non-optimising economic actors and places an effective natural limit on actions that do not maximise the value of production.

Prevailing economic appraisals of carbon markets, such as those surveyed in the Introduction, are anchored in the Pigouvian–Coasian economic ideology of nature, and reflect its shortcomings. Pigou's ideas underpin the preoccupation with evaluating carbon markets by quantifying least cost emissions reductions in an otherwise socio-ecologically undifferentiated manner (Anderson & Maria 2011; Ellerman et al. 2010; Martin et al. 2016). Because the climate change problem is defined in terms of deviations from the optimal level of pollution, the primary concern is quantifying how much, rather than how, emissions are reduced. Yet, how emissions are reduced matters because, as will be established, different sources of emissions are unequally implicated in the climate change problem. The displacement of the problem to unpriced emissions is evident in the distinctive method employed for calculating relative emissions reductions: once a limited number of known and quantifiable factors that reduce emissions are accounted for, it is assumed that any reductions in actual emissions from the counterfactual scenarios is due to the influence of the carbon price.

Coase's ideas underpin economic research with in-built biases against policies outside of the market-based framework. Somewhat contradictorily, how emissions are reduced becomes a matter of concern, but only if they are

1.2 Climate-Changing Capitalism

generated by renewable energy and energy efficiency policies. These policies are criticised for targeting particular types of climate action that do not represent least cost, as decided by, and dispersed through, the market (Böhringer 2014 pp. 10–11). This translates the abstract limits of the economic ideology of nature into concrete positions against a broad suite of policy options. Again, as will be established, evaluating the efficacy of climate policy cannot be restricted to questions of cost efficiency, and instead needs to consider the actors, institutions and relations under capitalism that shape the course of climate change.

1.2 Climate-Changing Capitalism

The alternative to the external-universal ideology of nature that hinders common economic approaches to climate change and carbon markets is to place carbon markets in the context of a 'climate-changing capitalism'. The notion of 'climate-changing capitalism' emphasises the co-production capitalism and climate change in two ways. First, it moves climate change from a problem that is external to markets to one that is produced by capitalism, which is quite literally changing the planet's climate. Second, it recognises that the very nature of capitalism is being changed by climatic conditions that are partly of capitalism's own making, but in an uneven and contested – not universal – manner. This formulation builds on different strands of critical literature on capitalist relations with, and within, nature, which are outlined and developed in this section.

Climate change represents one part of the broader production of nature under capitalism. The notion of the 'production of nature', developed by Marxist geographers including Smith, Harvey, and Swyngedouw, is built on an ontological position of the 'prior dissolution' of society and nature as 'coherent entities' (Harvey 1996 p. 140). Instead, society and nature are understood as 'intertwined in perpetually changing ways in the production processes of both society and the physical environment' (Swyngedouw 1999 p. 445). Unlike the universal conception of nature, produced nature is a 'differentiated unity' that is made and remade through labour processes that transform and retransform landscapes in ways that are shaped by dominant socio-ecological relations of production and reproduction. Here, produced nature is internally differentiated by the unequal character of those socio-ecological relations, as 'created ecosystems tend to both instantiate and reflect, therefore, the social systems that gave rise to them' (Harvey 1996 p. 185). This is not to say that capitalism transforms nature in an unbridled fashion; as is outlined below, climate change is a stark example of the uncontrolled character of the production of nature. Thus, the materiality of nature, as a constitutive part of the uneven development of capital, matters as 'both the product and the geographical *premise* of capitalist development' (Castree 1995 pp. 20–1; Smith 2008 p. 206 emphasis added). This line of thinking challenges ideologies of nature by emphasising that nature is not separate from or the same as society; it is 'socially produced' (Smith 2006 p. 28) as a hybrid form of 'socionature' (Swyngedouw 1999 p. 446) or 'created ecosystem' (Harvey 1996 p. 186). The changing climate can therefore be viewed as 'historical nature' which 'embodies chemical, physical, social, economic, political, and cultural processes in highly contradictory but inseparable manners' (Swyngedouw 1999 p. 447).

Moore (2015) elevates the purview of 'historical natures' to a world-historical process in advancing the 'world-ecology' paradigm. Significantly for our purposes, Moore (2015 p. 3 emphasis added) contends that 'capitalism as a world-ecology, join[s] the accumulation of capital, the pursuit of power, and the *co-production* of nature in dialectical unity'. Like Smith, Harvey, and Swyngedouw, society-nature dualisms, and especially, the external conception of nature, are key targets, in mainstream but also critical 'Green' thought. Moore's methodological starting point for addressing the problems of dualistic thought and method is the 'double internality' of 'capitalism-in-nature' and 'nature-in-capitalism'. 'Climate-changing capitalism' is an expression of this double internality that highlights the simultaneous ways capitalism develops within and through climate change, and climate change unfolds within and through capitalism. In one moment, that of capitalism-in-climate, capitalism produces climate change by organising nature for the appropriation of carbon by capital, which burns fossil fuels and emits greenhouse gases. In the other moment, that of climate-in-capitalism, the changing climate shapes capitalist development through direct climate impacts and the socio-political changes engendered by climate risks and uncertainties, including via the institution of carbon markets. These moments in climate-changing capitalism illuminate the 'internal relations' of capitalism and climate change (Bieler & Morton 2018).

The co-production of capitalism and climate change is mediated by capitalism's peculiar set of value relations. From a Marxist perspective, the substance of the specifically capitalist form of value is abstract social labour. In this formulation, value operates through abstractions from concrete labour processes, which are commensurated by the 'socially necessary labour time' embedded in commodities (Marx 1976 p. 129). This makes labour productivity the key metric of value determinations under capitalism. For many Marxists, this means that capitalism is historically distinguished in the sphere

1.2 Climate-Changing Capitalism 27

of production. Competition compels capitalists to constantly advance labour productivity, such as by investing capital in labour saving technologies, to reduce socially necessary labour time. This increases rates of exploitation, as workers, who are compelled to sell their labour power, produce more surplus value for capitalists. However, this class antagonism sets in motion, and emerges through, a much wider set of value relations that extend into spheres of reproduction.

Feminists studying the socio-ecological reproduction of capitalism, such as Federici (2014 p. 75), led the way in demonstrating that the accumulation of capital as self-expanding value depends on the 'devaluation and feminisation of reproductive labour'. As Mies (1986 p. 47) explains, 'labour can only be productive in the sense of producing surplus value as long as it can tap, extract, exploit, and appropriate labour which is spent in the production of life, or subsistence production which is largely non-wage labour mainly done by women'. Mies' (1986 p. 77) analysis proceeds to trace the 'underground connections' between the appropriation of the unpaid labour of women and the appropriation of non-human nature, often as part of colonial histories. In this vein, Salleh (2009 p. 4) proposes a model of value relations that understands the 'social debts' accrued through the exploitation of wage labour as internally related to the 'embodied debts' owed to unpaid workers and the 'ecological debts' owed to non-human nature. Value under capitalism thus expands through, yet requires limits on, processes of commodification (Fraser 2014a, 2014b).

Capitalist value relations are therefore conditioned by what Moore (2015) terms 'accumulation by capitalisation' *and* 'accumulation by appropriation'. Processes of capitalisation, where capital is invested in the sphere of commodity production to create cycles of expanded accumulation, depends on the appropriation of uncommodified labour, energy, and materials. When capital burns fossil fuels, it appropriates the use values of accumulated energy from the biogeochemical cycles that create coal, gas, and oil deposits over millions of years, which are not fully produced by wage labour within circuits of capital (Burkett 1999 pp. 70–1; Clark & York 2005 p. 402). The extraction, processing, transportation, and combustion of fossil fuels requires significant capital investments and labour time. Historically, these costs for capital have been outweighed by the labour productivity improvements delivered through the appropriation of fossil energy.

Coal, oil, and gas have several distinct advantages for capitalist production. First, fossil fuels are spatially flexible in the sense that they can be mined in one place and burned in another, supporting expanded scales of production and geographical concentration in the most profitable locations, while expanding the speed and scope of commodity circulation. Second, fossil fuels are temporally flexible in the sense that they allow capitalist production to be constantly in motion, while also giving capitalists the power to switch energy on when it is profitable and switch it off when it is not (Altvater 2006; Huber 2009; Malm 2016). The wide uses of fossil fuels across multiple commodity production processes, including electricity generation and heat, transportation and a range of manufacturing processes, such as cement, steel and aluminium production, leads Malm (2013 p. 51) to describe fossil fuels as 'the general lever for surplus-value production'. Third, fossil fuels indirectly support capitalist production in supplying energy for the unpaid work that reproduces labour power in households and across everyday life.

The close relationship between capitalism and fossil fuels is a historical rather than absolute one. That history extends back to before the industrial revolution and is only one aspect of capitalism's systemic appropriation of nature (Moore 2017). Indeed, in principle, capital only requires cheap energy, rather than cheap fossil fuels, and many of the advantages of fossil fuels are being eroded by the political, economic, and geophysical challenges facing coal, oil, and gas industries and the rise of renewables (Patel & Moore 2017 pp. 177–9). Yet, the historical legacy of an economy organised through the appropriation of carbon looms large in contemporary capitalism, creating a 'fossil fuel landscape' characterised by inertia (Carton 2017). One significant dimension of this was captured by the Governor of the Bank of England, who estimated that 'around one third of equity and fixed income assets' remains bound up in fossil fuel-intensive companies and, through this, the rapidly changing global climate (Carney 2015).

Capitalism's way of organising nature stands out historically because 'for the first time human beings produce nature at a world scale' (Smith 2008 p. 77). Climate change, where greenhouse gas emissions are transforming the systems that regulate climatic conditions globally, radically exemplifies the planetary scale of the capitalist production of nature. The magnitude of climatic and other related socio-ecological transformations is also captured in more recent concepts such as the 'Anthropocene', which posits the emergence of a new human-centred geological epoch (Castree 2014; Steffen et al. 2007). However, in the social sciences and humanities, the notion of the Anthropocene is often deployed in a manner that erases the centrality of capitalism in the nature and origins of planetary socio-ecological crisis (Malm 2016; Malm & Hornborg 2014; Moore 2016, 2017, 2018). In contrast, recognising the emergence of a 'climate-changing capitalism' places the capitalist relations, actors and institutions that drive climate change in sharp focus.

In a climate-changing capitalism, increasing concentrations of greenhouse gases in the atmosphere are products of an asymmetry between

1.2 Climate-Changing Capitalism 29

exploitation and appropriation that is integral to capitalist value relations. This asymmetry is captured by Salleh (2017 pp. 227–8) who argues 'capitalist patriarchal value is dissociated from bioreproductive processes … The price of an object on the market gets to be accepted as its value, and matter stripped of its kinetic pulse is laid waste'. In producing climate change, capital appropriates the labour productivity-enhancing properties of carbon without regard for the consequences of greenhouse gas emissions as dissipated energy. In Benton's (1989 p. 70, 84) terms, carbon pollution is outside of the 'value-maximising intentional structure' of capitalist production and therefore 'excluded or occluded by the forms of calculation available to economic agents'. Rather, the capacity of forests, oceans, and other parts of the biosphere to absorb and circulate carbon is simply 'presupposed' by the intentional structure of capitalist production (Benton 1992 p. 59; Clark & York 2005 p. 402). The combination of dependence on, but indifference to, these carbon cycling processes makes climate change a 'naturally mediated unintended consequence' of capitalist production (Benton 1989 p. 77).

Patterns of greenhouse gas emissions are integrally linked to uneven geographical, sectoral, and organisational patterns of carbon appropriation. Between 1750 and 2011, two-thirds of carbon dioxide emissions – the most prevalent 'human-induced' greenhouse gas in terms of atmospheric concentration – were from the combustion of fossil fuels. The other one-third are largely the result of land use changes, such as deforestation (Stocker et al. 2013 pp. 50, 56–7). Cumulative emissions are particularly concentrated in regions with the longest histories of advanced capitalist development. Between 1870 and 2013, 23 per cent of emissions from fossil fuels and cement originated in the then 28 EU member states – internally skewed towards the wealthier states of Germany, the United Kingdom, and France – just below the largest cumulative emitter, the United States, which was responsible for 26 per cent of emissions over the same period (Baumert et al. 2005 p. 32; Le Quéré et al. 2014 p. 37). Inside, and across these and other state borders, the bulk of historical greenhouse gas emissions are attributable to a relatively small number of entities involved in the primary, 'upstream', production of oil, gas, coal, as well as the manufacturing of cement. Only 90 'carbon majors' – privately owned corporations, state-owned enterprises and, historically, national governments – were cumulatively responsible for 63 per cent of carbon dioxide and methane emissions globally between 1751 and 2010 (Heede 2013). The uneven development of capitalism, therefore, organises greenhouse gas emissions unevenly, revealing unequal relations of capitalism-in-climate.

30   *Conceptualising Carbon*

The inequalities that give rise to climate change are matched by those constituting relations of climate-in-capitalism. Sea level rises, extreme weather events, desertification and other manifestations of climate change create threats to human capabilities that are historically and geographically differentiated by class, race, gender, not to mention threats to non-humans (Edenhofer et al. 2014; Pearse 2017a; Stocker et al. 2013 p. 50). These threats are bundled up with major and uncertain reorientations in patterns of accumulation, geopolitical conflicts, and forms of political organisation (Mitchell 2009; Parenti 2012). Regarding the latter, Mann and Wainwright (2018 p. x) contend climate change will fundamentally 'alter our world's basic political arrangements, processes we call "adaptation of the political"'. Their thesis envisages climate change-induced transformations in the very nature of 'the political' along two sets of intersecting coordinates: capitalism/anti-capitalism and planetary sovereignty/anti-planetary sovereignty. 'Climate Leviathan', a political economic order that extends both capitalism and planetary sovereignty, is nominated by Mann and Wainwright (2018 pp. 30–1) as the most likely pathway, and the current market-based climate paradigm is identified as a precursor. Carbon markets, therefore, represent one way that capitalism is being shaped by climate change, not as a universal force of nature that is externally imposed on society, but through contestation over state-instituted responses to climate change.

The centrality of the state in a climate-changing capitalism is foreshadowed by 'production of nature' and 'world-ecology' approaches. Smith (2006 p. 28) makes it clear that capital never controls the production of nature and instead 'can create accidental, unintended and even counter-effective results vis-à-vis nature'. Lack of capitalist control, however, does not mean that the production of nature, encompassing the production of climate change, is an unmediated process. Indeed, Smith (2008 pp. 72–3) notes that the state is the key institution that regulates the socio-ecological reproduction of capitalism, and that it is through the state that the 'contradictory character of the [capitalist] relation with nature, along with its complexity, begins to emerge more concretely'. Likewise, Moore's (2015 p. 150) emphasis on the *co*-production of nature by 'capital, science and empire' signals that nature's production is more than a capital affair. The latter two are especially significant in unlocking zones of reproduction for capital, which Moore (2015 p. 149) characterises as outside of circuits of capital but 'within reach of capitalist power'. The state is the critical institution of capitalist power. Its position in co-producing nature is most comprehensively developed by O'Connor (1998) through the notion of nature as 'condition of production'.

O'Connor integrated Marx's understanding of nature as 'condition of production' by developing Polanyi's (1944) idea of 'fictitious commodities'.

1.2 Climate-Changing Capitalism 31

Polanyi (1944 pp. 72–5) argued that land, labour power, and money shared a common feature in that capitalism depends on their commodification even though 'none of them are produced for sale', meaning they are not in his definition, true commodities. O'Connor (1998 p. 146) understands the significance of this Polanyian 'fiction' in Marxist value terms, as 'nature's contribution to physical production independent of (or abstracted from) the quantity of labour time (or amount of capital) applied to production'. What the Polanyian perspective brings is a focus on the institutions that both facilitate and restrict capitalist relations with, and within, nature (Polanyi 1944 p. 76). For O'Connor (1998 p. 148), 'this agency can be no other than the capitalist state that produces these conditions and/or regulates access to, use of and exit from labour power, land, raw material, and other markets for fictitious commodities which Marx called "production conditions"'.

The central place of the state in the production of nature is a corollary of the dependence of capitalist value relations on zones of reproduction that are outside of circuits of capital, which places natural conditions outside the sphere of capital's direct economic control. The state is required as the 'relatively autonomous' institution that ensures the 'politically guaranteed existence' of natural conditions in 'the desired quantities and qualities at the right times and places' (O'Connor 1998 pp. 148–9). Natural conditions are therefore conceived in relational terms as 'produced and reproduced (or made accessible) within definite property, legal and social relationships' (O'Connor 1998 p. 148). The combustion of fossil fuels in the accumulation process is mediated by states in a multitude of ways. Relations of capitalism-in-climate occur through state action including tax credits, licensing of fossil fuel reserves, state ownership, research and development funding, competition policy, and infrastructure provision. The subsidy value of state actions in EU energy sectors was quantified at €34 billion in 2011 (Alberici et al. 2014 p. 34). Examples such as this lead O'Connor (1998 p. 155) to argue 'it is clear that environmental destruction cannot be laid at the door of capital alone; the state is deeply implicated in the crisis of nature'.

Climate policy adds another layer to the integral role of states in climate-changing capitalism by mediating relations of climate-in-capitalism. Climate policy is a consequence of the structural position of states in regulating natural conditions. As articulated by Parenti (2015 p. 830), the state is an 'environment making' institution because 'capital's metabolic relationship with non-human nature is also always a relationship with the state, and mediated through the state'. While nature actively constitutes the production of value, the reproduction of nature is politicised and bureaucratised, directing contestation over nature towards the state. Conflicting interests between and within different arms and levels of states, sections of capital, and wings of environment movements (which contest nature not as conditions of production, but as 'conditions of human life – and of life itself' (O'Connor 1998 p. 155)), manifest in constant contestation over the goals and instruments of state regulation of nature. Decisions over the institution of environmental policies are always contingent on these bureaucratic and political factors, which 'affect state production and/or regulation of the conditions of production in highly complicated, often unknown, and sometimes unknowable ways' (O'Connor 1998 p. 153). Hence, the impact of carbon markets within a climate-changing capitalism is dependent on the agency and power of climate activists and environmental organisations, the bodies representing carbon-intensive and green industries, and heterogeneous state institutions.

The notion of a climate-changing capitalism replaces the externalising and universalising approach of environmental economics with a focus on the actors, relations, and institutions that organise the appropriation of carbon. This provides a much firmer basis to analyse carbon markets in terms of how processes of commodification and capitalisation relate to and potentially alter patterns of carbon appropriation. The next section examines concrete patterns of carbon appropriation in the historical and geographical context of the EU ETS in order to apply this approach to the European carbon market and its links with the Kyoto mechanisms.

1.3 Mapping the Appropriation of Carbon in the EU ETS

This section examines the appropriation of carbon within the EU ETS by mapping the socio-spatial distribution of greenhouse gas emissions along three dimensions: corporate groups, sites of production, and ownership structures. Each dimension is integrally related to the socio-ecological relations that create climate change. First, corporations are the key institutions through which capital appropriates carbon. Second, the materiality of fossil fuels shapes the scale of polluting labour processes at sites of production. Third, the division of ownership between private and public actors is a key factor shaping the capacity of the state to produce and mediate climate change. The analysis reveals that greenhouse gas emissions are organised in a highly unequal manner between different corporate groups and across different sites of production, reflecting the socio-spatial concentration and centralisation of carbon. States play a central role across both dimensions by wielding significant control over emissions through state ownership of polluting companies and infrastructure.

1.3 Mapping the Appropriation of Carbon in the EU ETS   33

The analysis draws on a database of polluting companies regulated by the EU ETS constructed by the author. This database also forms the empirical basis of analysis of the activities of companies and installations in the proceeding chapters, unless otherwise noted. It was constructed by matching available installation data (European Commission 2014e, 2014h, 2014k) with companies information in Orbis, an online database of company information, published by Bureau van Dijk, and exported on 16 July 2014 (Bureau van Dijk 2014).[1]

Adjusting for gaps in installation emissions and shareholding ownership data, 10,938 installations, owned by 7,003 companies, which released 14,943 Mt CO_2-e from 2005–12, were matched. As such, the database of companies covers 94 per cent of emissions released in the first two phases of the EU ETS (European Commission 2014e, 2014h, 2014k).[2]

1.3.1 The Social Organisation of Carbon

Mapping relationships between installations and the companies that ultimately own them reveals that a relatively small number of corporate and state actors are responsible for a relatively large share of emissions. Using a 50.01 per cent ownership path, which follows ownership through parent companies that own more than half of the shares in their subsidiaries until the ultimate owner is reached, there are 3,587 ultimate owners in the database of companies. Of these ultimate owners, just five (0.1 per cent of ultimate owners) were responsible for over a quarter of emissions, twenty (0.6 per cent) were responsible for more than half of emissions, and seventy-five (2 per cent) were responsible for more than three-quarters of emissions. Conversely, the bottom 3,512 ultimate owners (98 per cent) were responsible for 23 per cent of emissions. This too is heavily skewed to ultimate owners within the top 1,000; the bottom 2,587 ultimate owners (72 per cent) were responsible for just 2 per cent of 2005–12 verified emissions. Figure 1.1 breaks down these results so that each segment

---

[1] Three sources of installation data from EU authorities were matched in the following order. See Bryant (2016 pp. 309–10) for further details:

- Company identification numbers from the list of stationary (i.e. non-aviation) installations (European Commission 2014h).
- 'Operator' (company that controls the installation) information in 2008-12 National Allocation Plan (NAP) tables (European Commission 2014k).
- Operator holding account information, used for trading carbon allowances and credits, in the European Union Transaction Log (EUTL) (European Commission 2014e).

[2] Ultimate ownership of EU installations is constantly in motion. Most importantly for this analysis, E.ON separated its fossil fuel operations into a new company, Uniper, in 2016, and sold its stake to Fortum, in 2018. In March 2018, E.ON announced it would transfer its renewable generation assets to RWE, while taking control of RWE's Innogy as a grid and retail-focused company. GDF Suez also rebranded as ENGIE in 2015 (Storbeck 2018). The analysis in this book uses ownership information current at the Orbis export date of 16 July 2014, which is closer to the main period of EU ETS operation being studied (2005–12), unless otherwise stated.

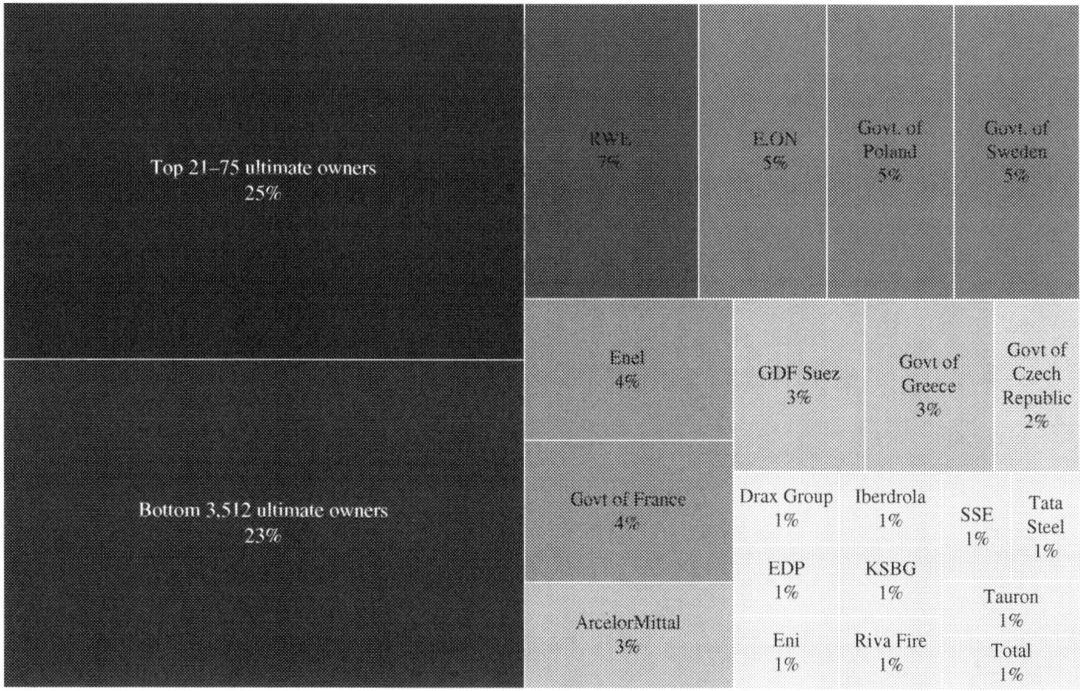

Fig. 1.1.   Proportion of emissions by ultimate owner (2005–12)
Sources: Own calculation using Bureau van Dijk (2014) and European Commission (2014b, 2014e, 2014h, 2014k)

1.3 Mapping the Appropriation of Carbon in the EU ETS

Table 1.1. *Top 20 polluting ultimate owners (2005–12)*

No.	Ultimate owner	2005–12 emissions (Mt CO$_2$-e)	Percentage 2005–12 emissions (%)	Main emissions sector
1	RWE	1,053	7	Electricity
2	E.ON	768	5	Electricity
3	Government of Sweden	742	5	Electricity
4	Government of Poland	674	5	Electricity
5	Enel	669	4	Electricity
6	Government of France	527	4	Electricity
7	ArcelorMittal	488	3	Iron and steel
8	GDF Suez	442	3	Electricity
9	Government of Greece	399	3	Electricity
10	Government of the Czech Republic	290	2	Electricity
11	Iberdrola	208	1	Electricity
12	Tauron Polska Energia	189	1	Electricity
13	Eni	188	1	Electricity
14	Tata Steel	186	1	Iron and steel
15	KSBG	180	1	Electricity
16	Drax Group	174	1	Electricity
17	SSE	170	1	Electricity
18	Total	168	1	Oil refining
19	EDP – Energias de Portugal	157	1	Electricity
20	Riva Fire	152	1	Iron and steel

Sources: Own calculation using Bureau van Dijk (2014) and European Commission (2014b, 2014e, 2014h, 2014k)

represents the proportion of emissions produced by the top 20 individual polluters, representing about half of emissions, on the right-hand side, and the remaining polluters, split into two groups of ultimate owners, each representing about a quarter of emissions, on the left-hand side. This illustrates the clustering of emissions among the top ultimate owners and comparatively low emissions from the vast number of ultimate owners.

Due to their disproportionate contribution to climate change, the top 20 EU ETS polluters are a major point of focus in the following chapters. Table 1.1 provides a list of the corporations and governments that made up the top 20 polluters in order of the magnitude of EU ETS emissions historically attributable to the installations they owned in the database of companies. Combined, these top 20 polluters were responsible for 52 per cent of 2005–12 emissions in the EU ETS. German energy company RWE tops the list by alone accounting for 7 per cent of 2005–12 emissions released in the

36 *Conceptualising Carbon*

EU ETS database of companies. All 20 top polluting ultimate owners account for at least 1 per cent of 2005–12 emissions. Sixteen out of the top twenty ultimate owners released their highest share of emissions from installations in the electricity sector, with the remainder in manufacturing: three in iron and steel production and one in oil refining. The uneven distribution of emissions by ultimate ownership reflects the socially concentrated and centralised structure of capital in these industries, which are dominated by relatively small numbers of large corporations (Domanico 2007 pp. 5067–8; Ecorys 2008 p. 23; European Commission 2010c pp. 35–6). Thus, in a climate-changing capitalism, greenhouse gas emissions are produced by capital 'in its own image' through the social concentration and centralisation of carbon (Smith 2008 p. 83).

1.3.2 The Spatial Organisation of Carbon

The uneven distribution of emissions according to ultimate owner is directly related to the number of installations they own and the size of those installations. Installations are greenhouse gas-emitting individual sites of production, such as power plants and factories, regulated by the EU ETS. Mapping the distribution of emissions between installations represents a second dimension of the uneven socio-spatial organisation of carbon appropriation. The top twenty ultimate owners were, in part, significant polluters because they owned a large number of individual installations. They represent less than 1 per cent of ultimate owners, but owned 14 per cent of installations. More significant is ownership of individual installations that release a large amount of carbon emissions in their own right. For example, Drax Group, the sixteenth largest polluter in the EU ETS, which was alone responsible for 1 per cent of all emissions in the database of companies, is the ultimate owner of a single power plant, fuelled by coal in the period being studied: the 4,000 MW Drax power station in North Yorkshire, England.[3]

The distribution of emissions in the EU ETS between greater and lesser polluting installations can be mapped using the European Environment Agency's (2014b p. 18) five installation sizes, based on the largest quantity of CO_2-e released in any one regulated year: zero (0 Kt), mini (0–25 Kt), small (25–50 Kt), medium (50–500 Kt), and large (500 Kt or more). Once again, the distribution of emissions is highly uneven between the large proportion of installations that release relatively low amounts of emissions and the small

---

[3] Drax began converting a number of its generators to woodchip-fired biomass units from 2013, supported by UK government renewable energy policy (Drax Group 2014).

proportion of installations that release significant amounts of carbon pollution. The vast majority of installations – 7,718, representing 71 per cent of installations – were zero, mini, or small in size. However, they were responsible for only 4 per cent of emissions. Conversely, 939 large installations, representing only 9 per cent of installations, were responsible for the vast majority of carbon emissions at 83 per cent. Figure 1.2 compares the proportion of installations with the proportion of emissions for each installation size to illustrate the disparities between different polluting units according to scale of emissions they release.

The zero-mini-small-medium-large breakdown of installation size conceals the high proportion of emissions that result from a smaller number of very large installations within the large category. Some installations were responsible for many times the 500 Kt of CO_2-e per year that is emitted by the smallest installations within the large category. For example, the most polluting installation, the state-owned 5,400 MW coal-fired Bełchatów Power Station in Łódź Province, Poland, released up to 35,000 Kt of CO_2-e per year, and was responsible for close to 2 per cent of EU ETS emissions in the first two phases (PGE Group 2015). Indeed, there were 83 very large installations which emitted more than 5,000 Kt CO_2-e per year, ten times greater than the smallest polluting installations within the large category. They accounted for less than 1 per cent of total installations but were responsible for more than one-third of total emissions in the database of companies. Sixty-seven (81 per cent) were fossil fuel-fired electricity generators, while fourteen (17 per cent) manufactured steel and two (2 per cent) were involved in refining oil.

The presence of the same sectors in the most polluting installations as the most polluting companies reflects a close connection between the social and spatial concentration and centralisation of capital in carbon-intensive industries. Indeed, in the electricity industry, the centralisation of control over operations within large, vertically integrated corporations often co-evolved with centralisation of generating capacity (Bridge et al. 2013 pp. 336–7). Centralised generation models are based on small numbers of large-scale power plants, often co-located around coal mining regions (where the spatial intensity of fossil energy extends to the subterranean level (see Huber & McCarthy 2017)), and connected by high-voltage transmission wires that carry electricity long distances for distribution to end-users. Despite increases in renewables, electricity generation in the EU remains heavily reliant on fossil fuels largely organised through a centralised model. In 2015, 48 per cent of generation came from coal, gas and oil (Eurostat 2017). The organisation of capital in large-scale power stations is an expression of the material properties of fossil fuels in delivering labour productivity improvements by increasing the

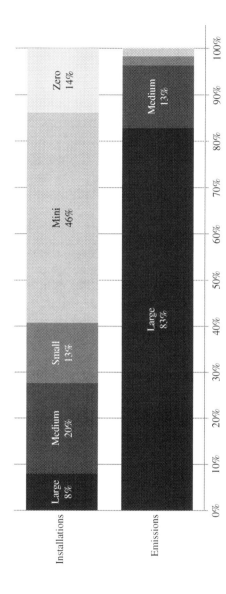

Fig. 1.2. Proportion of installations and emissions by installation size (2005–12)
Sources: Own calculation using Bureau van Dijk (2014) and European Commission (2014b, 2014e, 2014h, 2014k)

scales of production. The spatial concentration and centralisation of capital therefore occurs through a spatial concentration and centralisation of carbon.

1.3.3 States and the Socio-Spatial Organisation of Carbon

Both the most polluting ultimate owners and installations have a significant presence of states. Five out of the top ten highest emitting ultimate owners are nation states (in order, the governments of: Sweden, Poland, France, Greece, and the Czech Republic). Out of the eighty-three very large polluting installations, twenty-six were majority-owned by states. Aggregating emissions according to the ultimate owner type reveals a high degree of state ownership across the EU ETS. At a 50.01 per cent ownership path, 26 per cent of EU ETS emissions were directly controlled by states at the national, regional, or local level. Most of this came from the particularly large state-owned, coal-dependent power companies in the top twenty polluting ultimate owners. By this measure, states were the second most significant ultimate owning organisation type behind conventional, publicly listed, industrial companies.

However, the 50.01 per cent ultimate ownership path underestimates the extent of state control over emissions through direct ownership. While the measure is a necessarily conservative estimate of a controlling stake for the distribution of emissions between all ultimate owners in the EU ETS, states do not always operate like regular shareholders, particularly in formerly majority state-owned enterprises. Partial or even full privatisation often does not result in a relinquishing of government control due to special provisions for states, such as special voting rights (Bortolotti & Faccio 2009). Such rights may require government authorisation of, or limits to, private shareholders as well as the potential to shape or block management decisions through veto power or permanent representation on boards (European Commission 2005 pp. 5–6). Indeed, both GDF Suez and Enel were privatised in a way that granted their former state owners special powers to retain certain forms of control over their operation (Enel 2014 p.4; GDF Suez 2014 p.3).

Using a 25.01 per cent largest ultimate owner rule therefore better captures the extent of government control over emissions for some companies, whether it is being exercised, or could be exercised. It still misses other ways in which governments leverage minority ownership levels below 25.01 per cent, such as through single golden shares. Conversely, even if a greater than 25.01 and less than 50.01 per cent state ownership level does not come with any special provisions, it nonetheless constitutes a significant and potentially controlling stake depending on the relative equity of other shareholders. At this lower path, 40 per cent of emissions were from installations that were ultimately owned by states, fractionally less than emissions from industrial companies,

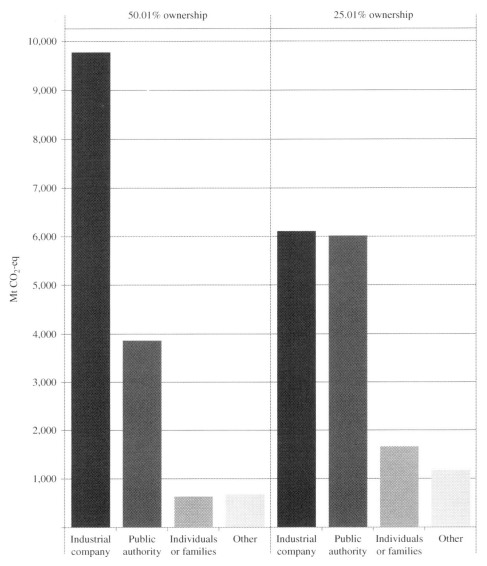

Fig. 1.3. Emissions by company type (2005–12)
Sources: Own calculation using Bureau van Dijk (2014) and European Commission (2014b, 2014e, 2014h, 2014k)

which controlled 41 per cent of emissions. This includes emissions from four other top twenty ultimate owners – GDF Suez (France), Tauron (Poland), Enel and Eni (both Italy) – that have minority state ownership at levels above 25.01 per cent, and a total of forty-seven of the eighty-three very large installations, all of which are fossil fuel-fired power stations. Figure 1.3 compares emissions by company type at both 50.01 and 25.01 per cent ownership thresholds to illustrate the share of emissions between industrial companies, public authorities, individuals or families and other less prominent types.[4] Direct public ownership is, of course, just one way that states organise the appropriation of carbon unevenly, with the privatisation of formerly state-owned assets and the regulation of mergers and acquisitions through competition policy being other, significant, factors (Bryant 2016).

Conclusion

The socio-spatial concentration and centralisation of carbon in the EU ETS demonstrates the need to place analysis of carbon markets within a climate-changing capitalism. In contrast to the externalising and universalising impulses of dominant economic discourses, it signals that climate change is internally, and unevenly, produced by capitalism. The uneven organisation of carbon appropriation matters, in turn, for analysing the socio-ecological efficacy of carbon markets. The EU ETS is constituted by many actors that have made marginal contributions to climate change, and a few actors that have made, and continue to make, a significant contribution to the problem. Thus, drawing on the empirical foundation of the database of companies, the next two chapters focus on the impact of the EU ETS and its links with offsetting mechanisms on the patterns of appropriation by the large-scale polluting installations and major polluting corporations that disproportionally transform the climate.

Conceptually, the focus on relations of carbon appropriation in this chapter is a necessary step to evaluating the evolution and outcomes of carbon markets in the following chapters. Bridge (2011 p. 822) argues that critical perspectives on the 'carbon economy' have been too narrowly focused on the trading of carbon dioxide-equivalent in carbon markets, and states:

Limiting the label 'carbon' to this downstream portion is unnecessarily restrictive. There is an 'actually existing' carbon economy that extends backwards from the point of greenhouse gas emissions all the way upstream to the site of fossil fuel extraction … It is desirable, therefore, to extend the idiom 'carbon' beyond its conventional association with greenhouse gases to examine the installation and maintenance of contemporary fossil-fuel intensive forms of social life, and the cultural and political forms to which they give rise.

---

[4] 'Other' includes insurance companies, financial companies, banks, foundations, mutual and pension funds, trusts, private equity firms, and employee-owned companies, which each individually control a relatively insignificant level of emissions.

This chapter has begun to conceptualise the different meanings and sites of carbon in terms of the capitalist relations with, and within nature, they represent. The starting point has been the actors, institutions, and relations that organise the appropriation of carbon to support the expanded accumulation of capital in fossil fuel industries. The next two chapters extend this conceptualisation by examining how the appropriation of carbon is represented, and potentially reconfigured, by the commodification of carbon in the EU ETS and its links with the Kyoto mechanisms.

2

Internalising Carbon

Introduction

The socio-spatial inequalities that characterise the EU ETS, discussed in the previous chapter, represent just part of a wider set of inequalities underpinning climate change. The relationship between inequality and climate change has been most extensively studied with reference to the disproportionate costs of climate change faced by communities in poorer regions (e.g. Hsiang et al. 2017; Lobell et al. 2008). Similarly, studies of the origins of greenhouse gas emissions have tended to focus on the disproportionate responsibility of wealthier individuals leading high-consumption lifestyles (e.g. Chancel & Piketty 2015; Gore 2015). All these dimensions of inequality are elided by the dominant economic framing of climate change, which displaces attention from inequalities in the production of climate change and imposes principles of market equality in its preferred solution to the problem.

This chapter and Chapter 3 examine the first contradiction of carbon markets in a climate-changing capitalism. This is the contradiction between the substantively unequal relations of carbon appropriation that underpin the climate change problem and the formally equal relations of carbon commodification that structure the carbon market solution. Conceptually, the focus is on the relationship between the appropriation and commodification of carbon, as the next step to developing an understanding of the commodification of nature as a mediator of internal relations between accumulation by appropriation and accumulation by capitalisation. This chapter focuses on the processes of carbon commodification and trading that are *internal* to the boundaries of the EU ETS, while the next focuses on the *external,* but linked, Kyoto mechanisms of the CDM and JI. Combined, these chapters evaluate the efficacy of carbon markets in addressing climate change as a socio-ecological crisis.

44 *Internalising Carbon*

The first section provides an account of the development of the EU ETS in terms of debates and decisions over the scope of carbon commodification. Representations by key government, industry, and NGO actors at national, EU, and international levels show that the design of the EU ETS was the product of contestation that was heavily shaped by the view that a formally equal carbon market would 'level the playing field'. The second section analyses precisely how the regulatory basis of the EU ETS works to represent unequal relations of carbon appropriation in commodity form. It reveals processes of commodification that excavate variegated relationships between certain 'installations' and 'emissions' and equalise differences between them. The third section presents a case study of the trading strategy of the biggest polluting corporation in the EU ETS, and the greatest buyer of allowances: multinational German energy utility RWE. By reconstructing the carbon allowance flows between RWE's most polluting coal-fired power station and other installations, the section illustrates how abstractions in carbon commodities create the potential for polluters to exploit inequalities in carbon commodities, and thus trade less for more effective forms of climate action. The distinctive understanding of carbon commodification in this chapter and the next provides a basis to evaluate the socio-ecological efficacy of carbon markets, not in terms of the cost-efficiency of emissions reductions, but by considering whether and how the EU ETS affects the unequal organisation of carbon appropriation.

2.1 The Development of the EU ETS

The formal development of the EU ETS began with an initial proposal by the European Commission's (the Commission) Directorate-General for the Environment in 1999 and a subsequent Green Paper in 2000. The scheme was officially drafted as a Directive in 2001, which was finally agreed on by the European Parliament (the Parliament) and Council of the European Union (the Council) in 2003 (Bailey 2010; Braun 2009; Wettestad 2005 pp. 4–8). This legislative process was shaped by international, EU, and national contexts and contestation by government, industry, and NGO actors. It delivered a European carbon market over alternative policy approaches and a policy design favouring free allocation and wide sectoral coverage. The interplay between policy choice and policy design reflects what Bailey and Maresh (2009) refer to as the competing 'regulatory' and 'territorial' logics of emissions trading. From this perspective, the regulatory logic of cost-efficiency advantages emissions trading as a choice of policy, while the design of a scheme is determined by a territorial logic where actors aim to defend their own interests within the policy framework. These

2.1 The Development of the EU ETS

competing logics were folded into a winning political argument advanced by corporate and state actors, despite challenges from some climate advocates, to create a policy that would ostensibly 'level the playing field'.

2.1.1 *International, EU, and National Contexts*

Developments in UN climate negotiations, where European support for an international climate framework outweighed initial opposition to market mechanisms, created the international context for a European carbon market. As discussed in more detail in Chapter 3, European negotiators originally opposed US proposals for market mechanisms at the 1997 UN climate conference in Kyoto, before acquiescing to international carbon trading and offsetting mechanisms in order to get an agreement (Christiansen & Wettestad 2003; Damro & Luaces Méndez 2003). The inclusion of flexible mechanisms in the Kyoto Protocol's emissions reduction framework was an important step towards the adoption of a market-based framework in the EU. Despite initial doubts about the market-based approach by European governments, an EU-level carbon market was consistent with the main goals of European negotiators at Kyoto: meeting binding targets, safeguarding the Internal Market project and taking a leading role in international climate policy (Damro & Luaces Méndez 2003 pp. 88–90). EU opposition to emissions trading turned out to be less strong than it first appeared when European governments recognised the synergies between the instrument and the burden sharing arrangements used to distribute responsibility for meeting Kyoto targets between EU countries (Newell & Paterson 2010 p. 100). Finally, once President George W. Bush announced the withdrawal of the United States from the Kyoto process in 2001, European countries that were most opposed to the market-based approach were given political space to throw their support behind emissions trading, justified on the basis that it was necessary to ensure the viability of the Kyoto Protocol, which required a minimum share of world emissions to come into force (Skjærseth & Wettestad 2009 pp. 112–13).

At the EU level, the EU ETS was adopted following a period of stagnation in the implementation of climate policy. From the early 1990s, proposals for energy and carbon taxes were continually frustrated by lack of agreement among member governments. The institutional structure of the EU gave proposals for emissions trading an advantage over taxation. Firstly, fiscal matters, such as taxation, require unanimity from member states in the Council, whereas environmental matters, such as emissions trading, go through the ordinary legislative procedure of qualified majority support from the Council and Parliament (European Union 2012b Article 192). Wettestad (2005 pp. 17–18) argues that while the procedure for taxation empowered states opposed to the measure to block consensus, the procedure for emissions trading forced them to engage constructively in the policy process with a view to extracting concessions, because they could find themselves in a minority position and unable to prevent the passage of the legislation.

Secondly, the Commission is the sole EU institution that can propose legislation (European Union 2012a Article 17). This placed a market-oriented bureaucracy at the centre of the legislative process. The Commission indeed played an influential role in driving and managing the entire progression of the EU ETS into legislation (Wettestad 2005 pp. 11–15). Its Green Paper set the terms of the debate by drawing heavily on economic arguments on the efficiency of carbon markets in achieving emissions reductions at lowest cost. For example, the paper included economic modelling that estimated the costs of meeting emissions targets at €9 billion annually by 2010 without an emissions trading scheme, compared with €6 billion per year with an emissions trading scheme covering all major sectors (European Commission 2000a pp. 27–8). Politically, the Commission set out to build a coalition in favour of emissions trading by convening a working group on flexibility mechanisms involving representatives of different Directorates-General of the Commission, national governments, industry groups and environmental organisations, as well as holding a series of broader stakeholder meetings (European Commission 2000b, 2001a).

At the member state level, events in the United Kingdom provided some early impetus towards the EU ETS. As outlined in the Introduction, in the late 1990s, two of the world's largest fossil fuel companies, BP and Shell, instituted internal carbon trading systems, which was followed by a limited and voluntary domestic emissions trading system in the United Kingdom that commenced in 2002 (Betsill & Hoffmann 2011 p. 93). BP's initiative was motivated by opposition to taxation and direct regulation-based climate policies and was intended to demonstrate the viability of market-based schemes as an alternative to those options (Victor & House 2006 p. 2101). The UK scheme developed out of a proposal from the Emissions Trading Group, formed by BP and made up of oil and gas producers, power companies, and energy-intensive manufactures (Bailey & Rupp 2004 p. 242; Nye & Owens 2008 pp. 5–6). Again, the polluting companies were motivated by opposition to taxation and other regulatory measures, initially the Climate Change Levy, but more importantly, according to Nye and Owens (2008 p. 10), to the threat of more onerous future policies needed to meet national emissions targets (see also Paterson 2012 pp. 84–5). The development of the UK scheme hastened the formation of a pro-carbon market coalition of industry at the EU-level and placed pressure on EU institutions to develop a European carbon trading scheme to avoid the development of nationally fragmented climate policies (Christiansen & Wettestad 2003 p. 7; Meckling 2011 p. 111; Voß 2007 p. 337).

2.1.2 Government, Industry, and NGO Positions

These international, European and national level contextual factors provided supportive conditions for a convergence of governments, industry groups, and environmental organisations over support for an EU ETS in general. Within this overall consensus, debate continued over design details such as whether emissions caps would be absolute or relative, whether trading would occur at the installation or member state level and whether emissions liabilities would be incurred upstream or downstream (i.e., point of extraction or pollution) and directly or indirectly (i.e., point of commodity production or consumption). Ultimately, a consensus around a downstream scheme with absolute caps covering the direct emissions of installations emerged. Debates over the coverage of the scheme and the allocation of allowances were more drawn out.

Governments and companies with prior domestic experience in emissions trading were initially the strongest advocates for an EU ETS. However, support remained cooler from other governments and companies that preferred voluntary approaches. Initial negotiations were led by the governments of the United Kingdom and Denmark, which were setting up national level schemes, along with the Netherlands, Sweden, and Ireland (Skjærseth & Wettestad 2008 pp. 88–91). They were joined by BP, Shell, UK electricity companies, and EDF as prominent proponents (Meckling 2011 p. 112). Meckling (2011 p. 104) argues that the pro-carbon trading coalition of industry and government that spread from the United Kingdom 'acted as Europe's backdoor for emissions trading'. They were met with resistance, in particular, from the German government, which initially opposed the idea because it would undermine its domestic system of voluntary climate agreements with industry (Skjærseth & Wettestad 2008 pp. 92–4). The preference for voluntary agreements reflected the position of most of German industry, especially the electricity and chemicals industries. Energy-intensive manufacturing industries across Europe also tended to oppose a mandatory scheme on competitiveness grounds, arguing that they would be forced to relocate production to countries without a carbon price (Meckling 2011 pp. 118–20).

Industry opponents of emissions trading were outmanoeuvred by the pro-carbon trading coalition. German power companies were sidelined within the European electricity industry association, EURELECTRIC, and manufacturers, such as the steel and chemical industries, were too fragmented in their campaigning (Meckling 2011 pp. 118–9). EURELECTRIC had begun to shift their support behind emissions trading as an alternative to taxation in the aftermath of Kyoto, conducting simulated emissions trading between its members in 1999 and 2000 to test different market designs to inform their lobbying (Cartel et al. 2017). The majority of electricity generators and oil and gas producers that were in favour of emissions trading were also joined by a rapidly forming carbon trading industry that added political and economic weight to the proposal. Between the signing of the Kyoto Protocol and the passing of the EU ETS Directive, large banks set up carbon trading desks and new boutique carbon trading firms emerged, a pro-carbon market industry organisation in the International Emissions Trading Association (IETA) was founded, and a number specialty trade conferences and service providers appeared (Newell & Paterson 2009 p. 89).

Environment groups started their engagement with the proposed carbon market from the oppositional stance they took on market mechanisms at Kyoto, arguing that such policies did not mandate sufficient climate action (Meckling 2011 p. 114). However, some of the most influential groups shifted their position to what Meckling (2011 p. 117) describes as 'quality managers' over the environmental effectiveness of emissions trading. This was particularly true of the World Wide Fund for Nature (WWF) and Climate Action Network (CAN) Europe, which were part of the Commission's working group. In the process, these two groups, along with Friends of the Earth Europe, which remained more hostile to carbon markets, aligned with clean industry groups from renewable energy and energy efficiency-based businesses to counter polluting industries by advocating for stringent rules for any emissions trading scheme alongside a suite of other climate policies (Bokhoven et al. 2001). The gradual shift towards cautious support for emissions trading is reflected in the following statement by CAN Europe, the umbrella group for the largest environmental organisations, released in the lead up to the debate on the EU ETS Directive in the Parliament:

NGOs are generally sceptical of a cap and trade system, as an instrument that is relatively untried on such a scale. However, in view of the wide nature of the emission cuts needed and the lack of other strong EU level policies for heavy industry sectors, most environmental groups have taken a cautiously positive view of this proposal. Yet, unless certain key features are agreed, this system will not be a credible element of the EU's domestic action strategy and NGOs will oppose it. (Climate Action Network Europe 2002)

The key features nominated by CAN Europe were threefold: the need for mandatory participation, that allowances should be auctioned rather than given away for free, and that there should be no international linkages with Kyoto mechanisms. International linkages are the focus of Chapter 3. The other two features were major points of contention.

Free allowance allocation was instituted as the norm for the opening years of the EU ETS. CAN Europe's advocacy against free allocation found some support from the Parliament, which proposed amendments for enhanced use of auctioning. Relatedly, the Parliament also favoured greater EU control over the quantity and distribution of allowances, rather than devolving the decision to national governments (Skjærseth & Wettestad 2008 p. 136). However, on both issues, Parliament was unable to withstand the weight of government and industry pressure in favour of a regime of free allocation, which was devolved to the member state level (Skjærseth & Wettestad 2009 p. 117). The positions of Parliament and CAN Europe were successful only in extracting some concessions. In the final Directive, member states had the option to auction a small number (5 per cent in phase one, 10 per cent in phase two) of allowances and the allocation plans of member states were subject to approval by the Commission on the basis of their consistency with Kyoto targets – a clause that subsequently resulted in protected disputes (Bailey 2007 pp. 436–9; Bailey & Maresh 2009 pp. 451–3; European Parliament and Council 2003 Article 10, Annex III).

CAN Europe was more successful in securing mandatory participation against the opposition of energy intensive industries and the German government. A voluntary scheme was a second best option for energy industries that, like the German government, were less enthusiastic about emissions trading, such as the chemicals industry, represented by CEFIC, and the steel industry, represented by EUROFER (Economist Intelligence Unit 2002; European Report 2002; Markussen & Svendsen 2005). The Commission and Council pushed for the exclusion of the chemicals sector, despite the opposition from Parliament and NGOs, in order to quell overall German industry opposition to emissions trading that had been led by the German Chemical Industry Association (VCI) (Skjærseth & Wettestad 2008 p. 124). The chemicals sector lobby was successful in achieving voluntary participation for most of its own members. Process emissions from chemicals manufacturing, as well as the aluminium sector, were excluded from the first two phases of the scheme. The steel industry, however, was included (European Commission 2015a p. 18).

2.1.3 Creating a 'Level Playing Field'

Debates over the design of the EU ETS occurred within a policy space that was dominated by the economic rationale for emissions trading. Following one of its stakeholder meetings, the Commission summarised that 'somewhat paradoxically, on allocation industry's main preoccupation was to preserve and enhance a "level playing field". This was notwithstanding that the voluntary approach advocated by many could make it harder to ensure this' (European Commission 2001a p. 3). What was paradoxical for the Commission represented a two-pronged strategy from industry actors that sought favourably differentiated treatment for themselves and, failing that, equal treatment for other actors. A close examination of the positions of industry shows that the economic logic of emissions trading was used to both support the policy model in general and to achieve territorial concessions in the interests of certain actors. In framing interventions in terms of the need to 'level the playing field', polluting actors actually revealed material interests in exploiting unequal climate relations.

Fossil fuel-intensive capital appealed to the economic rationale of efficiency to support their united preference for carbon trading over alternative climate policies. In its summary of submissions to the Green Paper, the Commission stated that energy and carbon taxation was 'widely opposed by industry' and that businesses argued they 'should be exempt from other policies and measures' in return for supporting emissions trading (European Commission 2001c pp. 1, 3). The position is captured by the submission of the European Round Table of Industrialists, which is made up of the CEOs of about fifty of the largest Europe-based multinational corporations. Among them, around the time of the submission, were (antecedents of) corporations in the top twenty EU ETS polluters, including Total, Iberdrola, E.ON, and GDF Suez (Apeldoorn 2000 pp. 162–3). The organisation asserted that:

Emissions trading should not be seen as supplemental to existing fiscal measures, or to regulation. To realise the benefits of trading it should be introduced as an alternative to other measures, ensuring that the signals to business are unambiguous. (European Round Table of Industrialists 2001 p. 2)

The reasons for this position were fleshed out in more detail by the Industrial Energy and Power Industry Association (VIK), representing German energy-intensive industry. While advocating for voluntary agreements, the organisation argued more vehemently against climate policy moving 'in the direction of dos and don'ts'. Thus, VIK expressed a preference for an emissions trading system where 'all considerations are subordinated to the primacy of reducing costs' (VIK, 2001 p. 6 (translation)). This reluctant support for carbon trading was part of a defensive strategy that aimed, if voluntary agreements could not be preserved, to avoid regulatory and taxation approaches. These approaches were opposed on that basis that they

2.1 The Development of the EU ETS

discriminate between industries and corporations by factoring in broader socio-ecological considerations, which would violate the goal of the 'level playing field'.

The preference for the free allocation of allowances based on historical emissions by industry was also supported by appealing to the formal equality of the market. The Commission noted that 'industry, with only very few exceptions, preferred grandfathering as a method of allocation' (European Commission 2001c p. 3). A central argument against auctioning was a concern for equal treatment between industries. For example, EURELECTRIC, the body representing the European electricity industry, framed its position on allocation in terms of 'maximising equity' between companies and 'avoid[ing] discrimination' between states (EURELECTRIC 2000 p. 6). It argued that the vast majority of allowances should be given away for free because 'an auctioning system applicable to all or a large portion of permits could, compared to grandfathering, redistribute costs in an unforeseeable way and risk causing severe economic dislocation' (EURELECTRIC 2000 p. 6). This concern with the redistribution of costs makes it clearer that demands for a 'level playing field' sought to preserve the status quo and therefore, the uneven organisation of emissions. By freely allocating allowances based on historical emissions levels, grandfathering rewards established polluting companies for their disproportionate responsibility for climate change.

Lastly, the regulatory logic of efficiency and equal treatment was mobilised to support arguments in favour of maximising the coverage of the carbon market. Industry consensus on the latter was communicated in the final report of the Commission's working group on flexibility mechanisms, which recommended that 'a trading system should be designed with a view to extending it to as many sectors, entities, and greenhouse gases as possible' (European Commission 2001b p. 5). Despite campaigning, partially successfully, for exemption of its own members, CEFIC maintained, using the regulatory logic of carbon trading, that the scope of the scheme should be as broad as possible. The representatives of the chemicals industry effectively argued that if their industry was required to participate, others should too, stating: 'the greater the number of participating companies the greater the scope for cost effective emissions reductions' (CEFIC 2001 p. 7). The steel industry, which was not granted voluntary participation, although would subsequently benefit from favourable levels of free allocation, explained that maximising the scope of the scheme was in the interests of participants because it maximised the potential to source allowances from other actors rather than reduce their own emissions. From the perspective of EUROFER, the inclusion of 'all relevant sectors, not only [heavy] industry' was necessary because with 'energy efficiency close to the theoretical limit' in the steel industry, emissions reductions were 'not possible' (EUROFER 2001 pp. 1–2).

Similarly, RWE and E.ON drew on the least cost regulatory logic of emissions trading to make it clear why maximising scope was necessary in economic terms. Their joint position advanced the 'principle of equality of treatment' by warning that 'by only selecting energy-intensive sectors with a *similar* amount of marginal abatement costs, the *heterogeneity* of the trading partners and, consequently, the scope of trading is reduced' (RWE and E.ON 2001 p. 2 emphasis added). Hence, maximising the scope of the carbon market was explicitly nominated as useful for large polluters because it increased the levels of differentiation in forms of carbon appropriation between regulated actors that could be exploited through trading. The political upshot of this position was made clear by the Federation of German Industries (BDI). While the organisation argued for a voluntary scheme, it also favoured maximum scope because 'only involving large-scale emitters in the [emissions trading] system throughout the Community would perpetuate the idea that industry is mainly responsible for emissions, apparently diminishing the responsibility of other groups in society' (BDI, 2001 p. 5). The next section turns to what, and how, unequal relations are represented in commodify form.

2.2 The Carbon Commodity

2.2.1 Commodifying Nature

Research on the commodification of carbon is part of a broader set of literature analysing the marketisation of environmental governance (Newell 2008; see for example Bumpus 2011; Descheneau 2012; Knox-Hayes 2013; Lohmann 2005, 2011b; Lövbrand & Stripple 2012; MacKenzie 2009a; Paterson & Stripple 2012; Stephan 2012; Cooper 2015). Key sites of investigation include efforts to marketise water supply and quality (Bakker 2003, 2005; Bieler 2015; Swyngedouw 2005), bank wetlands (Robertson 2000, 2004, 2006, 2007, 2012), rationalise trees and forests (Demeritt 2001a; Prudham 2003), patent genes and biotechnology (McAfee 2003; Prudham 2007), offset biodiversity, forest carbon and other ecosystem services (Collard & Dempsey 2013; McAfee 1999; Osborne 2015; Osborne & Shapiro-Garza 2018; Sullivan 2013), apply fishing quotas (Mansfield 2004; St Martin 2005), privatise nature through free trade agreements (McCarthy 2004), and license wildlife hunting (Robbins & Luginbuhl 2005), to name

2.2 The Carbon Commodity 53

just some examples. The insights in this literature have been synthesised directly, in terms of the commodification of nature (Castree 2003; Prudham 2009), and indirectly, as aspects of the neoliberalisation (Castree 2008a, 2008b; Heynen et al. 2007; Heynen & Robbins 2005; McCarthy & Prudham 2004), or privatisation (Mansfield 2008), of nature. Together, this work assists the development of an understanding of the carbon commodity that is grounded in capitalist relations with, and within, nature.

Three key processes of commodification, which Castree (2003) characterises as individuation, privatisation, and abstraction, are expressly involved in the representation of unequal relations of carbon appropriation as commodities in the EU ETS. The commodification of nature firstly requires boundary drawing to separate a relation or substance from its socio-ecological context and to objectify it as a distinct thing (Castree 2003 p. 280). This physical and/or representational *individuation* can be seen in efforts to commodify genes. McAfee (2003 p. 204) argues that patenting genes as 'discrete entities' is 'reductionist in that it treats nature and its components as quantifiable and as separable, at least conceptually, from their contexts in living nature and society'. Similarly, using the language of wetland banking practitioners, Robertson (2012 pp. 393–4) identifies processes of 'unbundling' particular ecosystem services from ecosystems as a whole. The denial of the complex socio-ecological, political, and economic production of things like engineered genes and wetland ecosystems is, according to Prudham (2007 p. 414), a 'necessary fiction' for private control over the commodities.

The relationship between commodification and *privatisation* is a second key concern (Castree 2003 p. 279). Bakker (2005 p. 543) uses the failures of water commodification following privatisation in England and Wales to argue that privatisation is distinct to commodification. The distinction is important and could be made for other commodification processes. For example, Demeritt (2001a) shows how processes of individuation 'enframe' forests for use in the statistical records of state resource managers. Privatisation (or individuation) should therefore not be completely reduced to commodification but instead considered as 'relational moments in specifically capitalist commodification' (Prudham 2007 p. 411). This becomes clearer when privatisation is defined not just in terms of the formal transfer of resources from state or community to private institutional ownership (e.g. Heynen & Robbins 2005 p. 6), but any instance of the 'creat[ion of] new objects of property' (Mansfield 2008 pp. 5–6). McCarthy (2004 p. 337) illustrates this dynamic in the case of free trade agreements. Such agreements have privatised nature not through the direct transfer of ownership, but by

54 *Internalising Carbon*

creating what is effectively a 'brand-new private property right for specific firms' by protecting corporations from any adverse environmental regulation that impinges on profits.

Third, commodities are produced for exchange, which requires a measure of equivalence that *abstracts* from the particular qualities of individuated and privatised goods and services (Castree 2003 p. 281; Prudham 2009 p. 125). While money serves this function for commodities in general, markets in environmental management require specific forms of commensuration between objects of regulation that meet specific regulatory goals. Efforts to reproduce the generalised commodity logic for specific environmental commodities have been extensively documented by Robertson in the case of wetlands banking. In these systems, individuated ecosystem services in one location are made commensurable with different ecosystem services in another through the abstraction of 'units of incremental ecological function' (Robertson 2004 p. 367). This '(scientific) abstraction to functional categories' and 'spatial abstraction of already-abstracted functional categories' is necessary to create a very specific form of regulatory equivalence that is germane to carbon trading: trading the degradation of one wetland for the restoration of another (Robertson 2000 p. 468).

2.2.2 The Installation–Emissions Relationship

In the European carbon market, states have underpinned the commodification of carbon by instituting regulations that separate, objectify and equalise uneven relations of carbon appropriation. A close look at the 2003 EU ETS Directive and subsequent amendments reveals that the object of commodification in the EU ETS is a *relationship* between 'installations' and 'emissions'.[1] The relational basis of carbon allowances is often underappreciated in critical accounts of carbon markets that identify the object of commodification as pollution or the atmosphere (e.g. Lohmann 2005 p. 204, 2011a p. 100).

The EU ETS Directive codifies the commodification of installation–emissions relationships in its definition of an EUA. An EUA is defined as 'an allowance to emit one tonne of carbon dioxide equivalent during a specified period'. It is therefore defined in terms of the process of 'emitting'. Emitting, in turn, is defined in relation to the 'installation' as 'the release of

---

[1] The following discussion, and the analysis throughout this book, is limited to 'stationary' installations, which excludes the aviation sector. Aviation was partially included in the EU ETS from 2012 for commercial intra-EU ETS flights. The sector exists under a different set of rules for allocation and surrender due to the particular circumstances arising from emissions from aircraft and the international context of the industry (European Commission 2015a pp. 89–91).

2.2 The Carbon Commodity

greenhouse gases into the atmosphere from sources in an installation' (European Parliament and Council 2014 Article 3). The forms of carbon appropriation commodified in carbon allowances are determined by the categories of 'installation' and 'emissions'. The EU ETS Directive defines non-aviation installations as 'stationary technical unit[s] where one or more activities listed in Annex I are carried out'. Emissions are measured in units of 'one metric tonne of carbon dioxide (CO_2) or an amount of any other greenhouse gas listed in Annex II with an equivalent global warming potential' (European Parliament and Council 2014 Article 3).

The state enforces the commodification of carbon as a representation of installation–emissions relationships through a permit system administered by national states. Permits grant operators of installations 'authorisation to emit greenhouse gases from all or part of an installation'. Permits also come with 'an obligation to surrender allowances ... equal to the total emissions of the installation in each calendar year' (European Parliament and Council 2014 Article 6). This is enforced by a requirement that states ensure 'no installation carries out any activity listed in Annex I [discussed below] resulting in emissions specified in relation to that activity unless its operator holds a permit' (European Parliament and Council 2014 Article 4). The commodification of carbon in the EU ETS therefore involves processes of both individuation and privatisation. It separates and objectifies installation–emissions relationships from the broader production and market processes in which they are embedded. This process of individuation is underpinned by a partial privatisation of the climate system that both secures and restricts access to carbon sinks for certain installations.

The two aspects of individuation – separation and objectification – underpin the advantages of emissions trading over direct regulation and taxation for the interests of carbon-intensive capital. Separating installation–emissions relationships from the contexts in which they are embedded negates regulation of contextual factors that embed carbon pollution. This was most clearly illustrated in amendments enacted as part of the EU ETS Directive to the Integrated Pollution Prevention and Control (IPPC) Directive, the then primary EU-wide regulatory tool for emissions. The amendments removed any absolute limits imposed by the IPPC on greenhouse gas emissions for installations regulated by the EU ETS (European Parliament and Council 2014 Article 26). This was necessary because absolute limits for individual installations make allowance trading impossible; the entire rationale of cap and trade systems is that some actors can increase their emissions provided they can purchase excess allowances from other actors within the overall cap. In the process, the amendments also displaced the regulation of factors other than an installation's emissions, such as technology standards, which the IPPC regulates with reference to

56 *Internalising Carbon*

industry best practice (European Parliament and Council 2008 Article 1). The objectification of the installation–emissions relationship as a commodified thing is what differentiates carbon trading from other forms of carbon pricing, such as taxation, for fossil fuel-intensive industry. The taxation of emissions also requires the separation of the relationship between installation (or similar entity) and emissions. But rather than imposing a charge on the relationship, as with taxation, the commodification of the relationship becomes something that can be privately controlled. This objectification underpins the potential to exploit the uneven appropriation of carbon because it makes free allocation and trading of allowances possible.

2.2.3 Equalising (Some) Difference

The act, and impacts, of carbon trading are structured by the forms of abstraction that define the relational substance of the carbon commodity. Not all relationships between polluters and pollution become installation–emissions relationships as represented in carbon commodities. A range of tools are used to delimit precisely what greenhouse gases, production processes, scales of pollution/production, location, and timescales are included in installation–emissions relationships. Each tool works to equalise different forms of carbon appropriation through types of functional, process, scalar, spatial, and temporal abstraction. At the same time, defining the scope of abstraction also excludes other forms of carbon appropriation from commodification. Table 2.1 summarises the processes of abstraction involved in the

Table 2.1. *EUA abstraction*

Question	Target	Scope	Tool	Type
What?	Greenhouse gas	CO_2, N_2O, PFCs, other opted-in	Global warming potential	Functional
How?	Production process	Primarily electricity and manufacturing sectors	List of 'activities'	Process
How much?	Installation size	No absolute minimum	Capacity and output thresholds/opt-out provisions	Scalar
Where?	Location	Member states of the EU plus Norway, Iceland, Lichtenstein	EU treaties	Spatial
When?	Timing	2005–7 (phase 1) 2008–onwards (phases 2, 3, etc.)	Banking and borrowing	Temporal

commodification of carbon in the EU ETS in terms of five questions on the nature of installation–emissions relationships that determine what falls inside and outside the carbon commodity. Each question – what?; how?; how much?; where?; when? – targets a different aspect of installation–emissions relationships and utilises different tools to define a different scope of commodification, representing a different type of abstraction.

The tool of 'global warming potential' (GWP) abstracts from *what* greenhouse gases are included in commodified installation–emission relationships. GWP makes the different greenhouse gases emitted from installations equivalent by comparing their contribution to climate change over a certain period. The attempt to measure greenhouse gases in terms of their climate impacts makes GWP a form of functional abstraction. The tool has a scientific and political history that is prior to the direct history of carbon markets. The notion of GWP was developed by scientists, primarily working within the Intergovernmental Panel on Climate Change (IPCC), in response to the need for a single measure of climate impact that could structure both climate models and global climate agreements (Paterson & Stripple 2012 p. 571). Its use in these areas, and in carbon markets, has also been criticised for the significant uncertainties, the arbitrariness of the 100-year time period commonly used, the reductionism of measuring climate impacts in terms of 'radiative forcing' alone, and erasing the history of cumulative emissions (Demeritt 2001b pp. 316–17; Frame 2011 p. 142; MacKenzie 2009a p. 446).

Despite calls from industry for all six Kyoto Protocol greenhouse gases to be included, for largely practical reasons the EU ETS was limited to carbon dioxide in the first phase (European Parliament and Council 2014 Annex I). From 2008, states could also opt-in other gases, which was taken up for N_2O by the Netherlands, Italy, United Kingdom, Austria, and Norway in phase two (European Commission 2015c; European Parliament and Council 2014 Article 24). The original Directive also declared an intention to include further gases and this was realised from phase three, with amendments that mandatorily included N_2O from the chemicals sector and PFCs from the aluminium sector (European Parliament and Council 2014 Annex I). GWPs provide a means to commensurate, and thus equalise, different quantities of these different greenhouse gases. EU ETS regulations assign 100-year GWPs that make 1 tonne of N_2O, or 1 tonne of the two relevant PFCs, tetrafluoromethane and hexafluoroethane, equal to 298, 7,390, and 12,200 tonnes of CO_2, respectively (European Commission 2014c). Extensive critical attention has been given to the commensuration of different greenhouse gases (e.g. MacKenzie 2009a). However, the relatively limited scope of gases regulated by the EU ETS makes other types of abstraction, on the installation side of the commodified installation–emissions relationship, more significant.

The list of activities in Annex I of the EU ETS Directive is the tool that abstracts from *how* different production processes constitute installation–emissions relationships. In the first phase, this tool set the scope of process abstraction to include combustion, oil refining, coke oven baking, metal ore roasting and sintering, steel production, cement production, glass manufacturing, ceramic firing, and pulp, paper, and board production. As flagged above, while originally excluded, various activities from the chemicals and aluminium sectors along with carbon capture and storage, were ultimately included from 2013, but other production processes such as transport remained excluded, to make a total of twenty-five stationary activities (European Parliament and Council 2014 Annex I). The shares of EU ETS emissions between activities indicates that different production processes also appropriate carbon in highly uneven ways. For the EU ETS as a whole, 73 per cent of 2005–12 emissions were from combustion installations, 21 per cent were from cement, oil refining, and iron and steel installations, while the other activities, plus other opted-in installations, accounted for just 5 per cent of emissions. A sectoral breakdown reveals that combustion installations are dominated by electricity and gas supply installations, which accounted for 65 per cent of emissions.

The installation sizes captured within EUAs are determined by capacity and production thresholds as well as limited opt-out provisions, which set the scope of scalar abstraction for *how much* pollution is released in relationships between installations and emissions. For combustion installations, a capacity threshold is set at 20 MW of installed capacity, which was an increase in the scope of the scheme from the Commission's original proposal for 50 MW (European Commission 2000a p. 14). Thresholds for other activities are expressed in terms of production output. For example, for steel installations, the threshold is set above 2.5 tonnes of production per hour. Other activities, such as mineral oil refining, have no thresholds at all (European Parliament and Council 2014 Annex I). The amended Directive also allows states to opt-out installations emitting less than 25 Kt of CO_2-e per year (European Parliament and Council 2014 Article 27). As shown in Chapter 1, the majority of installations release less than 25 Kt of CO_2-e per year, indicating opt-out provisions have not been utilised in many cases. The prevalence of 'mini' installations suggests the tools of capacity and output thresholds produce a high level of scalar abstraction. This is evident when different levels of installed capacity in combustion installations are compared. The 20 MW threshold is 0.3 per cent as large as the of 5,400 MW

2.2 The Carbon Commodity

installed capacity of the Bełchatów power plant, the largest polluting installation in the EU ETS (PGE Group 2015).

The location *where* commodified installation–emissions relationships occur is a product of the broader political economy of European integration and expansion, rather than particular struggles over the coverage of the EU ETS (see Bieler & Morton 2001; Bonefeld 2001). All EU member states are automatically part of the EU ETS, while Iceland, Norway, and Lichtenstein joined in phase two through their membership of the European Economic Area. The tool of spatial abstraction is the EU ETS Directive requirement that states ensure 'allowances issued by a competent authority of another Member State are recognised for the purpose ... of meeting an operator's obligations', which is backed up by EU law that makes Directives binding on member states (European Parliament and Council 2014 Article 12; European Union 2012b Article 288). The geographical scope of the EU ETS expanded significantly as a result of the accession to the EU of new member states, mostly in Central and Eastern Europe, from 2004. This added some countries with both high absolute emissions, such as Poland (the fourth highest in the EU) and high per capita emissions, such as Estonia (the second highest in the EU). Overall, however, new EU members are mostly below average in terms of both absolute and per capita emissions (European Environment Agency 2015a). Thus, the differentiation in absolute and per capita emissions between states equalised in the carbon commodity was also increased with the accession of new member states. The Brexit vote in 2016 created uncertainty over whether the United Kingdom would leave the EU ETS, thus reducing the geographical scope of the scheme for the first time, or continue participating on a similar basis as other non-EU states (Tol 2018).

Lastly, banking and borrowing provisions in the Directive are tools for temporally abstracting from *when* installation–emissions relationships occur. The tools allow operators of installations to keep current allowances for future use and draw on future allowances for current use. The latter is possible because allowances are allocated each year before the deadline for surrendering allowances for the previous year's emissions, which means operators of installations have the next year's allocation in their possession at compliance time (European Parliament and Council 2014 Articles 11 and 12). Despite industry calls for maximum flexibility, banking and borrowing were restricted in phase one to years within that phase (2005–7) (European Parliament and Council 2003 Article 13). From phase two, banking and borrowing was extended by amendments that require unused allowances to be reissued in each new phase, thus indefinitely extending the effective eligibility of allowances for surrender in future years and phases (European

60 *Internalising Carbon*

Commission 2014i Article 13). Increasingly, therefore, the carbon commodity has made installation–emissions relationships in one-year equivalent to installation–emissions relationships in other years. Yet, year-to-year, the conditions determining emissions levels also differ. The clearest example of this was in the depths of the economic crisis in 2009, when controlled for new entrants, EU ETS emissions fell 11 per cent from 2008 levels (European Environment Agency 2015a). Each of these types of abstraction have been put to use through the trading of carbon allowances by RWE.

2.3 Trading Carbon Allowances

2.3.1 *RWE's Trading Strategy*

Equipped with an understanding of the socio-ecological relations represented within carbon commodities, this section presents a case study of the trading practices of German energy utility RWE to investigate how carbon markets reorganise the appropriation of carbon. RWE is a useful case study because it is the ultimate owner with both the highest 2005–12 verified emissions and the largest allowance allocation deficit. This makes RWE the company that made the largest contribution to climate change in the EU ETS, and the company whose response to climate change has been most mediated through the carbon market.

RWE's large share of emissions was fashioned through a series of takeovers of other energy utilities based in Germany and other parts of Europe (Bryant 2016). Between 2005 and 2012, RWE owned polluting EU ETS installations in Germany, Belgium, the Czech Republic, the United Kingdom, Hungary, the Netherlands, and Poland, with 71 per cent of its EU ETS emissions coming from its home country. RWE also owned four of the ten most polluting installations, all of which are in Germany, including the 2,800 MW Niederaussem power plant, in Bergheim, North Rhine-Westphalia, first commissioned in 1963, and second largest polluting installation in the EU ETS between 2005 and 2012 (RWE 2014b).

RWE shares common characteristics with most of the other ultimate owners with the ten largest allowance deficits, which are listed in Table 2.2. Like RWE, nine out of ten ultimate owners primarily polluted in the electricity and gas sector, and eight out of ten are in the top twenty overall polluters. The deficits for eight out of ten companies, including RWE, represented less than half, and in most cases much less, of their total allocations, indicating that free allowance allocations covered the vast majority of emissions for even the biggest deficit holders.

2.3 Trading Carbon Allowances 61

Table 2.2. *Top 10 2005–12 allowance deficits by ultimate owner*

Ultimate owner	EU ETS polluter ranking	Sector	2005–12 allowance deficit (Mt CO$_2$-e)	Deficit as percentage of 2005–12 allocation (%)
RWE	1	Electricity	237	29
Government of Sweden	3	Electricity	159	27
E.ON	2	Electricity	112	17
Enel	5	Electricity	91	16
Drax Group	16	Electricity	83	91
GDF Suez	8	Electricity	58	15
Government of Norway	43	Mining	43	168
Government of France	6	Electricity	42	9
Iberdrola	11	Electricity	41	24
Gas Natural	26	Electricity	37	49

Sources: Own calculation using Bureau van Dijk (2014) and European Commission (2014b, 2014e, 2014h, 2014k)

RWE's overall deficit of 237 Mt CO$_2$-e represented just over a quarter of its overall allocation. All deficit companies have three options for compliance: (1) bidding for allowances in open auctions, (2) sourcing offset credits from CDM and JI projects, or (3) purchasing allowances from other privately and publicly owned corporations regulated by the EU ETS. As noted above, auctioning was limited to 5 and 10 per cent of allowances in the first two phases of the EU ETS, respectively. In practice, states only reserved 0.13 and 3 per cent of allowances for auction in their phase one and two national allocation plans, which limited the potential of the first option for the period being studied (Ellerman et al. 2010 p. 62). The second option, the sourcing of carbon credits from the CDM and JI, is the focus of Chapter 3. This section focuses on the third option, which was the method primarily used by RWE to meet the gap between its free allocation and verified emissions. In total RWE covered 212 Mt CO$_2$-e of pollution above its allocation, representing 89 per cent of its allowance deficit, by surrendering EUAs. This was the most EUAs surrendered by any ultimate owner in excess of their free allocation, which means a case study of RWE also provides the most empirical scope to explore trading activity that is internal to the EU ETS.

The European Union Transaction Log (EUTL) makes it possible to follow the physical trading (i.e., actual transfers of carbon commodities) of carbon allowances and offset credits (European Commission 2014e). The EUTL logs trades between a range of account types including accounts linked to installations for the purposes of receiving allocations and surrendering

62   *Internalising Carbon*

Table 2.3. *Trades logged in EUTL by account type, 1 January 2005–30 April 2013*

Selling account type	Buying account type	Number of trades	Quantity traded (Mt CO_2-e)	Percentage of trading volume (%)
Installation	Installation	15,122	970	4
Trading-only	Trading-only	293,988	18,630	76
Installation	Trading-only	38,858	2,657	11
Trading-only	Installation	27,591	2,329	9

Source: European Commission (2017)

allowances, and trading accounts that may be controlled by polluting companies or purely financial actors.[2] Between the beginning of phase one on 1 January 2005 and the last day of phase two compliance on 30 April 2013, the EUTL logged a total of 375,559 physical trades between installation and/ or trading only accounts. The vast majority, constituting 76 per cent of total trading volume, were between trading-only accounts, as outlined in Table 2.3. These trading-only accounts have been matched with their ultimate owners using the same process outlined in the previous chapter.[3] In total, 95 per cent of the 4,357 trading-only accounts listed in the EUTL on 8 September 2017 were matched with their ultimate owners in Orbis on the same date (Bureau van Dijk 2017; European Commission 2017).[4]

RWE's installation accounts received 311 Mt CO_2-e worth of allowances and offset credits during the period for which trading data is available. Almost all (91 per cent) were acquired internally by accounts owned by RWE, as shown in Table 2.4. The 6 per cent from steel corporations HKM and ThyssenKrupp were also effectively internally acquired because they are allowances passed on to RWE as part of waste gas transfer agreements between the companies (Elsworth et al. 2011). Of RWE accounts supplying carbon commodities to RWE installations, 96 per cent were trading-only accounts. These accounts were controlled by RWE subsidiaries such as RWE Supply & Trading, RWE's specialised energy trading desk, which also engaged in power, gas, coal, freight, oil, weather, and renewable energy certificate trading. RWE Supply & Trading's carbon market involvement

---

[2] Installation-linked accounts are called 'operator holding accounts' and trading-only accounts are called 'person holding accounts'.

[3] The precise order of matching being: company ID in EUTL, person holding account name in EUTL, operator holding account name in database of companies.

[4] Trading-only account matches were conducted at a later date to installation accounts because trading data is subject to a three-year delay (European Commission 2013c).

Table 2.4. *Sources of carbon allowances and credits for RWE installations, 1 January 2005–30 April 2013*

Ultimate owner	Allowances and credits (Mt CO_2-e)	Percentage of total acquired (%)
RWE	311	91
HKM	14	4
ThyssenKrupp	13	4
EnBW	2	1
Others	0.1	0.03
Total	341	100

Sources: Own calculation using Bureau van Dijk (2014, 2017) and European Commission (2014b, 2014e, 2014h, 2014k, 2017)

extended beyond internal compliance to third-party trading of spot and futures contracts, EUA-CER swaps, and sourcing CERs from CDM projects (RWE Supply & Trading 2014). It is the activity of trading accounts, such as those controlled by RWE Supply & Trading, that is most relevant in discovering the external sources of allowances surrendered by RWE installations because it is these accounts, rather than installation accounts, that mostly trade outside the boundaries of the corporation.

Table 2.5 shows the top twenty external ultimate owners that RWE's trading-only accounts acquired carbon commodities from. Eleven were financial institutions that either provided carbon exchange platforms or actively engaged in carbon trading, and nine were polluting companies, or governments that own polluting companies, owning installations regulated by the EU ETS, but with substantial financial operations. NYSE Euronext owned the carbon exchange Bluenext (closed in 2012), and Deutsche Börse and Nasdaq own the carbon exchanges European Energy Exchange (EEX), and Nasdaq OMX commodities, respectively. RHJ International, Deutsche Bank, UBS, Barclays, the Bank of America, BNP Paribas, Morgan Stanley, and Citigroup are financial institutions that engage directly in carbon trading on behalf of clients and/or for their own gain. The broader financial activities of these actors are the subject of Chapter 4. This section charts their role as intermediaries between installations. The presence of some the biggest polluting ultimate owners in the EU ETS in the top twenty suppliers to RWE, despite many of them appearing in the top ten deficit holders, is reflective not of their surpluses, but rather of the orientation of E.ON, GDF Suez, EDF, and Vattenfall towards active and direct participation in financial markets.

64　　　　　　　　　　　　　*Internalising Carbon*

Table 2.5. *Top external sources for RWE trading-only accounts, 1 January 2005–30 April 2013*

Ultimate owner	Form of participation	Allowances and credits (Mt CO$_2$-e) sold to RWE	Percentage RWE's externally acquired allowances and credits (%)
RHJ International	Financial	34	10
Deutsche Bank	Financial	33	9
Deutsche Börse	Financial	32	9
UBS Group	Financial	32	9
Bluenext	Financial	26	7
Barclays	Financial	19	5
E.ON	Regulated	19	5
Government of Sweden	Regulated	19	5
Government of France	Regulated	17	5
KSBG	Regulated	10	3
Bank Of America Corp	Financial	10	3
GDF Suez	Regulated	9	2
Morgan Stanley	Financial	8	2
BNP Paribas	Financial	7	2
Centrica	Regulated	7	2
EnBW	Regulated	6	2
BP	Regulated	5	1
Citigroup	Financial	5	1
Royal Dutch Shell	Regulated	4	1
Nasdaq	Financial	4	1

Sources: Own calculation using Bureau van Dijk (2014, 2017) and European Commission (2014b, 2014e, 2014h, 2014k, 2017)

2.3.2 *RWE's Allowance Trading*

Identifying the internal and external sources of RWE's allowances sheds light on the different forms of commodity abstraction and trading methods involved in the EU ETS. The remainder of this chapter outlines four examples that each combine two of these factors. The first involves scalar abstraction between different installation sizes with an example of internal trading from a medium-sized installation owned by RWE. Then it moves on to functional abstraction between different greenhouse gases with an example of broker-mediated trading involving BNP Paribas and a nitrous oxide installation. Following this, spatial abstraction between countries is illustrated with an example of an exchange-mediated trade involving EEX and a Lithuanian installation. Lastly, a bilateral trade between polluters, from Shell's energy desk, on behalf of its own oil refinery, shows process abstraction between different production methods. The role of temporal abstraction is also highlighted across all trades.

The extent to which RWE could exploit unevenness between different pollution scales, greenhouse gases, locations, and production processes by trading carbon commodities is illustrated by comparing the source of allowances with the company's Niederaussem power plant. As RWE's largest installation, the Niederaussem power plant also had RWE's largest single allowance deficit of 63,244,650t CO_2-e. This represented 39 per cent of its total allocation and the deficit was closed entirely by surrendering EUAs. In trading for the first two phases of the EU ETS, the Niederaussem power plant sourced all of its allowances from accounts controlled by RWE. 93 per cent of allowances bought were from RWE trading-only accounts (European Commission 2017). The different forms of abstraction and types of trade at different stages of these reconstructed EUA commodity flows are illustrated in Figure 2.1.

Due to limitations in the available data, commodity flows can only be reconstructed rather than precisely mapped. It is not possible to trace an individual carbon allowance across multiple trades to its ultimate surrender because unique EUA serial numbers were hidden from public view in the EUTL following security breaches. What the available data does establish is the existence of trading relationships between accounts, including when and how many EUAs were transferred. Carbon commodity flows can therefore be reconstructed to concretely illustrate the socio-ecological relations of carbon appropriation that are substituted through the act of carbon trading.

RWE's overall deficit meant the company needed to buy allowances from other companies. However, its deficit installations could also trade internally to surrender allowances from RWE installations with surpluses. In net terms, large installations, such as the Niederaussem power plant, experienced a deficit of allowances and all non-large installation sizes experienced a surplus of allowances. Table 2.6 breaks down the surpluses and deficits of RWE's installations according to installation size. It shows that RWE's 74 zero, mini, small, and medium-sized installations had a net surplus of allowances while the company's twenty-four large installations had a net deficit. This replicates the pattern in the broader database of companies, also shown in Table 2.6. RWE's internal trading between installation–emissions relationships differentiated by polluting scales is therefore illustrative of the exploitation of the uneven appropriation of carbon in the EU ETS as a whole.

One of the non-large-sized installations that enjoyed an allowance surplus was RWE's own Heidelberg cogeneration plant. The installation provides heat, steam, and cooling for Heidelberg Hospital in Germany (RWE Innogy 2014). It recorded an allocation surplus each year between 2005 and 2012, and had a total phase one and two surplus of 104,811 allowances. This surplus was further extended by the 84,416 CERs the installation surrendered

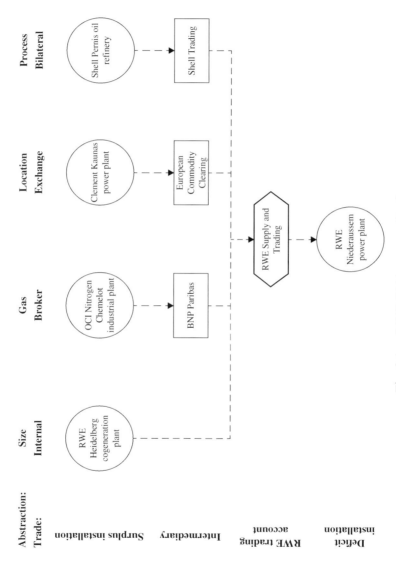

Fig. 2.1. RWE EUA commodity flows

2.3 Trading Carbon Allowances

Table 2.6. *RWE and EU ETS 2005–12 allowance surplus/deficits by installation size*

Installation size	RWE installations	RWE 2005–12 surplus/deficit (Mt CO_2-e)	EU ETS installations	EU ETS 2005–12 surplus/deficit (Mt CO_2-e)
Zero	3	0.05	855	35
Mini	36	1	5,333	127
Small	8	0.4	1,530	103
Medium	27	9	2,281	408
Large	24	−247	939	−369
Total	98	−237	10,938	304

Sources: Own calculation using Bureau van Dijk (2014) and European Commission (2014b, 2014e, 2014h, 2014k)

between 2005 and 2012, despite not requiring additional credits for compliance. It transferred a total of 92,121 allowances during these phases to other trading accounts owned by RWE (European Commission 2017).

The Heidelberg cogeneration plant shows how the carbon market enables substitutions between installation–emissions relationships with very different scales of pollution. The plant's maximum yearly verified emissions of 73,394t CO_2-e in 2010 made it the 2,864th biggest polluting installation in the EU ETS from 2005 to 2012. By comparison, this represents 0.2 per cent of the maximum 31,252,670t CO_2-e released by the Niederaussem power plant in 2007. However, RWE's non-large sized installations covered only 4 per cent of the deficit of large-sized installations, limiting the potential for internal trading of this kind.

RWE was also able to meet its deficit through trades involving functional abstraction between greenhouse gas emissions. Prior to 2012, this was made possible by the decisions of the governments of the Netherlands, Austria, Norway, the United Kingdom, and Italy to opt in ten nitrous oxide emitting installations (European Commission 2015c). The opted-in installations were also granted a substantial allowance surplus. In 2012 – the year by which they had all been opted-in – the nitrous oxide emitting installations registered a surplus of 2,785,231 EUAs, representing 41 per cent of their total allocation.

Three Dutch installations were the first to be opted-in from the beginning of phase two. One of them was the Chemelot industrial chemical park at Geleen. The park is operated jointly by a number of companies, including OCI Nitrogen, which produce nitric acid, used in the production of ammonia and fertiliser (Chemelot 2014). The park was already an EU ETS installation for its carbon dioxide emissions, but the inclusion of nitrous oxide emissions was rewarded, based on the benchmarking of historical emissions, with an increased allocation of 1,607,512 allowances over the course of phase two. This accounted for around half of the installation's 2008–12 surplus of 3,396,434t CO_2-e (European Commission 2008, 2009).

The connection between RWE and Chemelot was via the carbon brokering activities of a financial institution. Following the opt-in of nitrous oxide, the installation's account sold allowances totalling 141,000t CO_2-e to French investment bank BNP Paribas in phase two of the EU ETS (European Commission 2017). BNP Paribas operates as a carbon trader both for proprietary gain and on behalf of clients (BNP Paribas Corporate and Investment Banking 2014). The surplus allowances sold by Chemelot to BNP Paribus could then be sold to deficit companies such as RWE. BNP Paribus was the 16th highest external supplier of carbon commodities to RWE, selling 7,053,000 allowances to the company for the first two phases of the EU ETS (European Commission 2017).

The intermediation services provided by BNP Paribus made it possible for RWE to exploit differentiation in the GWPs of greenhouse gases, which are the basis of functional abstraction in the commodification of carbon. The Niederaussem power plant was only regulated for carbon dioxide, but was able to surrender allowances from an installation that was also regulated for nitrous oxide. The GWP of nitrous oxide is 298, indicating the relative potency of any given tonne of N_2O vis-à-vis CO_2. Yet, by this measure, carbon dioxide remains the most prevalent greenhouse gas: carbon dioxide accounted for 82 per cent of total CO_2-e emissions across the EU in 2012, compared with 7 per cent for nitrous oxide (European Environment Agency 2014a p. 11). Thus, RWE was also exploiting unevenness in the overall contribution of different gases to the production of climate change.

Spatial abstraction is part of all carbon trades, but is most evident in the standardised emissions contracts sold by financial institutions providing carbon exchange services – what Paterson and Stripple (2012 p. 578) describe as 'Walmart' carbon. As outlined above, RWE's third largest supplier of carbon commodities was Deutsche Börse, which owns EEX and its subsidiary clearing house, European Commodity Clearing (European Commodity Clearing 2014). European Commodity Clearing sold 24,146,225 allowances to RWE in phases one and two. The allowances originated from thirteen countries, including Germany, Lithuania, the Netherlands, Czech Republic, the United Kingdom, Slovakia, Poland, Portugal, Denmark, Sweden, Spain, Italy, and Luxemburg (European Commission 2017). This underscores the extent of spatial abstraction involved in exchange-mediated trades.

The presence of Lithuanian-allocated allowances in purchases by European Commodity Clearing illustrates the origins and implications of

2.3 Trading Carbon Allowances

spatial abstraction. European Commodity Clearing acquired 140,000 Lithuanian allowances in December 2005 from the Kaunas Combined Heat and Power Plant (European Commission 2017). The Kaunas plant was able to sell allowances to European Commodity Clearing because it registered a 2005–12 surplus of 1,379,324 allowances, representing 25 per cent of its total free allocation. This was indicative of a general pattern of over-allocation in Lithuania, which was enabled by the sharp decreases in emissions from 1990 following the dissolution of the Soviet Union, which is also the baseline year for Kyoto targets. The country had an overall surplus of 21 Mt CO_2-e in phase one and two, representing 32 per cent of its total free allocation.

The Kaunas plant's surplus contributed to the pool of allowances that European Commodity Clearing drew on to sell allowances to RWE, and thus allowed RWE to exploit spatial unevenness abstracted in the carbon commodity. However, spatial unevenness translates to unequal contributions to climate change. Lithuania's emissions were dwarfed by RWE's Niederaussem power plant alone, which between 2005 and 2012 released over four times more emissions than all of Lithuania's installations combined. This inequality extends to per capita emissions in the national and regional spaces in which the respective plants sell power. In 2012 Germans released 12 tonnes of CO_2-e per capita compared with 7 tonnes of CO_2-e per capita for Lithuanians (European Environment Agency 2015a). The equalisation of these differences in commodity form is most evident when compared to North Rhine-Westphalia, the state where the Niederaussem power plant is located, which has per capita emissions of almost twice the German average and, therefore, over three times higher than Lithuania's (Energie Agentur NRW 2010).

Lastly, RWE's trading relationship with Shell illustrates the potential to trade between differentiated production processes, this time via bilateral trading between polluters. Shell is involved in the EU ETS as both the owner of fifteen installations – oil refineries and associated power plants – and as a major carbon trader through its Shell Trading energy desk (Shell Global 2015). The 4,279,000 allowances and credits Shell sold to RWE could therefore have been drawn from its own 2005–12 surplus allocation of 13,508,784 EUAs and/or external trading activity (European Commission 2014e). Over half of Shell's surplus, totalling 7,464,684 allowances, was from a single installation: the Pernis oil refinery in Rotterdam, the Netherlands. The refinery, the largest in Europe and the 69th biggest polluting installation in the EU ETS, produces 404 thousand barrels of crude oil per day. The installation transferred a total of 7,823,979 allowances to trading-only accounts operated by Shell Trading in the first and second phases of the EU ETS (European Commission 2014e; Shell Netherlands 2015).

70 *Internalising Carbon*

The potential for trading between the Pernis and Niederaussem installations shows how process abstractions in the carbon commodity that enable substitutions between different production processes – oil refining-to-power generation – involve quite different sources of greenhouse gas emissions. In contrast to emissions from the Niederaussem power plant, the majority of on-site emissions from oil refineries such as Pernis are not from electricity production, but rather various process-based emissions (Ecofys 2009 pp. 4–6). Sectoral differences were central to Pernis' allowance surplus. Governments over-allocated oil refinery installations across the EU ETS because they were deemed exposed to international competition in a way that combustion installations in the electricity industry were not (Ellerman & Buchner 2007 pp. 74–5; Wettestad 2009 pp. 309–10). Between 2005 and 2012, the mineral oil refining 'activity' had the third greatest surplus after steel and then cement.

As with all the cases, installation–emissions relations at Pernis and Niederaussem do not represent equivalent contributions to climate change. Shell is a major global emitter – the sixth highest 'carbon major' according to Heede (2013) – and has a large responsibility to act on climate change. However, its contribution to climate change is largely from the Shell oil burned by other actors in the transport, and other, sectors, which is not commodified in the Pernis installation–emissions relationship. In contrast, the Niederaussem power plant, which sells electricity, not fuel, to other actors, is the direct source of its emissions. Shell has reported a number of efforts to reduce energy and process emissions at the Pernis plant (Royal Dutch Shell 2012; Shell Global 2008). However, such actions, while welcome, cannot reduce the carbon footprint of its supply chain in the same way that RWE could by replacing electricity generated at Niederaussem with renewable energy, or working with consumers to reduce their demand.

Finally, all four trading examples involve a degree of temporal abstraction. Many of the trades identified occurred in the early years of phase two of the EU ETS, when emissions were declining as a result of the economic crisis. These trades delivered allowances that RWE could surrender at any point in phase two, three, or beyond, owing to banking rules. Banking rules are based on the assumption that it is immaterial when installation–emissions relationships occur. Yet, studies of the non-linear nature of relationships between economic activity and emissions levels shows that 'history matters' (York 2012 p. 163). In short, greenhouse gas emissions decline at a slower rate in times of economic crisis than they increase in times of growth. Emissions reductions achieved during times of economic downturn are therefore temporary in nature and don't represent a pathway towards a climate solution. All four surplus installations discussed in this section experienced reduced emissions in 2008 and/or 2009, during the worst of the economic recession. These reductions, in line with crisis-induced emissions falls in these years in the EU ETS as a whole (European Environment Agency 2015a), contributed to the surplus allowances the installations sold, which could be surrendered by RWE and other polluters in lieu of reducing their own emissions.

Conclusion

This chapter has shown that the uneven socio-spatial organisation of carbon appropriation revealed in Chapter 1 is underpinned by multiple axes of internal differentiation, according to scale, location, timing, production process, and greenhouse gas. Carbon is commodified in the EU ETS by separating and objectifying relationships between installations and emissions and equalising difference between them. This enables polluting corporations to exploit internal differentiation by substituting one form of carbon appropriation for another to pollute above levels of free allocation. As the EU ETS has developed, levels of free allocation have contracted while the scope of the scheme has expanded, making substitution via commodity trading increasingly important. Rather than internalising externalities for efficient climate action, the EU ETS has enabled fossil fuel-intensive capital to internalise the inequalities of climate change for its own benefit.

The RWE case study illustrates how allocation and trading practices in the EU ETS can maintain the existing patterns of carbon appropriation and therefore fail to effectively address the production of climate change. Indeed, the Niederaussem plant maintained its emissions within a small band above and below 2005 levels throughout phase one and two. Buying allowances to sustain emissions aligned with RWE's corporate strategy of defending its existing fossil fuel generation assets rather than investing in renewables (Bontrup & Marquardt 2015). The strategy was reflected in the very low share of renewable energy in RWE Generation's (the part of the company that operated generation assets in its main markets of Germany, the United Kingdom, and the Netherlands, before renewables assets were moved into Innogy in 2016) asset portfolio at the end of the period studied in this chapter. In 2013, only 2 per cent of the electricity produced by RWE Generation was produced with renewables, compared to 81 per cent for fossil fuels (RWE 2014a p. 25). This is well below the average share of renewables in electricity production in each country, which in 2013 was 26 per cent in Germany, 14 per cent in the United Kingdom, and 10 per cent in the Netherlands (Eurostat 2015). RWE's Chief Executive, Peter Terium, acknowledged this poor record in saying 'we were late entering into the renewables market – possibly too late' (Steitz 2014).[5]

The economic logic that provides the policy rationale for the EU ETS is neutral on what, how, how much, when, or where RWE, or any other regulated entity pollutes, provided it is within the overall cap. Conversely, it has been argued in this chapter that the internal differentiation equalised in commodity form is reflective of uneven contributions to climate change. Compared with the installations linked to intermediaries that sold allowances to RWE, the Niederaussem power plant is responsible for a larger scale of emissions, of a more prevalent greenhouse gas, in a location with higher absolute and per capita emissions, and through a production process that is closer to the core of the organisation of emissions in the EU ETS. Therefore, efforts to reduce emissions from the Niederaussem power plant would have delivered a more effective response to climate change than the 'emissions reductions' represented in allowances surrendered by RWE. The point is not that reducing the appropriation of carbon at the other end of RWE's trading relationships is not important or necessary, but instead to question whether such actions should be able to maintain the emissions of one of Europe's largest corporate polluters.

RWE's reconstructed commodity flows illustrate how the EU ETS can engender the substitution of more marginal for more transformative efforts to address climate change. The EU ETS therefore risks entrenching the existing organisation of emissions, limiting its capacity to operate as an efficacious policy in addressing the production of climate change. A fuller exploration of the effects of carbon commodification on the efficacy of the EU ETS first requires consideration of its links with the Kyoto mechanisms, which is addressed in Chapter 3.

---

[5] RWE's relatively low share of renewables is set to change with its planned acquisition of E.ON's renewables assets, announced in March 2018, as part of a deal that envisages Innogy become a retail and grid company owned by E.ON (Storbeck 2018).

3

Externalising Carbon

Introduction

Opportunities to exploit differentiated forms of carbon appropriation are not limited to the relationships between installations and emissions that are commodified within the EU ETS. From 2008, European carbon allowances could be supplemented by carbon credits produced in offset projects that are part of the Kyoto Protocol's 'flexibility mechanisms'. While the Kyoto mechanisms have a longer history, the analysis of the CDM and JI in this chapter is developed out of an understanding of the limits to the internal trading within the EU ETS. Indeed, following the initial development of the CDM and JI, the evolution of the Kyoto mechanisms has been largely driven by their links with the EU ETS. By focusing on the interactions between the EU ETS and the Kyoto mechanisms, this chapter enables a more complete evaluation of the relationship between carbon markets and climate change as a socio-ecological crisis. It achieves this by extending the conceptualisation of carbon commodification to the spatio-temporal constitution of carbon offset credits that represent relationships between offset projects and emissions reductions. The chapter argues the external 'fix' carbon offsetting has provided for corporations and states within the EU ETS works by incorporating more unequal forms of carbon appropriation within the carbon commodity. This intensifies contradictions created by the formal equality of carbon trading in a climate-changing capitalism.

This chapter builds on the main strands of critical research questioning the socio-ecological outcomes of carbon offsetting. As mentioned in the Introduction, there is extensive critical literature with strong ties to radical movements on the negative local impacts of offset projects, and thus, the limits of the CDM, in particular, in realising its 'sustainable development' goal (Boyd et al. 2009). This is complemented by critical perspectives on the

73

74   *Externalising Carbon*

credibility of the 'additionality' claims of offsetting projects – the measure by which emissions reductions are demonstrated and quantified (Schneider 2009). Reflecting on these themes in research on carbon offsetting, Bumpus and Liverman (2008 pp. 148–9) propose a research agenda that 'would include detailed empirical studies of carbon reductions in particular places and through different networks and value chains, and further theoretical work on the commodification of carbon, the spatial relations of emissions trading, and the role of non-nation-state actors'.

The first section provides an overview of the background and institutional design of the CDM and JI through an account of negotiations that took place as part of the Kyoto process and the Linking Directive. The second section then responds to calls for a focus on the spatial relations of emissions trading by drawing on Harvey's (2001b, 2006) work on the historical-geography of capitalist crisis and its displacement. It does so by conceptualising the commodification of carbon in the Kyoto mechanisms as a 'spatio-temporal fix' for corporations and their polluting installations in the EU ETS. The third section responds to calls for detailed empirical studies of carbon commodity networks by constructing a case study of the trading relationships of German energy company E.ON, to illustrate the operation, and assess the implications of, the link between the EU ETS and the Kyoto mechanisms.

3.1 The Development of the CDM and JI

3.1.1 The 'Kyoto Surprise'

The CDM and JI are products of the United Nations international climate regime. Alongside emissions trading they represent two out of three flexibility mechanisms that formed a crucial part of the 1997 Kyoto Protocol. The United States was the strongest advocate for emissions reduction flexibility through market mechanisms from the signing of the UNFCCC in Rio de Janeiro in 1992 to the final agreement at Kyoto. A flexibility principle was included in the UNFCCC, developed by US negotiators but originally proposed by a Norwegian think tank, that contained provisions for developed countries to meet the non-binding aim of stabilising emissions at 1990 levels 'individually or *jointly*' (Newell & Paterson 2010 pp. 78–9; UNFCCC 1992 Article 4 emphasis added). Developing countries tended to oppose the idea on the basis that it would dilute the responsibility of developed countries to cut their own emissions and blur the lines that excluded developing countries from such responsibilities (Paterson 1996 p. 66). This opposition meant that the first concrete manifestation of a joint provision in the 1995

3.1 The Development of the CDM and JI 75

Berlin Mandate was a pilot, voluntary scheme that allowed measures between countries but did not produce credits that would count towards the targets of developed countries (Grubb et al. 1999 p. 45). The scheme was named 'activities implemented jointly' to make it clear that it was the particular projects, not the commitments, that were jointly held between developed and developing countries (Matthews & Paterson 2005 pp. 66–7; Oberthür & Ott 1999 p. 152).

Several key countries shifted their support towards the adoption of flexibility mechanisms in the lead up to the Kyoto conference. The United States adopted a 'binding but flexible' approach that made the adoption of concrete emissions reduction targets and timetables, which they had successfully opposed in the UNFCCC, conditional on the inclusion of market mechanisms (Grubb et al. 1999 p. 88; Newell 2000 p. 15). The United States was joined by other members of the 'JUSSCANNZ' group of negotiators, which included Japan, Switzerland, Canada, Australia, Norway, and New Zealand in this position. As flagged in Chapter 2, European negotiators, to the contrary, had been less enthusiastic about the use of such mechanisms and instead favoured stronger domestic measures. Within the EU there were differing positions, particularly between Northern and Southern European countries, where the former tended to be more in favour of stronger measures. Such differences were, however, dealt with by the demand for an EU-wide cap that would allow the target to be distributed between EU countries (Newell 2000 p. 14). European negotiators as a whole responded to the US position, following a decision of the Council of the European Union, by indicating a willingness to accept market mechanisms if they were 'supplementary to domestic action' in the interests of reaching an agreement (Skjærseth & Wettestad 2008 p. 67).

A similar movement in both directions, making support for climate action conditional on market mechanisms, and support for market mechanisms conditional on climate action, emerged among industry groups, on the one hand, and NGOs, on the other. From its formation in 1989, the Global Climate Coalition was the most influential industry group opposing the adoption of emissions targets and policies. It represented oil, gas, electricity, and carbon-intensive manufacturing companies, primarily based in the United States but included European companies. The organisation's key strategy was to question climate science and emphasise the negative economic impacts of climate action (Levy & Egan 2003 p. 819; Newell & Paterson 1998 p. 683). This 'do nothing' position was opposed by environmental groups such as Climate Action Network (CAN) International, a coalition of the major environmental NGOs originally from developed countries but subsequently expanding internationally, which was also formed in 1989 (Alcock 2008 pp. 81–2; Newell 2000 pp. 126–7). CAN International's position at Kyoto was for a binding emissions reduction target of 20 per cent below 1990 levels by 2005, to be made domestically and without the use of market mechanisms (Betsill 2002 p. 53).

Actors from industry and NGO groups emerged to form a coalition that supported the combination of binding emissions targets and market mechanisms. UK oil corporation BP formally split from the Global Climate Coalition in 1996 and US NGO Environmental Defense departed from the official position of CAN and worked with BP on market mechanisms (Meckling 2011 pp. 82–3). Charting a course that would later be replicated by business in the negotiations for the EU ETS, BP, joined by chemicals company Dupont and other companies represented by the International Climate Change Partnership, threw their support behind market mechanisms primarily as a defensive strategy against less favourable policies (Meckling 2011 pp. 84–5). Other industries that hoped to directly benefit from climate policy, such as clean technology industries, represented by the Business Council for Sustainable Energy, and the insurance industry, which was potentially threatened by the prospect of large payouts for climate change-induced events, were also broadly in favour (Levy & Egan 1998 p. 346; Newell & Paterson 1998 p. 696).

A framework for JI, although it was not explicitly named as such, was the first offsetting provision agreed to in negotiations for the Kyoto protocol, because it bypassed the more difficult North–South politics that structured UN climate negotiations. China, and most other developing countries operating under the 'Group of 77' (G77) banner, had maintained their opposition to North–South flexibility mechanisms in the lead up to the Kyoto negotiations. Again, there were notable exceptions, such as Costa Rica, which saw potential domestic benefits of forestry offset projects. The framework for JI became Article 6 of the Kyoto Protocol with relative ease because it limited the location of projects, and the users of credits, to developed countries listed in Annex I of the UNFCCC (Grubb et al. 1999 p. 89). Developing countries supported this arrangement because all countries involved would have emissions targets. Therefore, any credits produced by projects in one country and surrendered in another would result in a reduction in the host country's emissions cap. Former Soviet bloc countries were heavily in favour of JI because, given the significant decrease in their emissions levels following the collapse of industrial production in the 1990s, they could afford deductions from their emissions cap and benefit from project investment and the sale of credits (Grubb et al. 1999 p. 97; Oberthür & Ott 1999 pp. 153–5).

3.1 The Development of the CDM and JI

Remarkably, a North–South flexibility mechanism in the form of the CDM was also agreed to. As briefly outlined in the Introduction, the CDM emerged out of a proposal by the Brazilian government for a 'clean development fund'. This fund was to be financed by penalties for developed countries that breached their emissions targets. The proposal was strongly supported by the G77 but opposed by many developed countries that had, like the United States, objected to what they viewed as rigid and punitive approaches (Grubb et al. 1999 pp. 101–2; Oberthür & Ott 1999 p. 166). The United States, however, responded to the proposal proactively, arguing that it could be made consistent with a market logic by flipping its design. Rather than a redistributive fund, the United States reframed the proposal as an investment mechanism. The projects that Brazil envisaged would be supported by a 'penalty for not complying' would instead be considered as 'contributing to compliance' (Grubb et al. 1999 p. 103). With some compromises – including adaptation funding provisions from CDM project revenues, as demanded by the Alliance of Small Island States (AOSIS), and provisos that the use of offset credits would be 'supplemental' to domestic action, as urged by the European Community – the framework for the CDM was enshrined in Article 12 of the Kyoto Protocol. In a subsequent speech, the Chairman of the Kyoto Conference, Raúl Estrada Oyuela, reflecting on the CDM's role in securing the overall Kyoto agreement and its unconventional evolution as a market mechanism, memorably described the CDM as the 'Kyoto surprise' (Werksman 1998 p. 147).

Developments following agreement at Kyoto were significant for the implementation of both Kyoto mechanisms. The text of the Protocol provided an overall framework for the CDM and JI, but many of the details, such as the project approval process, the eligibility of sectors such as forestry, and governance arrangements were decided and outlined in the Marrakech Accords of 2001 (Boyd & Schipper 2002 pp. 185–6). Paterson and Stripple (2012 pp. 572–3) point out that the Marrakech Accords were the first time CERs and ERUs, the commodities of the CDM and JI, respectively, were reified as units of CO_2-e. Despite achieving the inclusion of flexibility mechanisms, 2001 was also the year that President Bush formally withdrew the United States from the Kyoto Protocol, in line with the pre-Kyoto demands of the US Senate not to accept an agreement that didn't also include developing country targets (Meckling 2011 pp. 134–5). Chapter 2 noted that this was one of the international factors that contributed to the development of the EU ETS. The EU ETS, in turn, became the driving force behind the growth of the Kyoto mechanisms, following the negotiation of the Linking Directive that established connections between the two schemes.

78   *Externalising Carbon*

3.1.2 The Linking Directive

International linkages with the Kyoto mechanisms were major parts of the debate over the scope of, and allocation in, the EU ETS. However, the issue was largely excluded from the negotiations for the EU ETS Directive. At the time of the Commission's proposal for a European carbon trading system, the rules for the CDM and JI had yet to be finalised, and opposing views on the mechanisms, especially between industry and environmental groups, threatened to derail the rest of the EU ETS Directive (Skjærseth & Wettestad 2008 p. 46). The clear intention of the EU ETS Directive was, nonetheless, to connect the schemes. It stated that 'linking the project-based mechanisms, including Joint Implementation (JI) and the Clean Development Mechanism (CDM), with the Community scheme is desirable and important' and foreshadowed the adoption of a parallel directive in this direction (European Parliament and Council 2003 Article 30). This process was kicked off with a proposal for the Linking Directive from the Commission the day after the Council agreed to the EU ETS Directive in July 2003. The progression from proposal to adoption of the Linking Directive in 2004 was faster than for the EU ETS Directive. Once again, within this overall direction towards adoption, contestation continued over similar issues that vexed debates over the EU ETS Directive, including the quantitative distribution of offsets and qualitative boundaries on eligible offset types.

The Commission's attempts to impose quantitative and qualitative limits on offset use were generally opposed by member states. Contestation over the quantitative distribution of offset credits focused on whether the Kyoto Protocol's 'supplementary' provision would translate to a cap on offset credit use and at which level – national state or EU – this would be decided. The Environment Directorate-General of the Commission initially favoured an EU-determined cap. After opposition from the Enterprise Directorate-General, member states, and industry, the proposal became a mechanism that would trigger a review on the need for a cap once offset use reached 6 per cent of the total allowance allocation (European Commission 2003). Most member states, with the notable exceptions of Germany and the Netherlands, opposed caps to promote flexibility, reflecting the shift to a more positive view of market mechanisms. Central and Eastern European states that were in the process of acceding to the EU also actively opposed caps because they wanted to host JI projects in their non-EU ETS sectors and sell ERUs to installations in Western European countries (Flåm 2009 pp. 28–9). Similarly, the Commission's proposals for qualitative limits on offsets from certain projects, including a ban on forestry and nuclear offsets, and social and environmental safeguards on hydroelectric dam projects, were each opposed by various configurations of EU states (Skjærseth & Wettestad 2008 pp. 116–7). The positions of polluting corporations and their industry groups outlined in the previous chapter thus translated to demands to maximise use of offset credits.

Environmental groups took a different position on international linkages compared to their approach to the EU ETS. While willing to accept a tightly regulated EU ETS, NGOs continued their Kyoto position on carbon offsetting by opposing the use of CERs and ERUs in the EU ETS. Indeed, one of CAN Europe's conditions for supporting an EU ETS was that 'links to the project mechanisms should also not be made, as they will unnecessarily inflate the [carbon] budget and divert attention away from domestic reductions' (Climate Action Network Europe 2002). Despite a position that opposed the Linking Directive, CAN Europe and many of their prominent member organisations, including Greenpeace and WWF, again adopted a 'quality control' approach as a secondary strategy, arguing for strict caps on offset use, limiting projects to renewable energy and extra social safeguards (Climate Action Network Europe 2004).

Throughout the debate, most of the Parliament was in favour of imposing quantitative and qualitative restrictions but acquiesced on the issue of caps in return for more limited bans on certain project types (Skjærseth & Wettestad 2008 p. 47). In the final Linking Directive, prospects for an EU-level cap gave way to an initial system where member states had control over determining allowable offset use for each installation, although their decisions would be overseen by the Commission for consistency with Kyoto 'supplementary' requirements as part of the national allocation plan process (European Parliament and Council 2004 pp. 20, 23). Forestry and nuclear offsets were banned and hydroelectric power projects over 20 MW in size needed to adhere to the social and environmental guidelines set out by the World Commission on Dams (European Parliament and Council 2004 p. 21).

Overall, agreement on the Linking Directive delivered polluting companies the capacity to surrender significant quantities of CERs and ERUs in lieu of EUAs from almost all project types (although further restrictions on CERs were introduced from 2013, considered in detail in Chapter 5). Commission oversight did subsequently result in a tightening of allowable offset use by installations in the many countries – some by up to half – that had their national allocation plans rejected for overgenerous offset caps (Flåm 2009 p. 31). Eventually, a loose cap was instituted at 50 per cent of total EU ETS emissions reduction efforts between 2008 and 2020 (European Parliament and Council 2014 Article 11a). Before analysing the use of CERs and ERUs

80 *Externalising Carbon*

in the EU ETS overall, and through a case study of E.ON, the next section conceptualises the spatial and temporal dynamics of the Kyoto mechanisms by bringing in Harvey's insights on the history and geography of capitalist crisis.

3.2 The Spatio-Temporal Fix

3.2.1 *Capitalist Crisis and the Spatial Fix*

According to Marxist political economy, crises of capitalism inevitably develop out of contradictions within the accumulation process. Competitive pressures and class relations demand constant improvements in labour productivity through technological and institutional changes that are necessary to maintain profitability but lead to the overaccumulation of capital (Harvey 2001b pp. 313–6). Particular types and combinations of fixed capital, workforces, state regulation, and infrastructure support 'certain kinds of production, certain kinds of labour processes, distributional arrangements [and] consumption patterns' that eventually become barriers to the profitable reinvestment of surplus value needed to sustain capital accumulation (Harvey, 2006: 428). All else being equal, the ensuing crisis can only be resolved through a wholesale devaluation of capital.

However, Harvey (2006 p. 425) stresses that all else is not equal and accordingly seeks to 'integrate the geography of uneven development into the theory of crisis'. The perennial restructuring of the organisation of capitalist production contributes to uneven development. Harvey conceptualises this dynamic in terms of the contradiction between 'fixity' and 'motion' in the circulation of capital (see also Brenner 1998). Paradoxically, 'spatial organisation is necessary to overcome space' because the circulation of capital as 'value in motion' depends on social and physical infrastructures that are relatively immobile (Harvey 2001b p. 328). These organisational arrangements see certain individual capitals, sectors, and regions develop at the expense of others.

Harvey (2006 p. 424) considers how this 'framework of uneven geographical development, produced by differential mobilities of various kinds of capital and labour power', both contributes to endemic crises of capital accumulation, and contains possibilities for crisis displacement. Capital, Harvey argues, can make use of uneven spatial configurations by 'switching' to underdeveloped capitals, sectors and regions with greater capacity to absorb surpluses and therefore sustain capital accumulation for a time. Such moves are coordinated by a range of 'nested hierarchical structures of

3.2 The Spatio-Temporal Fix 81

organisation' including institutions such as states, corporations, and money that link – and produce – various local, regional, national, and international scales (Harvey 2006 p. 422). These include credit markets and state policies that coordinate the movement of capital, creating opportunities for more profitable endeavours. While this is not a costless exercise, 'the geography of uneven development helps convert the crisis tendencies of capitalism into compensating regional configurations of rapid accumulation and devaluation' (Harvey 2006 p. 428).

The limits of this strategy of crisis displacement are also explored by Harvey who develops Hegel's dialectic of inner and outer transformations aimed at resolving the internal contradictions of civil society. While conditions of uneven development within a particular region provide possibilities for crisis displacement, 'options for the internal transformation of capitalism become increasingly limited' by those very conditions (Harvey 2001b p. 328). For example, the centralisation of capital both increases the extent of uneven development, and therefore, the advantages of switching, and limits opportunities to do so because it reduces the domain of the market needed to make the switch (Harvey 2006 p. 141). Such limits to internal transformations see the inertia of existing fixed social and physical infrastructures, and with it, the threat of devaluation, resurface (Harvey 2001b p. 300). However, Harvey (2006 p. 427) also argues that the exploitation of uneven development is not limited to a given territory, and that the threat of devaluation 'is, of course, exactly the kind of "inner dialectic" that forces society to seek relief through some sort of "spatial fix"'.

Outer transformations that Harvey terms 'spatial fixes' are vital for restoring conditions for capital accumulation in the face of limits to inner transformations. Spatial fixes use 'geographical expansion, spatial reorganisation and uneven geographical development' to find profitable outlets for surplus capital in external regions in order to defer the devaluation of capital in internal regions threatened by crises of overaccumulation (Harvey 1995 p. 2). Geographical expansion through the spatial fix has been critical for the survival of capitalism and depends on many of the same nested hierarchical structures, such as states, the financial system, and corporations, that facilitate internal reorganisation. The exact form of spatial fix depends on how crises of overaccumulation manifest, whether as too many commodities relative to demand, idle production capacity or shortages in labour power and natural conditions (Harvey 2001a pp. 25–6). Thus, spatial fixes range from opening up new markets for consumer goods, to the export of productive capital, and securing access to new workers and raw materials, whether through economic contract, political agreement, or military force (Harvey

82 *Externalising Carbon*

2001b pp. 335–8, 2006 pp. 432–8). Harvey (2003a p. 141) stresses that while capitalism requires an 'outside' to achieve spatial fixes, it 'can make use of some pre-existing outside' or, more regularly, 'it can actively manufacture it'. Boundaries are therefore necessarily fixed but constantly recreated (Harvey 2006 p. 427).

3.2.2 Carbon Offsetting as a Spatio-Temporal Fix

Harvey's framework for understanding capitalist crisis and its displacement through the spatial fix can be usefully applied to understand carbon offsetting mechanisms as an external response to the internal limitations of emissions trading within the EU ETS. Ekers and Prudham (2015, 2017, 2018) have laid the groundwork for this application by extending Harvey's notion of the spatial fix through the notion of the 'socio-ecological fix'. This formulation seeks to understand the spatial fix as an inherently metabolic process, constituted by the co-production of nature and space, which seeks to temporarily resolve capitalism's manifold socio-ecological crises. It also seeks to place the development of socio-ecological fixes within political contestation over the legitimacy of different ways of reproducing capitalism's conditions of production. Ekers and Prudham's (2017, 2018) primary focus is on fixed capital formation as a socio-ecological fix, but the concept has also been extended to insurance markets (Johnson 2015), renewable energy (McCarthy 2015), and biodiversity regulation (Dempsey 2015) among other issues. The latter resonates with other work on regulatory 'fixes' by governments responding to environmental challenges, often through market-based mechanisms (Castree 2008b; Cohen & Bakker 2014).

The account of carbon offsetting as a socio-ecological fix in this section builds on Ekers and Prudham's framework in two ways. The first is to extend analysis of the political-regulatory dimensions of the socio-ecological fix as involving 'shifts in the social regulation of productions of space and nature in response to real and perceived crises of legitimacy' (Ekers & Prudham 2015 p. 2438). Carbon offsetting as a spatial fix involves investment in fixed capital at offsetting projects, but the more significant 'fix' for capital is to the regulatory constraints imposed by the EU ETS. The CDM and JI offer a regulatory fix to these constraints through the political construction, or 'fixing', of boundaries between spaces that are internal and external to the EU ETS, which makes outward expansion possible. Carbon offsetting projects are less about providing investment space to sink surplus capital and more about providing regulatory space to sink surplus emissions, to maintain carbon-intensive accumulation by capital within the EU ETS.

3.2 The Spatio-Temporal Fix

The second is to draw out the temporal dimensions of carbon offsetting spatial fixes to more squarely pose socio-ecological fixes as spatio-temporal fixes. Carbon offsetting expands the scope of carbon commodification, and thus, levels unevenness in linked carbon markets, through the commodification of relationships between projects and emissions reductions that are constructed using differentiated scenarios *over time*.

The regulatory fix provided by the Kyoto offsetting mechanisms maps on to Harvey's (2003b pp. 65–6) metaphorical meaning of 'a fix' as a temporary resolution. In the metaphorical sense, the CDM and JI provide a spatial 'fix' for companies or governments that would otherwise need to reduce emissions within the EU ETS or domestically. Just as the uneven development of capital creates limits for internal restructuring, the uneven appropriation of carbon by a small proportion of privately and state-owned corporations and their large-scale installations limits the scope for sourcing carbon allowances from other, smaller actors within the EU ETS. An outward fix to source carbon offsets in lieu of carbon allowances was therefore necessary to preserve or expand the value produced by carbon-intensive capital regulated by the EU ETS. The Kyoto mechanisms achieve this by creating the possibility to switch between unevenly developed forms of carbon appropriation. The CDM and JI, and its links to the EU ETS, represent additional nested hierarchical structures for the commodification of carbon that connect installation-emission relationships with project-*emissions reduction* relationships.

The regulatory fix is dependent on another meaning of 'fix' identified by Harvey (2003b pp. 65–6): the material idea of spatial 'fixity'. Spatial fixity in the CDM and JI goes all the way down to the local level where projects are fixed in particular places, leading to socio-ecological dispossession and displacement (Bryant et al. 2015). On a larger scale, the spatial fix is dependent on the political 'fixing' of global difference into internal and external spaces to restructure the geographical management of greenhouse gas emissions and carbon sinks. The instrument creates a boundary between an external space in the South where representations of the appropriation of carbon are produced and an internal space in the North where those commodities are consumed. The difference the CDM builds upon is the general socio-spatial divide between developed and developing countries that characterised early UN climate conferences and was codified as Annex I and non-Annex I countries to the UNFCCC. The spatial fix is underpinned by the differentiated emissions targets between developed and developing countries that resulted from this distinction. It is this regulatory unevenness that allows the operators of projects in any non-Annex I country that has ratified the Kyoto Protocol to be credited for their emissions reductions. As with spatial fixes to crises of overaccumulation that seek relief from external territories in addressing internal constraints, the CDM allows polluters to draw on commodified representations of project-emission reduction relationships that are external to the EU ETS to maintain their emissions within the boundaries of the scheme.

The co-production of space and nature through the linking of the EU ETS with JI is somewhat different. As mentioned above, unlike with the CDM, both host and investor countries participating in JI projects had Kyoto targets. The institution of the EU ETS and its links with the Kyoto mechanisms created a new set of boundaries internal to Annex I countries between the forms of carbon appropriation that are, and are not, represented within the EUA. The Linking Directive produced this boundary by stating that 'no ERUs or CERs are issued for reductions or limitations of greenhouse gas emissions from installations falling within the scope of [the EU ETS] Directive' (European Parliament and Council 2004 p. 21). Thus, the external space of the JI became constituted by non-EU ETS Annex I countries, as well as projects involving greenhouse gases, production processes or pollution scales within EU ETS countries but outside the scope of the EUA. This means that the internal and external boundaries of the spatial fix were not simply about facilitating geographical expansion to new locations, but also about finding new socio-ecological relationships that could be represented within CER and ERU commodities.

The spatial fix expands the scope of abstraction within carbon commodities to new greenhouse gases, production processes and scales, temporalities, and geographical locations through quite different commodification processes compared to those involved in carbon allowances. In contrast to the commodification of relationships between installations and actual emissions, carbon offsetting instruments commodify relationships between projects and emissions that do not materialise (Bumpus 2011 p. 620; Knox-Hayes 2013 p. 117; Paterson 2014 p. 577). At the 'project' end of this relationship, this is defined by UNFCCC regulations, although as mentioned, the EU ETS imposes restrictions on some project types. Each type of abstraction is much broader than the EU ETS. In contrast to the EU ETS, JI and CDM projects can reduce any of the six types of greenhouse gases, including methane and hydrofluorocarbons, which are not part of the EU ETS, can be involved in production processes in the transport, agricultural, extractive, and waste sectors, which are also largely excluded, and can be located in any country that has ratified the Kyoto Protocol (UNFCCC, 1997 Annex A). By commodifying relationships between projects and emissions reductions involving these factors, the CDM and JI significantly increased levels of differentiation that can be exploited by polluters in the EU ETS.

3.2 The Spatio-Temporal Fix 85

The expansion offered by the link to the CDM and JI is facilitated by a simultaneous 'temporal fix' that commodifies representations of emissions reductions over time periods that are longer than the temporal abstraction that exists within the EU ETS. Spatial fixes associated with fixed capital always have a temporal component, whether it be the role of infrastructure in decreasing turnover time or, conversely, as a long-term investment (Jessop 2006 p. 149). Carbon offsetting more closely accords with temporal fixes created through financial markets, which defer crises of overaccumulation in the short-term by borrowing from, and shaping, the future. Harvey conceptualises this using Marx's term 'fictitious capital', being a 'claim exercised by money capital over a share of future surplus value production' (Harvey 2006 p. 267). Chapter 4 questions whether financial capital is indeed fictitious; what is important for the purposes of this chapter is that carbon offsetting works by commodifying relationships between projects and emissions reductions that rest on expectations of future emissions. As with 'fictitious' capital, the greater the expectation for future growth in emissions, the more carbon credits are issued.

At the centre of temporal fix is the notion of 'additionality' that is used to define and calculate the 'emission reduction' side of the offset relationship. What matters is not that emissions are reduced by a project absolutely, but that emissions levels are relatively lower than they would have otherwise been, and thus 'additional'. The 2001 Marrakech Accords defined emissions reductions from CDM projects as additional 'if anthropogenic emissions of greenhouse gases by sources are reduced below those that would have occurred in the absence of the registered CDM project activity'. An almost verbatim definition of additionality was also adopted for JI (UNFCCC, 2001 pp. 61, 83).

A range of related tools are used to measure additionality by comparing emissions released with and without the project. In the CDM, these include 'barrier analysis', which identifies financial, technological, policy, or other barriers to the project, 'investment analysis', which compares the profitability of different scenarios and 'common practice analysis', which considers whether a project goes beyond industry norms in the host region (Schneider 2009 pp. 243–50). A baseline emissions scenario is then constructed using these tools that takes account of a combination of historical emissions levels with existing barriers, the most profitable path available for the project developer and/or common technological practices in relevant parts of the economy (Paulsson 2009 p. 68). Emissions reductions are calculated out of the difference between the baseline scenario and actual emissions. These methodologies extend the more limited temporal abstraction of carbon

86 *Externalising Carbon*

allowances discussed in the previous chapter, especially for CDM projects, which have a total crediting period of up to twenty-one years.

The inner relationship between the spatial and temporal axes of crisis displacement and deferral is recognised by Harvey (2003b p. 64) in the conceptualisation of the 'spatio-temporal fix'. The coupling of the spatial and temporal aspects of the CDM and JI is critical to the fix for carbon-intensive companies in the EU ETS. As spatial fix, the CDM and JI expand the different forms of carbon appropriation covered by carbon markets. As temporal fix, the CDM and JI represent relationships between projects and emission reductions over a period of time in commodity form. The equalisation and exploitation of increased levels of difference between the internal and external spaces through the trading of carbon credits from offset projects to EU ETS installations is analysed and illustrated in the final section of this chapter.

3.3 Trading Carbon Credits

The CDM/JI spatial fix primarily benefited companies and their installations in the EU ETS. Of the just over 2 billion offset credits issued to CDM and JI projects by 1 May 2013, the day after the final phase two compliance date, 52 per cent had already been surrendered by installations in the EU ETS (European Commission 2013b; UNEP DTU 2018a, 2018b). These 1.059 billion surrendered CERs and ERUs allowed EU ETS installations to release 1,059 Mt CO_2-e more greenhouse gas emissions than the total emissions cap between 2008 (when CERs and ERUs were first permitted to be surrendered in the EU ETS) and 2012. Mostly due to the combined effects of the economic crisis and the over-allocation of allowances, total phase two emissions were well below free allocation levels, although surpluses and deficits were unevenly distributed between installations (European Environment Agency 2015b). Therefore, the main uses of CERs and ERUs in phase two were threefold: to provide deficit installations additional regulatory space to cover their excess emissions, to reduce the overall costs of complying across the EU ETS because of the lower price of CERs and ERUs, and to provide a fix to companies' post-2012 emissions caps by supporting the enhanced banking of EUAs.

The benefits of the spatio-temporal fix were concentrated among the top polluting companies. Table 3.1 shows the ten ultimate owners that surrendered the highest quantity of offsets in phase two in absolute terms. Germany energy utility E.ON is at the top, surrendering 53 Mt CO_{2-e} worth of CERs and ERUs. All except one were top twenty EU ETS polluters. The table also reports the relative use of offsets as a percentage of phase two surpluses or deficits. This shows offsets allowed many large polluting companies

3.3 Trading Carbon Credits

Table 3.1. *Top 10 EU ETS offset users 2008–12*

Ultimate owner	CERs (Mt CO$_2$-e)	ERUs (Mt CO$_2$-e)	Total offsets surrendered (Mt CO$_2$-e)	Phase 2 surplus/deficit (Mt CO$_2$-e)	Offsets as percentage of (surplus)/deficit (%)
E.ON	41	12	53	−76	70
Enel	45	1	46	−39	116
ArcelorMittal	33	12	45	155	(29)
Government of Poland	35	4	39	−26	151
RWE	12	13	25	−223	11
GDF Suez	18	6	24	−47	51
Government of Greece	10	10	20	−21	94
ThyssenKrupp	6	13	20	33	(59)
Government of Sweden	17	2	19	−156	12
KSBG	10	7	17	−11	152

Sources: Own calculation using Bureau van Dijk (2014) and European Commission (2013b, 2014b, 2014e, 2014h, 2014k)

to increase their emissions well above their allowance allocation levels. E. ON used offsets to cover 70 per cent of its allowance allocation deficit. Offset use ranged from 11 and 12 per cent of phase two allocation deficits for RWE and the Swedish Government (which owns Vattenfall), indicating a greater reliance on internal European allowances, to 151 and 152 per cent for German energy consortium KSBG and the Government of Poland (which owns PGE), respectively. Figures of greater than 100 per cent, also registered by Enel, indicate that installations owned by these companies surrendered offsets in excess of their allocation deficit. There are also two ultimate owners in the top ten offset users, steel producers ArcelorMittal and ThyssenKrupp, which had an overall allowance surplus.[1] All or some of the CERs and ERUs surrendered by KSBG, the Polish government, Enel, ArcelorMittal, and ThyssenKrupp, therefore enabled those companies to sell carbon commodities for profit or bank them for future use.

3.3.1 E.ON's Offset Strategy

This section follows the method employed in Chapter 2 by presenting a case study of the trading operations of E.ON. E.ON surrendered the most carbon credits of any company in the EU ETS in phase two, when the link to the

[1] Surpluses recorded for iron and steel companies are reduced by unrecorded transfers of allowances to power companies. Allowance transfers follow the transfer of waste gases for use in electricity generation, because the resulting emissions are apportioned to the generating installation. No robust and publicly available data exists to quantify this phenomenon.

Kyoto mechanisms began. As outlined in Chapter 1, E.ON was the second largest polluter in the EU ETS in the first two phases of the scheme. E.ON was established in 2000 through the merger of what were then the second and third biggest energy companies in Germany: VEBA and VIAG (E.ON 2015b; Millward 2008 p. 184). E.ON pursued a more aggressive internationalisation strategy than RWE, acquiring polluting assets that led to the company registering EU ETS emissions in Germany, Belgium, the Czech Republic, the United Kingdom, Hungary, the Netherlands, Poland, Denmark, Spain, Italy, France, Sweden, and Slovakia between 2005 and 2012. Among these assets were five very large installations, located in Germany, the United Kingdom, and the Netherlands. The largest installation was the 2,200 MW black coal-fired Scholven power plant in Gelsenkirchen, North Rhine-Westphalia, Germany. The plant, first commissioned in 1968, was the thirteenth largest polluting installation in the EU ETS between 2005 and 2012 (E.ON 2015f). E.ON moved its fossil fuel assets into a new company, Uniper, in 2016, and sold its stake in Uniper to Fortum (majority owned by the Government of Finland) in 2018 (Uniper SE 2018). E.ON also announced, in early 2018, that it would transfer its renewables assets to RWE (Storbeck 2018). The analysis in this section refers to E. ON as it was constituted before these changes because the period under examination is the second phase of the EU ETS.

Like RWE, E.ON installations directly sourced most of their carbon credits and allowances internally from specialist trading-only accounts associated with the financial operations of the company. Phase two trading data shows that accounts linked with E.ON installations secured 64 per cent of carbon credits and allowances internally, and the majority of these were associated with the company's speciality trading desk: E.ON Global Commodities (European Commission 2017). E.ON Global Commodities traded carbon alongside other commodities and derivatives including electricity, gas, oil, coal, and weather (E.ON 2014a). It claimed to have traded a total of 721 Mt of carbon in 2012, about equal to E.ON's total phase one and two emissions (E.ON 2014b).

There were two main ways for E.ON Global Commodities to source offsets that it could transfer to E.ON installations. The first way was the 'primary' offset market where carbon credits are sourced from direct participation in offset projects. The second way was the 'secondary' offset market where credits are purchased in over-the-counter or exchange-mediated contracts from third parties. E.ON Carbon Sourcing, a subsidiary of E.ON Global Commodities, described the former as its 'make' strategy, where the price of offsets is determined by the cost of production, and the latter as its

3.3 Trading Carbon Credits

'buy' strategy, where the price is determined by the market (Russo & Odeska 2009). The primary offset market can be further split up into different levels of participation, which can involve direct investment in the project or a purchase agreement with the project developer to simply purchase offsets directly.

E.ON surrendered approximately one-third of its carbon credits via the primary market route and approximately two-thirds of its credits via the secondary market route. Regarding the primary market, E.ON subsidiaries, including E.ON Carbon Sourcing, were named as 'project participants' in 21 registered CDM and three registered JI projects (UNEP DTU 2018a, 2018b; UNFCCC, 2014a, 2014b). Between 2008 and 2012, installations owned by E.ON ultimately surrendered CERs and ERUs produced by twelve of the CDM projects and one of the JI projects that they directly participated in. In total, E.ON installations surrendered 17,033,277 carbon credits from this primary market route, which represented 32 per cent of all offsets surrendered by the company (European Commission 2013b). Phase two trading data shows that the trading accounts of the E.ON subsidiaries that acted as project participants, such as E.ON Carbon Sourcing, sold 98 per cent their credits internally to E.ON trading accounts, which in turn traded with E.ON installation accounts and third parties (European Commission 2017).

3.3.2 E.ON's Offset Trading

The following case study of E.ON's offset trading is organised similarly to the RWE case study. It includes examples of the two kinds of primary market trading, and as well one example of a secondary market trade. Each example illustrates how the Kyoto mechanisms expand a different type of abstraction – scalar, functional, and process – to provide a fix to the limits of commodification in the EU ETS. Figure 3.1 represents the CER/ERU commodity flows in the three examples between various actors from the offset project that produced the credits to the EU ETS installation that finally surrendered the credits, in terms of the two axes of market segmentation and forms of abstraction highlighted. Offset commodity flows from these projects to installations can be much more precisely studied than with carbon allowances because the European Commission (2013b) publishes a complete list of the CDM and JI project IDs of carbon credits surrendered by EU ETS installations.

Linking the EU ETS to the CDM and JI provided polluters in Europe with a fix by expanding the scope of spatial abstraction beyond countries within the EU to less wealthy countries in the Global South and the former Soviet Union. Table 3.2 shows the countries of origin for offsets surrendered

90 *Externalising Carbon*

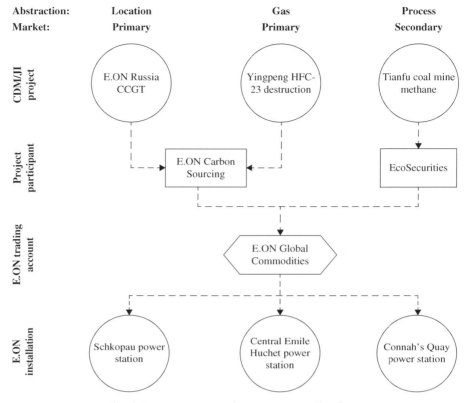

Fig. 3.1. E.ON CER/ERU commodity flows

by E.ON between 2008 and 2012. Just over half of offsets were produced by CDM projects in China, with South Korea, India, and Brazil also representing important sources of CERs. E.ON installations also made use of ERUs from JI projects, primarily from Russia and Ukraine. These two countries have dominated the JI market, representing 91 per cent of all issued ERUs and 99.8 per cent of ERUs surrendered by E.ON installations (European Commission 2013b; UNEP DTU 2018b). Though minor sources of ERUs for E.ON and the EU ETS as a whole, the presence of Lithuania, France and Estonia in Table 3.2 demonstrates the operation of the spatial fix within the EU, by projects that are outside the mandatory scope of the EU ETS.

The first example of a carbon credit chain ending with surrender by E.ON, illustrating abstraction from location, is a primary market trade from a JI project in Russia. For E.ON, this geographical expansion beyond the scope of the EU ETS didn't require trading relationships that went beyond the boundaries of the corporation. This was because E.ON's corporate

3.3 Trading Carbon Credits

Table 3.2. *Origin of offsets surrendered by E.ON installations 2008–12*

Country	Instrument	CERs/ERUs (Kt CO$_2$-e)	Percentage of offsets (%)
China	CDM	27,668	52
Ukraine	JI	8,406	16
South Korea	CDM	7,111	13
India	CDM	5,047	9
Russia	JI	3,437	6
Brazil	CDM	1,020	2
Mexico	CDM	214	0.4
Vietnam	CDM	154	0.3
South Africa	CDM	117	0.2
Argentina	CDM	106	0.2
Malaysia	CDM	44	0.1
Thailand	CDM	21	0.04
Lithuania	JI	18	0.03
France	JI	7	0.01
Pakistan	CDM	4	0.01
Estonia	JI	3	0.005
Egypt	CDM	2	0.003
Israel	CDM	1	0.002
Peru	CDM	1	0.002

Sources: Own calculation using Bureau van Dijk (2014) and European Commission (2013b, 2014b, 2014e, 2014h, 2014k)

boundaries also expanded beyond the EU. Indeed, one of E.ON Carbon Sourcing's JI projects, the Shaturskaya power plant in Shatura, Russia, was owned by E.ON Russia Power (Unipro 2018).

The project exploited geographical differentiation to construct and commodify a project-emissions reduction relationship. The project involved the construction of a new 400 MW combined cycle gas turbine power plant. It claimed additionality on the basis that without the project, electricity would be produced by other corporate actors from more polluting alternatives, such as coal-fired power (Global Carbon 2010 p. 3). This project-emission reduction relationship was commodified not because it replaced power from existing coal-fired stations, but because it replaced coal-fired power that would otherwise be needed to meet projected future increases in energy demand. This illustrates the capitalist teleology that underpins the formation of baselines (Lohmann 2011b p. 100). Less profitable possibilities, such as demand reduction, that could also avoid the need for more coal-fired power stations, are not considered in any of the alternative scenarios in the project design document (Global Carbon 2010 pp. 13–14). In assuming the need for

92 *Externalising Carbon*

new generation capacity, the choice of a combined cycle gas turbine was asserted as additional due to geographical differentiation in technology standards, as 'most of the new gas power plants in North America and Europe are of this type, whereas in Russia this is not the case' (Global Carbon 2010 p. 8).

The fix specifically benefited two E.ON installations that surrendered 416,887 ERUs from the project between 2008 and 2012: the 900 MW brown coal-fired Schkopau power plant in Saxony-Anhalt, Germany, and the 1,000 MW black coal-fired Ironbridge power station in Shropshire, in the United Kingdom (E.ON 2015c, 2015e; European Commission 2013b). This contributed to closing the phase two gap between allocation and emissions of 10,716,207t CO_2-e for the former, and increasing the latter's 1,655,724t CO_2-e phase two surplus. Two large installations not owned by E.ON, ThyssenKrupp's Duisburg steelworks in Germany and Riva Fire's Taranto steelworks in Italy, both also surrendered ERUs from the E.ON project. Thus, carbon offsetting also provided a spatio-temporal fix for E.ON beyond its own compliance requirements, through the profits it gained from selling credits to other companies.

Spatial abstraction in carbon offsetting is integrally linked to other forms of abstraction. The second example of a carbon credit chain leading to surrender by E.ON, also from within the primary market, adds abstraction from greenhouse gases with the commodification of carbon at a HFC-23 destruction CDM project in China. The main reason China sits at the top of Table 3.2 is that it has hosted 11 HFC-23 destruction CDM projects. These projects produced 41 per cent of the offsets surrendered by E.ON installations. Indeed, CERs from the destruction of HFC-23 dominated the CDM market as a whole, with 22 HFC-23 destruction projects out of a total of 7,792 registered projects producing 28 per cent of all CERs by the end of 2017, and an even greater proportion in the early years of the scheme (UNEP DTU 2018a). These CERs were made possible by the CDM expanding the scope of functional abstraction beyond the gases covered by the EU ETS to HFC-23, which is covered by the Kyoto Protocol as a type of hydrofluorocarbon. Expanding to HFC-23 also expanded the maximum scope of global warming potentials underpinning the carbon commodities circulating in the first two phases of the EU ETS from 298 for nitrous oxide, as discussed in Chapter 2, to 11,700 for HFC-23 (UNFCCC, 1995).

The largest single supplier of CERs surrendered by E.ON installations, representing 24 per cent of the total surrendered, was the Yingpeng HFC-23 destruction project in Yongkang City, Zhejiang Province, China (European Commission 2013b). E.ON sourced these credits on the primary market as a

3.3 Trading Carbon Credits 93

formal project participant through E.ON Carbon Sourcing. This form of participation was different to the Russian JI project; it was limited to a contractual arrangement to directly purchase CERs, rather than a direct investment and operational role. E.ON was only added as a project participant on 18 January 2010, after the registration and the beginning of the crediting period on 20 April 2009. It subsequently withdrew on 13 March 2013 following the ban on HFC-23 credits in the EU ETS, which is discussed in Chapter 5 (UNFCCC, 2014c).

The commodification of this project-emissions reduction relationship firstly depended on differentiation in the regulation of gases in China compared to wealthier countries. The Yingpeng project claimed to reduce greenhouse gas emissions by collecting and decomposing HFC-23 – a by-product of the production of HCFC-22, which is used as a refrigerant gas – into the less potent carbon dioxide and other substances (Climate Experts 2009 p. 2). China did not have emissions reductions requirements for HFC-23 under the Kyoto Protocol. Under the Montreal Protocol, which regulates HCFCs and HFCs as ozone depleting substances, China is grouped with developing countries, which have slower timetables for phasing out these gases (UNEP 2018). The differentiated treatment of China in these agreements is due to the recognition of lower historical responsibility for ozone depletion and global warming compared to wealthy countries. It also allowed the project to establish additionality by arguing that 'as a developing country, there are no regulations which require the destruction of the total amount of HFC23 waste in China at this moment or in the near future' (Climate Experts 2009 p. 9).

Second, the project uses China's rapid development to exploit its differentiated regulatory space to continue producing HCFC-22 and to not destroy HFC-23. The rapid increase in production of HCFC-22 supported a baseline scenario with high levels of HFC-23 emissions to reduce. HCFC-22 production capacity at the Yingpeng increased from 500 tonnes per year before 1997 to 25,000 tonnes per year in 2001 (Climate Experts 2009 p. 3). Following the standard HFC-23 methodology, the baseline scenario for the project, from which emissions reductions are credited, was based on ongoing HCFC-22 production at its maximum 2004 level of 23,269 tonnes (Climate Experts 2009 p. 11).

Third, the spatio-temporal fix from Yingpeng for E.ON installations was underpinned by the difference between the global warming potentials of carbon dioxide and HFC-23. Sixty installations owned by E.ON in the Czech Republic, Germany, Spain, France, the United Kingdom, Hungary, Italy, and Sweden ultimately surrendered 12,798,919 CERs from the project in phase two. Each E.ON installation is only regulated for carbon dioxide

94   *Externalising Carbon*

Table 3.3. *Project type of offsets surrendered by E.ON installations 2008–12*

Project type	CERs/ERUs (Kt CO_2-e)	Percentage of offsets (%)
HFCs	29,709	56
N_2O	10,791	20
Fugitive	5,083	10
Energy efficiency industry	3,471	7
Coal bed/mine methane	1,162	2
Hydro	804	2
Fossil fuel switch	727	1
Landfill gas	409	1
Methane avoidance	278	1
Energy distribution	200	0.4
Energy efficiency own generation	185	0.3
PFCs and SF6	167	0.3
Wind	122	0.2
Biomass energy	117	0.2
Energy efficiency service	69	0.1
Energy efficiency supply side	49	0.1
Cement	30	0.1
Landfill gas	6	0.01

Sources: Own calculation using Bureau van Dijk (2014), UNEP DTU (2018a, 2018b) and European Commission (2013b, 2014b, 2014e, 2014h, 2014k)

emissions. The E.ON installation that surrendered the most was the 1,873 MW coal and gas-fired Emile Huchet power station in Saint-Avold, Lorraine, France, which surrendered exactly 2 million Yingpeng CERs (E.ON 2011; European Commission 2013b). The difference in global warming potentials meant that the destruction of 171 tonnes of HFC-23 at Yingpeng substituted for the reduction of 2 million tonnes of carbon dioxide by E.ON's Emile Huchet power station.

The final example of a carbon credit chain leading to E.ON illustrates abstraction from location, greenhouse gas *and* production process in the CDM/JI spatio-temporal fix. Table 3.3 shows the wide range of project types that E.ON sourced carbon offsets from between 2008 and 2012. This includes several production processes that are outside the boundaries of installation-emissions relationships commodified in the EU ETS. Emissions from coal mining and landfill installations are not commodified in the EU ETS, which excludes methane. Methane is, however, covered by the Kyoto protocol, and the CDM provides opportunities for operators of coal mines, landfill, and other sources of fugitive emissions to commodify project-emissions reduction relationships in countries such as China.

3.3 Trading Carbon Credits

This final example is a secondary market trade from a project reducing fugitive emissions from coal mining processes. The largest supplier of such offsets to E.ON installations was the Tianfu project in the Beibei district of Chongqing, China. E.ON has never been a project participant and therefore acquired the CERs on the secondary market. The only project participant, other than the company that owns the mine, was Ecosecurities, which has participated in 354 CDM projects, making it the second most active project participant in the CDM (UNEP DTU 2018a). Ecosecurities was a specialist carbon market firm that was bought by investment bank JP Morgan Chase in 2009 and then subsumed into commodities trading company Mercuria in 2013 (Point Carbon 2013).

The Tianfu project produced carbon credits by capturing coal mine methane and using it to generate electricity for its own operations. Additionality came from avoiding the venting of methane and replacing more carbon-intensive electricity from coal-fired power stations that would otherwise supply the local network (EcoSecurities 2011 pp. 2–3). One installation owned by E.ON, the 1420 MW Connah's Quay combined cycle gas turbine power station in Flintshire, Wales, surrendered CERs from the project (E.ON 2013a). By surrendering 304,309 CERs produced by the Tianfu project between 2008 and 2012, the installation partly made up its phase two deficit of 2,628,829t CO_2-e (European Commission 2013b).

The three commodity chains outlined in this section demonstrate how processes of commodification in carbon offsetting risk entrenching unsustainable practices. All three examples involve projects that are based on the appropriation of carbon at different stages of the fossil fuel chain: Tianfu as miner, E.ON Russia as an electricity producer, and Yingpeng as an energy consumer. All make relative improvements from constructed scenarios, but none challenge the patterns of appropriation that underpin business-as-usual. The Tianfu case illustrates how such processes often fail to challenge fossil fuel-intensive accumulation. Abstracted from the production process creating the emissions, it is better for the climate to burn methane for electricity rather than vent it. But these emissions reductions depend on ongoing – and expanding, according to project documentation – coal mining (EcoSecurities 2011 p. 3). When Tianfu's full relationship with climate-changing capitalism is accounted for, it becomes clear that the project should support the phase out of coal mining. This is because, failing carbon capture and storage, 88 per cent of the world's known coal reserves, including 77 per cent of those located in China and India, need to remain in the ground to avoid global warming above 2 degrees Celsius (McGlade & Ekins 2015 p. 189). Yet, the rationale and design of commodification in carbon offsetting abstracts from this wider context that could inform, and necessitate, such actions.

Conclusion

Two related conclusions emerge from this chapter's consideration of the relationship between the EU ETS and the Kyoto mechanisms. First, the link with the Kyoto mechanisms has further impeded the capacity of the EU ETS to address climate change as a socio-ecological crisis, by providing an external fix that has offered additional means to sustain existing patterns of carbon appropriation beyond what is possible through carbon allowance trading alone. Second, by expanding levels of abstraction between differentiated forms of carbon appropriation that are equalised in carbon commodities, the substitutions involved in the trading and surrendering of offset credits are even less likely to represent effective forms of climate action, compared with trading within the EU ETS. Together, these conclusions show that rather than internalising externalities, the Kyoto offsetting mechanisms enabled fossil fuel-intensive capital to externalise climate action, with limited climate benefit.

In relation to the first conclusion, E.ON's heavy use of offsets to cover carbon pollution above its levels of free allocation supported the maintenance of a European energy mix only marginally better than RWE's, explored in the previous chapter. Excluding E.ON's hydropower assets, which were mostly built in the early to mid-twentieth century, only 6 per cent of E.ON's electricity was produced by renewables in 2013 – the year after a full phase of EU ETS trading allowing offset use (E.ON 2015a, 2015d pp. 36–7, 40, 43, 47). The poor climate performances of RWE and E.ON are significant in their own right because, together, they represented about one-eighth of both 2005–12 EU ETS emissions and 2013 EU electricity generation (RWE 2014a p. 17). Further, the experience of RWE and E.ON was shared by the other large polluting companies in the EU ETS. In 2012, after two phases of the EU ETS, the ten largest electricity companies in the EU by generation output – all of which, except EnBW, are also in the top 20 EU ETS polluters – were responsible for over half of total electricity production, but only 4 per cent of this was from renewables (Dallos 2014 p. 18). The Commission calculated that to meet the EU's own goal of an 80–95 per cent reduction in greenhouse gas emissions from 1990 levels by 2050, renewable energy needs to increase to as much as 97 per cent of electricity consumption, depending levels of energy demand management (European Commission 2011a pp. 6–7). Yet, the previous two chapters have shown that the EU ETS, including its links with the Kyoto mechanisms, has enabled companies responsible for large shares of emissions to avoid investing in renewables.

Secondly, at the other end of offset commodity movements, the offset projects discussed in this chapter are inadequate substitutes for structural change by large polluters in the EU ETS. Reiterating the conclusion of Chapter 2, this is not to say the activities of many CDM or JI projects are not useful in climate and/or community development terms. However, the experience of the trading relationships discussed are indicative of the inherent problems of using principles of formal market equality to address a substantively unequal climate problem. Carbon credits are produced by separating and objectifying project-emissions reduction relationships from their contexts and making them equal with installation-emissions relationships. The spatio-temporal fix of the Kyoto mechanisms and their links with the EU ETS is therefore delivered through different processes of commodification to those described in Chapter 2, but the fundamental principles are the same. In this respect, the primary distinction is the greater extent of the equalisation of difference embedded in offset commodities, which is evident in the uneven levels of technological, regulatory, and economic development between installations owned by E.ON and the offset projects it surrendered credits from. Thus, the first contradiction of carbon markets in a climate-changing capitalism – using market equality to address climate inequalities – is only intensified by carbon offsetting.

The last two chapters have assessed the EU ETS and its links with the Kyoto mechanisms in terms of whether the commodification and trading of carbon has reorganised the appropriation of carbon. The reconfiguration of time and space in the CDM and JI resonates with O'Connor's (1998 p. 167) notion that capitalist states tend to respond to socio-ecological crisis with attempts to '*restructure* production conditions with the aim of raising profits' (emphasis added). However, the defence of profits that this entails for the large polluters in the EU ETS has not, as flagged in the Introduction, translated to rising profits for other carbon market actors in financial markets. Chapter 4 adds the 'capitalisation' of carbon to this book's typology of capitalist relations with, and within, nature, to analyse contradictions in carbon markets as accumulation strategy.

4

Valuing Carbon

Introduction

The commodification of carbon brings climate policy firmly within the calculus of capitalist value relations. The focus of this chapter is on the nature of value relations in carbon markets to better understand the relationship between carbon markets and processes of capital accumulation. As outlined in the Introduction, crisis-ridden carbon markets have, to date, failed to create opportunities for accumulation on the scale anticipated by financial actors. Despite these developments, dominant political economic accounts are grounded in the notion that carbon markets represent an accumulation strategy for capital. The argument was most prominently described by Bumpus and Liverman (2008) as 'accumulation by decarbonisation'. As Böhm et al. (2012 p. 1630) explain, 'from a Marxist standpoint, carbon markets can be understood as a successful strategy for the creation of a new environmental commodity, introducing a new mechanism of capitalist legitimation and playing a crucial role in the creation of accumulation opportunities'. Significantly, assessments of the efficacy of carbon markets in addressing climate change have, in part, rested on the positive or negative effects of the opportunities for accumulation that they engender (Lohmann 2010, 2011a; Newell & Paterson 2009, 2010).

This chapter reconsiders dominant political economic analyses of carbon markets as accumulation strategy in light of the financial challenges faced by emissions trading and carbon offsetting schemes. Hence, its primary concern is the relationship between carbon markets and climate change as an economic crisis. To do so, it moves beyond the focus in Chapters 2 and 3 on the more concrete aspects of the commodification of carbon. Reflecting on the critical literature on the commodification of nature that informed the argument in those chapters, Robertson (2012 p. 387) warns that that 'we are often focused so intently on the bizarre diversity of forms in this new economy that we forget that they are united in this process of abstraction: at least in capitalism, what is circulating is not wetlands, not trees, not salmon, but *value*' (emphasis in original, see also Bigger & Robertson 2017). This chapter follows this conceptual move by analysing whether and how carbon commodities could become a new form of capital, as 'self-expanding value'. It therefore introduces and develops the notion of the 'capitalisation' of carbon to conceptualise the shift that occurs when the expansion of commodification makes areas of socio-ecological life that were formerly freely appropriated by capital the direct object of capital accumulation. The chapter identifies another contradiction of carbon markets in a climate-changing capitalism, which emerges from tensions between accumulation by appropriation and accumulation by capitalisation that are internal to the carbon commodity. The contradiction is that the carbon market accumulation strategy requires ongoing accumulation in fossil fuel industries.

The first section provides an overview of how carbon is traded and presents data to document the growth and decline of financial activity in the main global carbon markets, focusing on the impact of weak carbon prices. The second section revisits accounts of carbon markets as a state-driven accumulation strategy by comparing two contrasting approaches to understanding value relations in carbon markets: carbon as rent and carbon as capital. The third section analyses accumulation dynamics in carbon markets in terms of the extent to which carbon has or could become an emergent form of capital, assigning an active role to finance and nature in constituting capitalist value relations. Focusing on instances of carbon as capital in the form of credit, collateral, and risk, the chapter argues that states have thus far failed to navigate the necessary tensions between fossil fuel and financial interests in the carbon market accumulation strategy. It also argues, however, that the commodification of carbon, as 'meta-capital', contains the potential to bring the appropriation and capitalisation of carbon together in a singular accumulation strategy that would compare, and enforce, the profitability of carbon pollution.

4.1 Trading Carbon

4.1.1 The Financial Infrastructure of Carbon Trading

EUAs allocated or auctioned in the EU ETS, and CERs and ERUs issued to offset projects as part of the CDM and JI, are traded as commodities in futures, options, and spot markets. Carbon futures are contracts that arrange the delivery and payment of a certain quantity of allowances or offset credits at a specified future date, usually in December. Carbon options are contracts that give an actor the right, but not obligation, to buy (known as a call) or sell (known as a put) allowances or offset credits at a point of time in the future. Carbon spot trading involves the almost immediate purchase and physical delivery of allowances or offset credits (World Bank 2012 pp. 31–3).

These different carbon instruments are traded in a variety of settings, including exchanges, over-the-counter, and bilaterally. Exchange platforms offer generic spot, options, and futures contracts by acting as the direct counterparty for both buyer and seller, guaranteeing delivery of carbon allowances and credits or cash settlements (Ellerman & Joskow 2008 p. 50). Over-the-counter and bilateral trades tend to involve larger contracts that are more tailored to the parties involved, compared to exchange trading. In bilateral and over-the-counter trades, a contract for future delivery is known as a forward. Over-the-counter trades are mediated by financial institutions acting as carbon brokers, whereas bilateral trades occur directly between buyer and seller (Ellerman et al. 2010 pp. 131–2). The vast majority of carbon allowances are either traded in or cleared by exchanges (World Bank 2012 pp. 31–3). Due to the heterogeneity of offset projects, primary (i.e., the initial purchase of carbon credits from project developers) CER trades tend to occur over-the-counter or bilaterally and follow the terms set out in contracts known as emissions reduction purchase agreements (World Bank 2008 p. 65).

Carbon trading is driven by a number of factors, including state decisions over allowance allocation patterns and regulations determining the compliance cycle, which affect different actors unevenly. Power companies have tended to be allocated fewer allowances than they required, whereas manufacturing companies have tended to be overallocated compared to their actual emissions. This means that power companies mostly trade to secure carbon allowances and credits to cover future emissions, whereas manufacturing companies mostly trade to maximise profits from their surplus of allowances. This creates competing imperatives to hedge against the risk of carbon prices going up or down, encouraging trading in derivatives markets, which offer the potential to buy financial instruments that are linked to carbon price movements without necessarily needing to buy or sell actual carbon commodities (Neuhoff et al. 2012 pp. 2–3; World Bank 2012 pp. 34–6).

Carbon allowances and offset credits have also been bundled together as securities in structures that are shaped by the particularities of carbon markets. Securities have been developed that progressively deliver carbon allowances in yearly tranches to meet compliance requirements. Similarly, securities that pool together offset credits from a range of different project types and locations have also been developed to manage risks of purchasing agreements for credits from individual projects (see for example Camco 2009; Szabo 2010).

4.1.2 The Rise and Fall of Carbon Trading Profits

Polluting companies regulated by the EU ETS have made profits from carbon trading in a variety of ways. Companies that were overallocated allowances in the first two phases of the scheme could make windfall profits by engaging in the financial practices outlined above to sell surplus allowances. As mentioned, companies involved in manufacturing industries received the highest allocation levels relative to verified emissions. The uneven distribution of emissions translated to the uneven distribution of surplus allowances between companies, which saw many of the biggest polluters gain the biggest windfall profits.

Table 4.1 lists the ten ultimate owners that accrued the largest allowance surpluses in absolute terms between 2005 and 2012.[1] All are in the top seventy-five largest polluting ultimate owners. Combined, their 553 million surplus allowances represent 35 per cent of the total accrued to surplus ultimate owners across the whole EU ETS in that period, demonstrating a concentration

Table 4.1. *Top ten ultimate owners by 2005–12 allowance surplus*

Ultimate owner	2005–12 allowance surplus (Mt CO_2-e)	% of allocation	Sector
ArcelorMittal	215	31	Iron and steel
Tata Steel	82	31	Iron and steel
Lafarge	49	25	Cement
ThyssenKrupp	39	25	Iron and steel
SSAB	34	36	Iron and steel
Government of the Czech Republic	33	10	Electricity
HeidelbergCement	31	18	Cement
CEMEX	24	23	Cement
HKM	23	39	Iron and steel
Total	23	12	Oil refining

Sources: Own calculation using Bureau van Dijk (2014) and European Commission (2014b, 2014e, 2014h, 2014k)

---

[1] As flagged in Chapter 3, these figures are unadjusted for waste gas transfers. Efforts to estimate this phenomenon have still found significant allowance surpluses in the iron and steel industry (de Bruyn et al. 2016; Morris 2014).

102   *Valuing Carbon*

Table 4.2. *2005–12 allowance surpluses by general sector*

General sector	2005–12 net surplus/deficit (Mt CO_2-e)
Manufacturing	1,188
Electricity	−893

Sources: Own calculation using Bureau van Dijk (2014) and European Commission (2014b, 2014e, 2014h, 2014k)

and centralisation of surpluses. On average, the top ten surplus holders were allocated 25 per cent more allowances than their verified emissions. The sectoral breakdown reveals that eight of the ten are steel or cement companies.

Allowance surpluses generated significant profits for manufacturing companies, especially in the first and early part of the second phase of the EU ETS. The most overallocated company, Luxembourg-based steel company ArcelorMittal, illustrates the upper end of the magnitude of profits from selling surplus allowances for individual companies. Between 2009 and 2012, the company reported a total of US$508 million in net profits from the sale of carbon allowances and credits (ArcelorMittal 2010 p. 53, 2011 p. 40, 2013 p. 92). In the EU ETS as a whole, de Bruyn et al. (2016 p. 2) estimate that manufacturing and other overallocated companies, excluding those in the electricity sector, made €8 billion from selling surplus allowances between 2008 and 2014. These profits could also be bolstered by purchasing and surrendering CERs or ERUs and profiting from the spread between offset and EUA prices.

Demand for surplus allowances from ArcelorMittal and other manufacturing companies came from the generally under-allocated electricity industry. Table 4.2 compares the surpluses and deficits of the electricity and manufacturing industries, the two general sectors that account for 98 per cent of all EU ETS emissions, for 2005–12. Overall, the deficit of the electricity sector comprised 75 per cent of the surplus of manufacturers. Thus, although the electricity industry deficit was a source of windfall profits for the overallocated manufacturing sector, these profits were limited by the general surplus of allowances in the EU ETS as a whole.

Both over-allocated and under-allocated companies could also make indirect profits from passing on the costs of freely allocated allowances. The overallocation of manufacturing industries in the first two phases of the EU ETS was justified on the basis that those sectors were exposed to international competition and therefore could not increase their prices in line with EUA prices. However, both electricity and manufacturing industries (cement, iron and steel, and oil refineries particularly), have been able to pass on the price of carbon allowances to varying degrees (CE Delft & Öko-Institut 2015; European Commission 2015b p. 201). Moreover, for the first two phases of the EU ETS, there is no evidence that increased prices resulted in 'carbon leakage' – that is, a transfer of carbon-intensive production to locations without equivalent climate policies (Ecorys et al. 2013). De Bruyn et al. (2016 p. 20) estimate that passing on the notional costs of mostly freely allocated permits delivered manufacturing industries an additional €15–26 billion between 2008 and 2014. For the fossil fuel-based electricity sector, Ellerman et al. (2010 p. 326) calculated windfall profits from increased prices to be €11 billion in phase one of the scheme. Thus, in buying their carbon allowances, the power sector was not necessarily the source of manufacturers' profits; all regulated sectors derived profits in the carbon market from end consumers.

Both sources of profits for polluting industries – free allocation and passing on the nominal costs of carbon allowances – have diminished over time. First, as will be outlined in Chapter 5, the EU ETS has been reformed to reduce levels of free allocation. The EU ETS has gradually moved towards auctioning allowances, starting within the electricity sector in phase two, and extending to other sectors in phase three. While free allocation continues for many sectors, midway through phase three in 2016, all sectors except the cement industry were being allocated fewer allowances than they required for compliance (Buckley 2017 p. 34). When allowances are auctioned, increased prices from cost pass-through covers actual allowance costs, rather than 'opportunity costs'. Income from auctioning carbon allowances primarily accrues to states but some of this is returned to industry via compensation mechanisms. For example, Germany's compensation plan for 2014, approved by the European Commission, totalled €350 million. This is almost half of the €750 million in auctioning revenues the German government received in the same year (European Commission 2013f; Federal Ministry for Economy Affairs and Energy 2012; German Emissions Trading Authority 2015). Second, as a result of the lingering effects of overallocation, and the downturn in emissions following the global recession, the prices of carbon allowances and credits fell, minimising the effect of cost pass-through, and the profits to be made from selling surplus allowances. For example, ArcelorMittal's reported profits from selling carbon allowances and credits fell from an average of US$127 million per year from 2009 to 2012 to US$32 and US$14 million in 2013 and 2014, despite ongoing free allocation for the company (ArcelorMittal 2015 p. 90).

Figure 4.1 illustrates the volatile but overall downward price trajectory of major carbon allowance and offset credit contracts on the European Climate

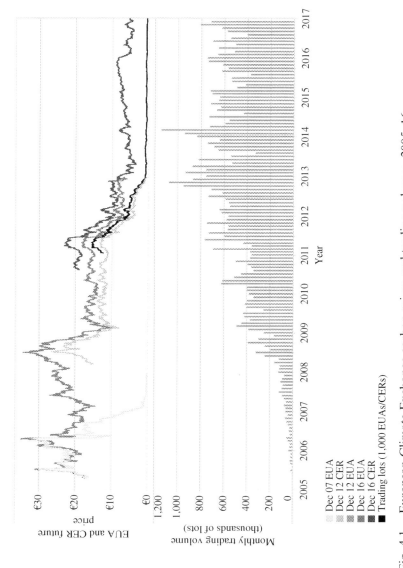

Fig. 4.1. European Climate Exchange carbon prices and trading volumes, 2005–16
Source: Intercontinental Exchange (2017). Note: from 2014 trading volumes include electricity and coal lots

Exchange from 2005 to the end of 2016. In phase one, EUA futures for delivery in December 2007 hit a high of €31.50 in April 2006. The contracts then halved in price in two weeks with the release of 2005 verified emissions data. With the endemic nature of the allowance surplus becoming clear, in the context of the inability to bank allowances into 2008, the price of EUAs hovered around €1 for most of 2007. In phase two, EUA futures for delivery in 2012 again reached highs of €34.38 in July 2008 before crashing over the European winter of 2008–9 to levels to as low as €9.43 because of the lower emissions that came with reduced production levels in a recessionary economy. After a short price recovery, EUA futures largely traded below €10 from 2012, and even greater levels of oversupply in offset markets saw CERs lose almost all value (Intercontinental Exchange 2017).

Declining carbon prices, which have reduced windfall profits from the carbon market for polluting industries, have had contradictory effects on opportunities for financial actors to profit. On one hand, Figure 4.1 shows that trading volumes on the European Climate Exchange steadily increased while carbon prices were falling. Trading on the exchange more than doubled each year in the first phase of the EU ETS and the first year of the second phase. Trading volumes on the exchange continued to grow by an average of over one-third per year for the remainder of phase two from 2009 to 2012. This volume of trading activity was maintained after 2012, when prices plateaued at a low level. The experience of trading on this exchange is consistent with available figures for global carbon markets as a whole, which is to be expected because around 85 per cent of exchange trading occurs on the European Climate Exchange (Pell 2014). According to the World Bank (2006 p. 14), in 2005, only 15 per cent of total allocated allowances were traded. In the four years to 2011, the rate of allowance turnover increased to 324 per cent of the total allocation (World Bank 2014 p. 73).

On the other hand, increasing volumes were not able to sustain the overall market transaction value of global carbon trading. This is represented in Figure 4.2, which shows Bloomberg's calculation of annual market transaction values (roughly, the volume of trades multiplied by the carbon price) in global carbon markets, almost all of which is associated with the EU and UN schemes. Increased trading volumes supported increasing market transaction values until 2011. The 2011 peak in the market transaction value of global carbon trading was achieved because the 22 per cent increase in trading volume outweighed the 10 per cent average decline in carbon prices that year (Bloomberg New Energy Finance 2012). Trading volumes surpassed 2011 figures by 23 per cent in 2012 and 16 per cent in 2013, but

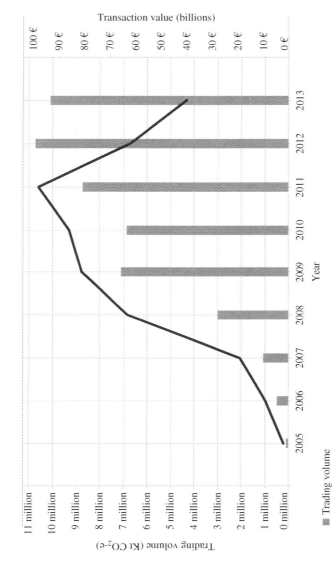

Fig. 4.2. Global carbon market transaction values and trading volumes, 2005–13
Source: Bloomberg New Energy Finance (2014)

this was unable to arrest the decline in market transaction value as a result of low carbon prices which, by Bloomberg's calculations, fell from €98 billion in 2011 to €62 billion in 2012 and €40 billion in 2013 (Bloomberg New Energy Finance 2014). Bloomberg ceased reporting these figures after 2013, but the most recent World Bank calculation, which put the total market transaction value of global carbon markets plus carbon taxation schemes in 2017 at US$52 billion (steady since 2015), indicates that the market has not recovered since then (World Bank 2017 p. 24).

Opportunities to make profits from trading carbon commodities in the EU ETS, and its links with the CDM and JI, have therefore not materialised to the extent that financial actors and institutions expected. In the early years of the EU ETS, the head of environmental markets at Barclays, for example, predicted that carbon would overtake oil as 'the world's biggest commodity market, and it could become the world's biggest market overall' (Kanter 2007). Similarly, the head of emissions trading at Merrill Lynch forecast that carbon markets could rival the world's largest financial markets, as 'one of the fasting-growing markets ever, with volumes comparable to credit derivatives inside of a decade' (Kanter 2007). However, even the peak yearly notional value of trading in global carbon markets, primarily made up of activity associated with the EU ETS, of €98 billion in 2011, remained dwarfed by the size of other markets that traders at Barclays and Merrill Lynch had hoped would be surpassed. By comparison, this figure is regularly surpassed on a weekly basis by trading in crude oil on CME Group exchanges alone and by trading in just one type of credit derivative: credit default swaps (CME Group 2016; International Swaps and Derivatives Association 2015).

The crash in the price of carbon and the value of trading had negative economic implications for financial institutions. Expectations of opportunities for the financial sector was reflected in advice from management consultancy firm McKinsey & Company on 'profiting from the low carbon economy', which stated:

To prosper, banks must determine the right time to commit to carbon trading and offset sourcing in order to build share in what is changing from a market of one-off, over-the-counter deals into a global flow business comparable to other large commodity markets such as oil...Exchanges are already moving quickly to help build this new market. Many of the big exchange groups, such as NYSE Euronext, through its Bluenext subsidiary, and Nasdaq OMX, through its NordPool operation, have launched spot and futures contracts. Volumes are growing smartly, and some exchanges are already turning profits. New brokerages are springing up to help create markets in EU emissions allowances [and] UN-backed certified emission reductions. (Hoffman & Twining 2009)

108 *Valuing Carbon*

However, since then, major financial institutions in the City of London, where the carbon trading industry is centred, have responded by voting on the carbon market with their feet. As mentioned in the Introduction, Deutsche Bank, Barclays, Morgan Stanley, and UBS, among other firms, all closed or scaled back their carbon desks (Straw & Platt 2013 p. 25). Negative implications have also followed for the various state and multilateral climate finance arrangements that were supposed to be funded by the growth of carbon trading (Bracking 2015b; Ervine 2013a, 2013b; Reyes 2011). This disjuncture between prediction and reality is somewhat replicated in critical political economic literature on carbon markets.

4.2 Finance, Nature, and Value in Carbon Markets

4.2.1 Carbon Markets as Accumulation Strategy

Political economic analyses of carbon markets as accumulation strategy highlight the profit-making opportunities created by the extension and multiplication of financial relations engendered by the commodification of carbon. Capitalist states, understood from a broadly Marxist perspective as institutions that secure the conditions for the expanded reproduction of capitalism, are central to this narrative (O'Connor 1998). The general argument is that states opted for the market-based policy route over alternatives because carbon markets promised to provide new opportunities for accumulation, benefiting financial actors, such as investment banks, brokerage firms, securities exchanges, and specialist carbon funds, and avoiding direct confrontation with, and, providing economic opportunities for, established fossil fuel interests (Böhm et al. 2012; Bumpus & Liverman 2008; Lohmann 2011a; Newell & Paterson 2009; Paterson 2010). This common analytical thread of carbon markets as state-driven accumulation strategy forms the basis of divergent assessments of the efficacy of carbon markets as climate policy.

Lohmann's (2010, 2011a) pessimistic assessment of carbon markets situates profits from the commodification of carbon within broader processes of financialisation, especially the proliferation of derivatives markets. Carbon markets, Lohmann (2011a p. 93) argues, rest on 'an open-ended dynamic of abstraction that helps expand the scope for accumulation in climate change mitigation … ma[king] possible a cascade of further profit-generating equivalences'. This serves as a warning, however, that carbon traders employ many of the same quantitative techniques of abstraction and equivalence that saw derivatives markets become disembedded from the risks that were purportedly being commodified, triggering and deepening the 2007–8 financial crisis.

4.2 Finance, Nature, and Value in Carbon Markets

Lohmann (2010 p. 238) sees parallel processes of disembedding at play in carbon markets, away from 'historical pathways and political and social movements involved in a transition away from fossil fuels'. This is said to generate new risks for those who are negatively affected by climate policy specifically and the climate crisis generally. Thus, Lohmann (2011a p. 98) draws a negative connection between carbon markets as accumulation strategy and the efficacy of the policy for combatting climate change, positing that accumulation in the carbon markets takes place not through 'decarbonisation' or 'defossilisation' but through the algebra of 'expropriation'.

Conversely, Newell and Paterson focus on the potentially positive political implications of opportunities for accumulation for the finance sector stemming from carbon markets. They argue that carbon markets were 'almost unstoppable once the newly dominant financial actors realised its potential as a new market, with its derivatives, options, swaps, insurance and so on, and thus as a profitable enterprise' (Newell & Paterson 2010 p. 28). As Paterson (2010 pp. 361–2) makes clear in response to complaints from business over the transaction costs created by carbon market regulation, opportunities for profits and accumulation in carbon markets derive from the very processes involved in creating a new commodity: 'It is precisely the methodology, and the bureaucratic steps followed, which create the value in the first place … going through stringent procedures thus creates value in the marketplace and enables a pattern of accumulation to proceed.' Although recognising the shortcomings of existing carbon markets and the obstacles facing the reform of market-based policies, Newell and Paterson (2010 p. 10) were cautiously optimistic about the policy approach because of the opportunities it creates for finance-led accumulation. As they explain, the carbon market, working in conjunction with initiatives such as carbon disclosure, shareholder activism, and fossil fuel divestment, 'creates the possibility of economic winners from decarbonisation. What's more, those winners – financiers – are rather powerful, and can support you as you build the policies which might produce decarbonisation overall'.

4.2.2 Carbon as Rent

Accounts of carbon markets as accumulation strategy are challenged by the declining economic opportunities from carbon markets. One line of critique is offered by Felli (2014) and Andreucci et al. (2017), who argued that the commodification of carbon is characterised by purely distributional rent relations. Felli (2014 p. 253) directly criticises the conceptual basis of the literature for 'tak[ing] the appearance of market mechanisms ("profit making") at

110 *Valuing Carbon*

face value, rather than questioning the social relations of production under-pinning them'. For Felli (2014 p. 275), carbon trading is 'predicated on a draw on surplus value' because no socially necessary labour time is involved in the creation of the carbon commodity (see also Vlachou & Pantelias 2017 p. 3). Andreucci et al. (2017 p. 31) extended this argument by drawing a clear distinction between rent as 'value grabbing' and accumulation as 'the creation of value', stating that 'pseudo-commodities' such as carbon 'yield profit for their owners primarily in the form of rent, rather than through the insertion of an asset as a productive force in the valorisation process'.

Marx's discussions of rent in volume III of *Capital* provide a basis to ela-borate this understanding of value in carbon markets as rent. In relation to land, Marx (1991 p. 959) argues: 'Just as the functioning capitalist pumps out surplus labour from the worker, and thus surplus-value and surplus pro-duct in the form of profit, so the landowner pumps out a part of this surplus-value or surplus profit in turn from the capitalist in the form of rent.' According to Marx there are two general conditions for the expropriation of rent. The first is whether the 'natural forces can be monopolised' and the sec-ond is whether they 'give the industrialist who makes use of them a surplus profit' (Marx 1991 p. 908). Monopolisation creates scarcity and excludabil-ity. If scarce and excludable natural conditions are to command a rent, their appropriation must be necessary to increase surplus value production.

In carbon markets, possibilities for the expropriation of value as rent fun-damentally depend on the relationship between the conditions of monopoli-sation creating scarcity and the contribution of nature to economic surpluses. Carbon commodities, as representations of the appropriation of carbon, give the companies that surrender them surplus profits because they enable fossil fuel-intensive production processes that produce surplus value by increasing the productivity of labour. In the EU ETS, the circulation of value as rent in carbon commodities is achieved through the monopolisation of relationships between installations and emissions by the commodification processes of individuation, privatisation and abstraction discussed in Chapter 2. These commodification processes create scarcity and excludability by limiting the quantity of carbon allowances and credits and compelling their surrender for each tonne of carbon dioxide-equivalent produced within regulated installation-emissions relationships.

From the perspective of carbon as rent, weaknesses in both conditions of carbon rent shed light on the challenges encountered by the carbon market accumulation strategy. The economic crisis reduced the underlying source of value in carbon markets by reducing opportunities for profits from the appropriation of carbon. For example, profits from electricity generation accruing to large EU electricity utilities dropped by 40 per cent between the onset of the crisis in 2008 and 2013, as demand and prices for electricity fell dramatically (McKinsey & Company 2014). By over-allocating allowances, and allowing too many offset credits into the system, states also failed to monopolise relations of carbon appropriation to support the circulation of carbon rents by setting a stringent-enough cap. Despite some reforms to withdraw allowances from the market, outlined in Chapter 5, at the end of 2015, the cumulative surplus was 1.8 billion allowances – approximately equivalent to one year of EU ETS emissions (European Environment Agency 2016 pp. 17–18). Once state subsidies via free allowance allocation were withdrawn, the devaluation of carbon rents offered little opportunities for profits in carbon markets.

4.2.3 Carbon as Capital

Understanding carbon as rent offers a framework for explaining the crisis of accumulation in carbon markets that relegates finance in processes of value creation to a distributive, and thus relatively passive, role. Carbon markets involve important conflicts over the distribution of value, but this does not discount the possibility that carbon commodities also have bearings on determinations of socially necessary labour time, and thus the production of value, beyond the labour embedded in their own creation. The remainder of this chapter considers the way nature and finance actively co-constitute value relations in carbon markets. In doing so, it responds, with an emphasis on the role of finance, to a question posed by Kay and Kenney-Lazar (2017 p. 296): 'What role does biophysical, material nature play in the process of producing value and enabling expanded capital accumulation?'

Recent interventions by critical geographers and other political economists have sought, albeit in ways that are not always in complete accord with each other, to understand how nature, finance, or both enter the calculus of value under capitalism. In relation to value and nature, Robertson (2012 p. 389) has led the way in warning against analyses that proceed according to sharp distinctions between actors and activities that do and do not produce value and consequently view new areas of nature's commodification as 'simply the search for profit in a fixed and existing world'. Robertson's (2012 p. 389) starting point is Marx's conception of labour, which he argues 'should be understood as a process that occurs between nature and the individual'. This conception of value-producing labour as a socio-ecological relation is echoed by Walker (2017 p. 55), who stresses that socially necessary labour time, the measure of value from a traditional Marxist perspective, 'includes the socially necessary amounts of natural inputs and natural forces' within its calculus.

Huber (2017, 2018) and Christophers (2016b), however, note that the role of finance in constituting socio-ecological relations of value has been given relatively less attention in the geographical literature. Like Robertson (2012), Huber (2018) points out the widespread existing literature on the commodification of nature tends to prioritise analyses that proceed at the level of nature's concrete specificities (for exceptions, see Labban 2010, 2014; Descheneau & Paterson 2011; Büscher 2012; Johnson 2013; Loftus & March 2015; Bracking 2015a; Kay 2017). Some critical studies of 'financialisation' in the broader political economic literature have indeed sought to consider the active role of finance in value relations but often in geographically anaemic and ecologically blind ways (Castree & Christophers 2015; Christophers 2012, 2013). At its best, this work has challenged dichotomies between unproductive finance and productive labour in ways that parallel interventions that critique the separation between unproductive nature and productive labour. One of the points of focus has been competing accounts on whether and how new forms of commodification in financial markets propel accumulation by creating new forms of capital, understood as a social relation of self-expanding value.

Contributions by Fine (2013), Leyshon and Thrift (2007), and Bryan and Rafferty (2006) nominate three different ways that finance can become integral to accumulation through processes of capitalisation. For Fine (2013), sustaining profits from the 'extensive' spread of finance into new spheres of life depends on the presence of 'intensive' practices that move beyond the redistribution of existing surplus value by creating new forms of interest-bearing capital. Fine (2013 p. 49) distinguishes between 'extensive' and 'intensive' financial relations by referring to Marx's distinction between money advanced as 'simple credit' and money advanced as capital 'requir[ing] the expansion of that wealth: production and realisation of surplus value in Marxist terms'. Leyshon and Thrift (2007) see a broader potential for the 'capitalisation of almost everything' in efforts to deliver income streams from new financial assets. They argue finance is engaged in 'a fresh round of tracing value to its source – or rather sources' by creating assets out of existing relations through processes of dis- and re-aggregation that can be used to leverage trading and investment (Leyshon & Thrift 2007 pp. 99–100). Finally, Bryan and Rafferty (2006) bring a deeper focus by looking at the transformation of capital itself within financial markets in derivatives. They argue that systems of derivatives, as 'meta-capital', intensify competition by enabling calculative practices that constantly compare and contest the relative performance of all circuits of capital, exerting disciplinary pressure on labour. Financial markets produce derivatives as commodified exposures to risk through processes of calculation and abstraction where 'capital itself is made homogeneous (capital in general) via the concept of return relative to calculable risk' (Bryan et al. 2015 p. 315).

Building on these perspectives by bringing in an appreciation of capital as a *socio-ecological* relation of self-expanding value illuminates specific contradictions for nature as accumulation strategy. Similar to perspectives on value and nature discussed above, Moore (2015 p. 57) argues, 'Marx's conception of value, already, entwines human and extra-human work and their constitutive relations.' Under capitalism, this occurs in a very peculiar fashion, where capitalist expansion is made possible by securing 'cheap nature', or 'unpaid work outside the commodity system' (see also Fraser 2014a, 2014b; Moore 2015 p. 17). This point is further developed by Collard and Dempsey (2017), who illuminate the varied 'orientations' of non-commodified nature that are produced and reproduced along different axes of hierarchical difference. Moore (2015) argues that free appropriation of this uncapitalised nature is an integral component of capitalist value relations because it places downward pressure on socially necessary labour time. Appropriation, in its different orientations, depends, in turn, on what Moore (2015 p. 62) terms 'abstract social nature': those knowledge practices that 'map, code, survey, quantify and otherwise identify and facilitate new sources of Cheap Nature'. Such practices, however, also allow socio-ecological relations to be commodified in ways that bring relations of appropriation directly into the orbit of relations of capitalisation. The sustainability of accumulation strategies based on the capitalisation of nature, such as in the case of commodifying carbon, therefore hinge on maintaining, and increasing, the appropriation of nature (Moore 2015 p. 95).

4.3 Capitalising Carbon

In the early stages of the EU ETS, surveys revealed great enthusiasm about carbon as a financial asset among corporate actors, including energy companies and financial institutions (e.g. Uhrig-Homburg & Wagner 2008). One year into the first phase of the scheme, there were signs that these expectations were beginning to materialise. For example, in January 2006, the head of environmental markets at Fortis Bank reported:

Yesterday gave us a real taste of the year to come. A minute fraction of the total pool of EUAs was monetised through a 14 month [repurchase agreement]. Simply put, a corporate net received about €50 million, to be used as working capital, for

114 *Valuing Carbon*

3.3 million EUAs, which they will get back in time for compliance in 2007 ... We can expect a reasonable percentage of first period allowances, worth some €150 billion, to be monetised and/or start serving as collateral. This is a turning point in the valuation of carbon. *Carbon is capital*, and well on track to become a European hard currency. (Walhain 2006 emphasis added)

In proclaiming 'carbon is capital', the banker heralded the subsumption of the carbon commodity to the logic of capitalist expansion in two key ways. In this first instance, the banker was referring to the capacity to monetise carbon, where the 'working capital' provided by the carbon market could take on the characteristics of interest-bearing capital (Fine 2013). Second, the banker was foreshadowing the use of carbon as collateral, where carbon could be leveraged for expanded capital accumulation (Leyshon & Thrift 2007). These two avenues toward the capitalisation of carbon, which have been attempted with varying and diminishing levels of success in the EU ETS, are examined in the first two parts of this section, paying particular attention to the contradictions facing states. The third part looks forward to the possibilities for capitalising carbon by considering how carbon could become a form of meta-capital, both as part of 'meta-nature' and 'meta-risk' (Bryan & Rafferty 2006).

4.3.1 Carbon as Credit

Strategies to monetise carbon use the annual compliance cycle of the EU ETS to create credit-like instruments that can become forms of interest-bearing capital (Fine 2013). Allowances are allocated in February each year but do not need to be surrendered for compliance until April in the following year. Companies therefore have allowances in their possession for fourteen months before they need to be surrendered. In the Fortis example above, the polluting company would have sold a portion of its allocated allowances for €50 million and agreed to buy the allowances back for a higher amount in time for compliance. Repurchase agreements such as this act like a short-term loan where the polluting company gains access to cash to use for investment or other purposes and the other party secures a return that is effectively interest.

The financial possibilities of this credit-like practice go much further than this particular arrangement in two important ways. First, the ongoing yearly overlap between allocation and surrender dates makes it possible to extend the practice on a longer-term basis. Polluting companies do not need to repurchase allocated allowances after fourteen months because they always receive the next year's allocation before the surrender date for the prior year's emissions. All allowances within a phase are equally valid for compliance purposes, regardless of the year in which they were allocated. To the extent

4.3 Capitalising Carbon 115

that their free allocation continues, polluting companies can make use of the money raised from selling their initial allowance allocation over multiple years, by continually using the next year's allocation to cover the prior year's emissions. Second, the practice can involve more parties than the two involved in a bilateral repurchase agreement. Polluting companies can buy allowances from different actors than those to which they sold them. This is because all allowances are also equally valid for compliance purpose, irrespective of the company to which they were originally allocated.

Making use of the carbon market compliance cycle to access a credit-like instrument became particularly significant in the context of the tight overall credit environment that developed with the onset of the financial crisis. Companies, especially those in the steel and cement industries that were hit particularly hard by the crisis, sold their 2008 or 2009 allocations on the spot market and bought 2012 (the end of phase two) options and futures, with a plan to roll over their yearly allocations for compliance purposes in between. Demand for these allowances was aided by the regulatory threat faced by the electricity generation sector. The sector anticipated that free allocation would end at the beginning of phase three, which encouraged power companies to buy up allowances (World Bank 2010 p. 10). Partly as a result of this practice (the other major factor being related to tax fraud), spot market trading increased by seventy-five times between the first half of 2008 and the first half of 2009 (World Bank 2010 p. 8).

For sellers of allowances, monetising 2008 and 2009 allowances on spot markets and purchasing 2012 contracts represented a more attractive loan than was otherwise available. Until November 2008, the premium paid for a carbon future to be delivered in 2012, compared to the price those companies received for selling their allowance allocation on the spot market, was below the Euribor interest rate at which banks lend to and borrow from other banks (CDC Climat 2009). For buyers of allowances, as other asset classes were experiencing significant write-downs, investors searching for yield were expecting to profit from steadily increasing carbon prices. This can be seen by the results of a March 2009 survey of banks and consultants involved in the carbon market. Respondents to the survey, which included Barclays, Citigroup, Daiwa, Deutsche Bank, Sagacarbon, Société Générale, Point Carbon, and UBS, on average, predicted that allowance prices would more than double to €25 by the end of 2012, compared to spot prices that had fallen to between €10 and €12 that month (Chestney 2009a; European Environment Agency 2012).

The benefits of this practice for both debtors and creditors dissipated over the course of the second phase of the EU ETS and did not recover. When spot trading for allowances opened at €21.05 in phase two, the combined market

116 *Valuing Carbon*

value of the 2008 total allowance allocation was €41 billion (European Environment Agency 2012, 2015b). On the last day of trading at the end of phase two in 2012, when spot prices for EUAs had fallen to €6.53, the total market value of that year's allocated allowances (which had increased in number by 5 per cent) had fallen by two thirds to €13 billion (European Energy Exchange 2012; European Environment Agency 2015b). For sellers of allowances acting as debtors, the potential amount of money that could be borrowed in this manner was drastically reduced. For buyers of allowances acting as creditors and searching for yield, carbon was not performing as an investment compared to 2008 and 2009 forecasts (European Energy Exchange 2012).

The structure of the compliance cycle in the European carbon market therefore creates possibilities for a new form of interest-bearing capital, which can support accumulation via what Fine (2013) termed 'intensive' financialisation. The potential to support accumulation in this way is integrally linked to the contribution of fossil fuels to the expansion of value, and the role of the state in regulating resulting emissions through the carbon market. The capacity to repurchase carbon commodities at a premium price in the future is aided by the production of surplus value through the appropriation of carbon. The need to make such a purchase is created by regulations that compel polluting companies to surrender EUAs or CERs to cover their emissions. Imperatives to create interest-bearing capital out of the carbon market compliance cycle decreased, however, with low and declining carbon prices.

4.3.2 Carbon as Collateral

Beyond efforts to monetise allowances, Fortis bank also indicated the potential to use carbon as collateral to leverage an expanded rate or scale of accumulation than would otherwise be possible (Leyshon & Thrift 2007). Collateral is an important form of capital because it is needed to access traditional lines of credit and to meet trading margin requirements. Leveraging the value of carbon as an asset and the income streams it creates, however, became increasingly difficult in both of these areas.

Collateral is required to access more traditional forms of credit needed to expand the surplus value produced in enlarged circuits of capital. Lenders demand collateral as security that can be seized in the event of a default on loan repayments. Borrowers use collateral to secure more favourable terms such as lower interest charges or increased loan amounts. Using expected income streams from purchase agreements for offset credits as collateral could encourage accumulation by financing new offset projects. There are some limited examples of this occurring, such as in the case of a loan granted by Spanish bank Banco Santander to the project developer of two wind farm CDM projects in Mexico. In this case, the purchase agreement to buy the offset credits was made with a group of state-owned development banks (NEFCO 2010).

More commercial carbon offset purchase agreements have been less readily accepted as collateral (Cox et al. 2010 pp. 32–3; Ellerman et al. 2010 p. 322; Padis 2011). This is not surprising when risks at both ends of such contracts are considered. At the seller's end, only about 31 per cent of CERs have been issued by national authorities in developing countries on time (Cormier & Bellassen 2013). In response to price crashes, buyers have also successfully renegotiated the terms of purchase agreements in their favour, to avoid buying CERs for multiple times their eventual market price (Szabo 2012; World Bank 2012 pp. 50–1). These moves reduce the security of carbon as collateral and frustrate opportunities to leverage accumulation in carbon markets.

Collateral is also required as trading 'margin' for parties that wish to trade in other forms of financial instruments. Margin is similar to collateral in credit markets in the sense that it protects the exchange facilitating a trade against one party not meeting its obligations. Margin is set at a portion of the market price of contracts, meaning that if traders can meet this requirement, they are able to leverage the collateral to enter into contracts, such as derivatives linked to commodities, bonds, shares, interest rates, or currencies, worth many times the margin value.

Intercontinental Exchange (ICE), which hosts the European Climate Exchange, accepts various financial instruments as collateral for margin, including those linked to government bonds, currencies, and previously, emissions allowances. ICE initially accepted EUAs as collateral for up to 30 per cent of margin requirements and CERs as collateral for up to 5 per cent of margin requirements, meaning that carbon could be leveraged to some extent (Intercontinental Exchange 2009). The margin value of collateral is determined by the haircut applied by ICE, reflecting its risk. Initially, allowances and credits were subject to a 25 per cent haircut on each of their values, but between February and June 2011, ICE gradually increased the haircut to 100 per cent (Point Carbon 2011). This made carbon completely worthless as collateral in the exchange.

As with the use of carbon as collateral for conventional loans, the use of carbon as collateral for trading margin was thwarted by regulatory risks that are specific to the carbon market, together with the general decline of carbon prices. The initial decision by ICE was triggered by the risks associated with the circulation of carbon allowances that had been stolen from national government registries (Point Carbon 2011). Despite the adoption of enhanced security arrangements with the creation of a central European registry and the publication of the serial numbers of stolen allowances by ICE, the 100 per cent haircut was maintained (Intercontinental Exchange 2015, 2016). Enhanced legal security was undermined by diminished security in the value of carbon commodities. On 1 June 2011, when the 100 per cent haircut was instituted, EUA and CER futures for delivery in December 2016 were trading at €22.08 and €14.82, respectively. Since then, these same contracts fell to as low as €3.15 for EUAs and €0.25 for CERs (Intercontinental Exchange 2017).

The commodification of relations of fossil fuel appropriation in carbon markets has not delivered the reliable income streams and asset prices that Leyshon and Thrift (2007) identified as the basis for 'capitalisation of almost everything'. There have, therefore, been limited opportunities to leverage value in carbon markets to create cycles of expanded accumulation in this way. Like efforts to create interest-bearing capital out of carbon markets, efforts to capitalise carbon as collateral have been frustrated by the collapse in carbon prices. With these difficulties becoming clearer, in 2009, just three years after announcing the arrival of carbon as capital, the same banker was describing the EU ETS as 'practically a joke'. The next year he reported that Fortis's commodities desk had shifted away from carbon, explaining, 'I don't see there is a proper business to be had in carbon' (Chestney 2009b, 2010).

How can we understand the failures of carbon as capital, whether as credit or collateral, beneath the proximate cause of low carbon prices? As Ervine (2017) notes, carbon prices express power relations in capitalism. Carbon prices crashed and have been held down by the massive surplus of allowances circulating in the EU ETS. The cumulative reduction in demand for allowances as a result of the impact of economic recession played an important role in this situation but this was not the only, or necessarily the major, factor (Koch et al. 2014). Ultimately, the persistent allowance surplus shows that states, which control the quantity of carbon allowances and credits in circulation, have instituted a weak carbon market by over-allocating allowances and insufficiently limiting international offset credits.

The failure of states to support opportunities for accumulation is comprehensible from the perspective of the contradictory value relations of carbon markets. As a creature of state regulation, the circulation of value through carbon commodities depends on the ongoing appropriation of carbon, without being determined by it. This is because burning fossil fuels produces greenhouse gas emissions that create compliance requirements and thus demand for allowances and credits. States face a paradox in supporting the circulation of value through carbon commodities at levels that are needed for 'accumulation by capitalisation'. The tension for states is that at a certain point carbon prices might raise costs of production to the extent that they create barriers to

4.3 Capitalising Carbon

'accumulation by appropriation' in fossil fuel industries, the maintenance of which is an integral component of the capitalisation of carbon.

4.3.3 Carbon as Risk

What are the prospects for states to mediate contradictions between relations of appropriation and capitalisation in the carbon market accumulation strategy? Research on financial derivatives, and financial risk more generally, as 'meta-capital', suggest possibilities at two levels.

First, characteristics of carbon commodities create possibilities to sustain accumulation by capitalisation in carbon markets by disciplining accumulation by appropriation in fossil fuel industries. According to Bryan and Rafferty (2006 pp. 12–13), derivatives, acting as a system, are meta-capital because they blend different forms of capital together and bind the future to the present. Similarly, carbon allowances and credits can be understood as 'meta-nature', because the abstractions involved in the commodification of carbon blend and bind greenhouse gases emitted in different production processes, in different places, at different points in time (Lohmann 2011b). By abstracting from the concrete specificities of carbon appropriation and simply allowing installations regulated by the EU ETS to emit greenhouse gases somehow, somewhere, and at some time, carbon markets are structured in ways that can exert pressure on all carbon-intensive production processes.

The processes of abstraction that go into the commodification of carbon enable calculative practices that scrutinise the use of fossil fuels by individual factories or power plants by comparing them to relations of carbon appropriation across the carbon market as a whole. If states implemented a more stringent emissions cap, the carbon market could enforce trade-offs in favour of more profitable forms of carbon appropriation, squeezing out more 'unpaid work' from labour processes involving the combustion of fossil fuels (Moore 2015). In this sense, carbon could emerge as meta-capital – a systemic socio-ecological relation of self-expanding value – by combining the appropriation and capitalisation of carbon within a singular accumulation strategy. In such an accumulation strategy, carbon markets operate as 'abstract social nature' to coordinate the contribution of fossil fuels to value relations of 'abstract social labour' (Moore 2015).

Second, as meta-capital, the blending and binding characteristics of financial derivatives go beyond processes of carbon commodification that commensurate different types of carbon appropriation. The calculations and abstractions that produce financial derivatives have the capacity to commensurate, and enable comparison and competition, between all forms of capital in circulation, regardless of explicit connections with fossil fuels and climate change. The key metric in these financial markets is much wider than fossil fuel-driven improvements in labour productivity: it is risk, or more precisely, risk-adjusted yield (Bryan & Rafferty 2013 p. 145). By 'open[ing] value analysis to the incorporation of risk', Bryan et al. (2015 p. 310) argue that that it is possible to see the emergence of commodified risk as a form of capital, where patterns of accumulation are created by constructing unequal relations of risk exposure and absorption. Derivatives markets in payments for housing and other essential, but illiquid, goods and services, are an important instance of this, because ongoing imperatives for social reproduction mean that households systemically absorb risk for broader processes of capital accumulation. While the financial crisis dramatically showed how this strategy can unravel, for capital, it underscored the need to better make and manage commodified risk exposures as capital, so that the 'chance of risk convergence in the context of crisis is minimised' (Bryan et al. 2015 p. 319).

What risk exposures are commodified in carbon markets, and how do these calculations relate to the broader operation of 'abstract social risk'? From the dominant economics perspective, carbon commodities, in theory, represent risks associated with the external social costs of climate change. In this formulation, carbon trading offers a means to manage those risks in an economically optimal fashion so that these costs equal the economic benefits of burning fossil fuels. In practice, carbon prices have been below even conservative economic calculations of the external social costs of climate change (Nordhaus 2017). The risk commodified in carbon markets is more political-economic in nature, as explained by Christophers (2016b p. 13):

The carbon credit is ultimately an instrument for commodifying the unknown future of greenhouse-gas emissions within the capitalist political economy. How stringently, in particular, will future emissions be regulated, how rapidly will society transition to alternative energy sources, and thus how will demand evolve for the 'right' to emit? This is a future shot through with risk – social, political, regulatory, technological, economic – and carbon markets are social mechanisms for congealing all such risk into current market prices.

Carbon prices are linked to levels of macroeconomic activity, energy prices, and weather conditions, the precise nature of which are debated in the econometric literature, and incorporated into competing financial models by corporations (Chevallier 2012; Zhu & Chevallier 2017). Yet, the calculation and abstraction of risk in carbon markets is always explicitly mediated by politics associated with decisions over regulatory design (Koch et al. 2016). Risk in carbon markets is therefore actively co-produced by the state and non-state actors that contest and shape the commodification of carbon. As Johnson

(2013, 2015) has demonstrated in relation to 'catastrophe bonds', assets with alternative climate risk exposures are attractive for financial actors. However, the weakness of the European carbon market made potential yields so low that the commodification of risk exposures became immaterial.

As with carbon becoming capital as meta-nature, enhanced state compulsion for fossil fuel corporations to buy and surrender allowances and credits is a prerequisite for carbon to become capital as meta-risk. This creates a regulatory equivalent to the social reproductive compulsion on households to pay their bills. The commodification of risk in carbon markets also depends on ongoing forms of carbon appropriation – without this, the future of fossil fuel-based accumulation would not be 'at risk'. Yet, as discussed above, and even more directly analogous to households, fossil fuel-intensive corporations do not pay if they can pass on costs to consumers. From this perspective, we can see the earlier evidence for carbon as rent in new light, representing a process of unequal risk absorption within processes of capital accumulation between active participants in carbon markets and those that ultimately pay.

Conclusion

Carbon markets have created new but diminishing economic opportunities for participants. The accumulation strategy has been frustrated by difficulties encountered in creating new forms of capital within the socio-ecological relations that are commodified in carbon markets. To date, carbon has become capital only occasionally, rather than systemically, due to persistently low and declining carbon prices. The promise of creating economic winners certainly made carbon markets an attractive option for policymakers. However, in practice, it is states that have undermined opportunities for accumulation. Political economic notions of carbon markets as accumulation strategy and, by extension, notions of 'nature as accumulation strategy' (Smith 2006) need to be more attuned to the tensions between relations of appropriation and capitalisation in the constitution of value and the contradictions this engenders for states in seeking to commodify new areas of socio-ecological life. Yet, these tensions and contradictions don't straightforwardly determine state regulation, which is heavily contested between and within different states, industries, and climate movements – the focus of Chapter 5.

This chapter has advanced an approach that asserts an active role of finance and nature within value relations. It has not sought to categorise emergent forms of capital within carbon markets as 'fictitious'. Paraphrasing Christophers's (2016a p. 144) conclusion on the problems of distinguishing the real and the fictitious with respect to land, to theorise carbon as real capital is to connect it to value and, thus, to labour. Labour is at the centre of the analysis of value relations in this chapter but not in a way that attempts to delimit value creation to certain 'productive' workers or discrete spheres of 'production', rendering carbon markets as simply redistributive. Instead, value is treated as a systemic phenomenon – a 'web of social relations' as Mann (2010 p. 181) puts it – that includes the work of fossil fuels and financial markets in determinations of socially necessary labour time and abstract social risk.

The analysis of possibilities for accumulation within carbon markets in this chapter leads to a subtly different conclusion about the relationship between accumulation and climate action in market-based policy compared to the existing political economy literature. A carbon market accumulation strategy in which the emergence of carbon as capital disciplines fossil fuel appropriation would indeed encourage emissions reductions at some less profitable factories and power plants that could not withstand the value determinations of carbon markets. Such disciplinary pressures would only increase if those value determinations were informed by comparison and competition with all forms of capital in circulation through the metric of risk. Yet, the carbon market would achieve this by substituting more profitable forms of pollution for these emissions reductions. Individual instances of climate benefit would be achieved while creating new synergies between the profits of fossil fuel and carbon trading industries. The danger here is that the appropriation of fossil fuels by the most politically economically powerful actors in the carbon market becomes further entrenched. This is the 'least cost' rationale of carbon markets in action and would make further steps toward decarbonisation that targeted these actors increasingly difficult. Thus, it is possible that states could successfully navigate the contradictions of carbon markets as accumulation strategy *for capital*. However, this would not resolve the central contradiction of carbon markets in a climate-changing capitalism identified in this chapter, as the economic opportunities from carbon markets would become more closely coupled with ongoing fossil fuel use.

Such a situation is a far cry from the experience of the European and UN schemes, which have supported unstainable patterns of accumulation through the breakdown, not realisation, of the carbon market accumulation strategy. Reversing this would require states to reinstitute carbon markets in a way that creates stronger carbon prices. In the next and final chapter of this book, the crisis of carbon markets is the backdrop for analysis of the political struggles over three proposals to reform the EU ETS. The prospects for climate action inside and outside the market-based paradigm depend on such struggles, which are discussed in terms of their implications for the circulation of value.

5

Contesting Carbon

Introduction

The financial problems that have engulfed the European carbon market have provided the context, and the impetus, for several rounds of EU ETS reform. Understanding the nature and outcomes of political contestation over these reforms is critical for understanding carbon markets in a climate-changing capitalism. The key question is whether carbon markets can address climate change as a political crisis by creating political and institutional conditions that are conducive to effective climate action. Responses to this question have focused on whether carbon markets themselves can be reformed. Critical scholars and radical activists have tended to argue that carbon markets cannot be reformed (Böhm & Dabhi 2009) and economists and policy makers have tended to emphasise the capacity for loopholes to be closed and ambition to be increased over time (Ellerman et al. 2016; Meckling et al. 2017). In addition to debates over what politics can do for carbon markets, such as achieving policy reform, it is just, if not more, important to consider what carbon markets have done to politics. This chapter therefore focuses on how the marketisation of climate policy, in the context of the crisis of carbon markets, has shaped the politics of climate change at the EU-level, and the implications of this for climate action inside and outside the EU ETS. Rounding out the argument developed in the previous chapters, the chapter highlights a third contradiction of carbon markets in a climate-changing capitalism: the singular logic of carbon pricing undermines the pluralistic policy debate necessary to develop a targeted and multi-pronged framework for climate action.

This chapter explores how carbon markets shape avenues and possibilities for contesting climate change across debates over three policy proposals for reforming the EU ETS: qualitative restrictions on industrial gas offsets,

123

124   *Contesting Carbon*

adjusting allowance supply through backloading and the market stability reserve, and the policy mix in the 2030 climate and energy package. It examines political contestation over each episode by engaging with two related but contrasting understandings of the politics of climate change that have been developed with special reference to carbon markets. On one hand, MacKenzie (2009a, 2009b) locates a 'techno-politics' within carbon markets that creates new possibilities for a 'politics of market design'. On the other hand, Swyngedouw (2010) argues carbon markets are part of a post-political shift that narrows potential pathways through depoliticisation. On the face of it, each of the three policy proposal episodes meets the stated conditions of both techno-politics and post-politics, as debates that took place within the narrow confines of EU legislative and regulatory processes over the technicalities of carbon market design. Equipped with the understanding of capitalist relations with, and within nature, developed over the course of this book, this chapter analyses the three proposals to reform the EU ETS as contests over the extent to which states manage climate change using the value determinations of carbon markets.

The first section gives an overview of the institutional landscape for reforming the EU ETS and key reforms that have taken place to allowance allocation and access to offsets since the institution of the carbon market. The next section reviews arguments on the techno-politics and post-politics of carbon markets before resituating these debates in the relations between value, nature, and the state under capitalism. The final section presents the three cases of debate over the EU ETS in chronological order, characterising each based on whether it concerns the reach, force, and priority of carbon market value determinations in climate policy. The section charts political contestation on each issue from initial proposals for reform to final policy outcome by focusing on the public contributions of key actors representing states, capital, and environment movements, drawn from government documents, submissions to consultations, press releases, and media reportage. The outcomes of contestation – real but limited reforms and a consolidation of the carbon market over alternatives – demonstrates tensions internal to states in market-based policy, constraints facing technocratic campaigning, and the ongoing politicisation of climate change.

5.1 Reforming the EU ETS

The design of the EU ETS, including its links with the Kyoto mechanisms, has been reformed in important ways since it began operation. The most significant reforms, spurred on by the crisis of the carbon market, have concerned the cap and distribution of carbon allowances, and the amount and types of carbon offsets that polluting companies in the EU ETS can access. In both cases, the general movement has been towards more stringent rules that have limited free allocation in favour of auctioning, reduced the total number of allowances, and placed restrictions on the use of carbon offsets. These developments ostensibly lend support to ideas that carbon markets offer a framework to move towards effective climate policy, despite inevitable teething problems. This section, in providing an overview of reforms to rules that govern use of and access to carbon commodities, shows that the trajectory towards reform in the EU ETS has indeed been real, but uneven and limited.

Reforms to the EU ETS occur at the EU level because, as mentioned in Chapter 2, it is an 'environmental', rather than 'fiscal', matter. Reforms occur through amendments to the EU ETS directive and its associated regulations. Most changes to these documents governing the EU ETS require a 'co-decision' legislative process where the European Commission (the public service) initiates a proposal, which can then be amended by, and requires the approval of, the European Parliament (representatives elected by citizens of member states) and the Council of the European Union (relevant ministers from member states). Other important institutions of EU ETS reform are the Environment, Public Health and Food Safety (ENVI) and Industry, Research and Energy (ITRE) Committees (part of the European Parliament), which express opinions on legislative proposals, and the Climate Change Committee (made up of Member state representatives) which the Commission consults regarding its implementation of Directives and Regulations (European Commission 2015a pp. 9–11). Headline policy directions, such as future emissions targets, are agreed to by the European Council (member heads of state) and then translated through the usual legislative procedure. These institutions have combined to reform the EU ETS in cycles shaped variously by the timing of EU ETS phases, one-off interventions, international climate summits, and EU climate and energy frameworks.

With the first two phases of the EU ETS revealing systemic over-allocation, efforts to reform the quantity and distribution of allowances in the scheme focused on arrangements for phase three. As outlined in Chapter 2, for phases one and two of the EU ETS, decisions over allocation were devolved to member states via national allocation plans, and almost all allowances were allocated for free. In 2007, the European Council agreed to an EU-wide 20 per cent emission reduction target by 2020 (for EU ETS and non-EU ETS sectors) from 1990 levels, which created the conditions for a more centralised system from phase three. Over the course of 2008 and early

2009, as the economic crisis leading to the carbon price crash was developing, the Commission, Parliament, and Council agreed to move to a lower, EU-wide allowance cap and greater use of allowance auctioning. The total EU-wide allowance cap would reduce by 1.74 per cent per year (the 'linear reduction factor') to deliver a 21 per cent reduction compared to 2005 levels across the EU ETS. Auctioning was made 'the basic principle of allocation', but in practice this only applied to electricity generation in wealthier states. Continued, though decreasing, free allocation was secured for poorer, fossil fuel-dependent states with limited connections to European grids, including Bulgaria, Cyprus, Czech Republic, Estonia, Hungary, Lithuania, Poland, and Romania, justified on the basis that it would assist those countries to 'modernise' and 'diversify' their generation supply. Free allocation for manufacturing and other non-electricity installations was also extended. Free allocation levels were, however, reformed to be reflect a declining proportion of industry-specific benchmarks based on best technology standards, rather than historical emissions. For installations assessed to be at risk of carbon leakage, full free allowance allocation was nonetheless guaranteed for the whole of phase three (European Commission 2015a p. 31; European Parliament and Council 2009). This meant both benchmark and leakage methodologies became new sites of contestation.

The same set of phase three reforms also made some limited restrictions to carbon offset use. Quantitative restrictions for total offset use from phase two were largely extended into phase three. The main change was a qualitative one restricting the timing of eligible carbon offsets. From 2015, only CERs and ERUs produced by CDM and JI projects that were registered before the end of 2012 would be eligible, unless it was a CDM project in a Least Developed Country. This change had important impacts for the distribution of new offsetting projects, given the large share of demand from the EU ETS (European Parliament and Council 2009). However, it had no impact on existing projects, which have crediting periods for up to twenty-one years, and therefore could continue supplying credits issued after 2013 to polluting companies in the EU ETS into phase three. However, by 2015, EU ETS installations had surrendered CERs and ERUs totalling 94 per cent of the total cap on offset use, and had mostly purchased enough credits to fill the remainder. This meant demand for credits from EU ETS installations, and by extension demand for Kyoto credits in general, had largely exhausted by this point (World Bank 2016 p. 36).

These changes to the EU ETS demonstrate some capacity for carbon market reform. Yet, contestation over the rules governing allowances and offsets continued before the phase three reforms came into effect, indicating the widespread recognition of their limits among states, businesses, and NGOs. The third section of this chapter focuses on important conflicts over proposed interventions in both areas (allowance supply and industrial gas offsets) that occurred outside of the periodic review processes, plus conflicts over a more regular review process (the policy mix in the 2030 climate and energy package). Debates over one-off interventions offer unique insights into the politics of specific elements of market design, while debates over the wider policy mix show how the overall logic of carbon markets relates to climate policy more generally. The next section discusses debates over the techno-politics and post-politics of carbon markets, with reference to Marxist understandings on value relations and state regulation of nature, as a framework of analysis for the three areas of contestation.

5.2 The Techno-Politics and Post-Politics of Carbon Markets

5.2.1 The (Techno-)Politics of Market Design

Carbon markets have provided fertile ground for critical research on the changing nature of political contestation (Blok 2011; Ervine 2017; Felli 2015; Kama 2014; Kuch 2015; Lövbrand & Stripple 2012; Rosewarne et al. 2014; Stephan & Lane 2015; Stephan & Paterson 2012). One of the most prominent examples of this comes from post-structuralist work highlighting contestation over the particular market devices that construct carbon markets. According to Callon (2009 p. 535), this contestation occurs 'between *in vitro* and *in vivo* experiments', meaning at the intersection of the policy instrument's design in the laboratory of economic theory (*in vitro*) and ongoing redesign and rearrangement in practice (*in vivo*). The implication of thinking about carbon markets in this way is that policy outcomes are contingent on the design of the experiment, thus providing opportunities for what MacKenzie (2009a p. 440) terms a 'politics of market design'. MacKenzie (2009b pp. 175–6) characterises this political terrain as 'techno-politics' because it is located not just in the formal political processes of representative democracy, but also in 'sub-political' realms, such as scientific and accounting bodies, where seemingly technical decisions are made that substantively shape the operation of carbon markets (Lovell & MacKenzie 2011; MacKenzie 2009a p. 453).

MacKenzie cites the experience of the US sulphur dioxide trading scheme as an exemplar of the capacity of the politics of market design to generate positive outcomes. When the scheme began in 1995, it had an overly generous emissions cap and allocation rules that saw emissions allowances largely distributed to polluters for free. This, according to MacKenzie (2009b pp. 145–6), was necessary to gain sufficient political acceptance of the scheme by industry and politicians. But within the negotiating process, actors with the goal of achieving greater stringency successfully inserted a so-called 'ratchet' clause that would introduce a tighter absolute cap on allocations from the second phase of the scheme, beginning in 2000. Following the end of the formal political process, bureaucrats at the Environmental Protection Agency tasked with implementing what had been negotiated used the ratchet to cancel out initial concessions for polluters by scaling back allowance allocations by 10 per cent (MacKenzie 2009b pp. 147–8).

MacKenzie interpreted some early reforms to the EU ETS, responding to the similarly loose cap of freely allocated allowances, as potentially containing the carbon market equivalent of the sulphur dioxide ratchet. As alluded to in the Introduction of this book, changes to the technical formulas governing phase two allocation were placed in this category. These two examples were used to support MacKenzie's (2009b p. 176) argument for a politics of climate change that 'focuses not just on the overall virtues and demerits of market solutions but on techno-political specifics such as the ratchet and [national allocation plan] formula. The need for such a politics is large'. Technocratic changes to carbon markets, and political contestation over this, are important subjects of study because they have made changes to elements of the design of carbon markets that have been focal points of criticism of the market-based policy approach. However, the systemic nature of the problems like over-allocation also suggests that the techno-political focus is missing major parts of the story. For Lane and Stephen (2015 p. 6), this is the 'elision of the broader institutional and structural context within which the markets develop'.

5.2.2 Post-Politics as De-Politicisation

The type of politics promoted by MacKenzie is given a less charitable treatment by Swyngedouw (2010 p. 225), who argues carbon markets are part of the 'de-politicisation' of climate change and a general shift towards a 'post-political' society and 'post-democratic' governing. In contrast to the 'proper democratic political', Swyngedouw (2010 p. 225) argues that post-politics is 'marked by the predominance of a managerial logic in all aspects of life, the reduction of the political to administration where decision-making is increasingly considered to be a question of expert knowledge and not of political position'. Rather than representing an expanded conception of politics that

5.2 The Techno-Politics and Post-Politics of Carbon Markets 129

brings new strategic possibilities, the reduction of politics to questions of 'administrative and techno-organisational means' is said to narrow the field of potential political pathways because it 'forecloses (or at least attempts to do so) politicisation and evacuates dissent' (Swyngedouw 2010 pp. 225–7).

Similarly, Bailey and Wilson (2009 p. 2325) argue that the carbon market paradigm 'exhibits a strong privileging of neoliberal and technocentric values that creates serious obstacles for the contemplation of alternatives, particularly more ecocentric ways of curbing greenhouse-gas emissions'. As with Swyngedouw, they link the institutionalisation of technocratic values embedded in carbon markets with path dependency effects that result in a 'narrowing and hardening of the "boundaries of the possible"' (Bailey & Wilson 2009 p. 2338). Felli (2015) adds to this critique, demonstrating that the depoliticising impulses of carbon markets have a long intellectual lineage running from key neoliberal thinkers to environmental economists.

As with the techno-political perspective, the insights of the post-political characterisation of carbon markets have been recognised as important yet partial (McCarthy 2013). Newell (2014), for example, illustrates a two-way, evolving relationship between political contestation and de-politicisation with the case of the CDM Policy Dialogue, an initiative designed to review and make recommendations to reform the UN's carbon offsetting instrument. Here, acute political contestation brought on and surrounded a process of 'disciplinary neoliberal participation' where the range of possible outcomes were heavily managed and controlled (Newell 2014 p. 215). In this manner, Lane and Stephen (2015 p. 12 emphasis added) call for a focus on 'depoliticising *and* repoliticising' movements because 'depoliticisation is never entirely complete, it cannot wholly close out the possibility of further debate and contestation of what is taken to be merely technical, objective or natural'. Responding to Lane and Stephen's critical engagement with techno- and post-political approaches, this chapter refocuses on states as the central institution mediating capitalist relations with, and within, nature and thus, setting key terms of contestation over carbon markets and climate change.

5.2.3 States, Value, and Nature

Capitalist states are always necessarily involved in delivering nature for, and regulating nature in, processes of capitalist valorisation. The previous chapter showed that states are centrally but uneasily located within processes of capital accumulation in carbon markets because they sit at the interface of socio-ecological relations of appropriation and capitalisation through their key role in the commodification of carbon. O'Connor (1998) argues that contradictions within the state regulation of nature unfold through a systemic tension facing capitalist states between imperatives for accumulation and legitimation. Parenti (2015 p. 830) directly links the former to the necessary position of the state in securing the contribution of nature to value relations, arguing: 'the state is central to the value form. If the utilities of non-human nature are important sources of wealth, which they are, then it is the state that delivers these to capital'. However, O'Connor (1998 p. 152) points out that this is complicated by imperatives for legitimisation because 'the capitalist state is a bureaucratic state within a formally democratic political system'. The state's bureaucratic organisation, comprising multiple apparatuses with their own objectives and constituencies, and competing democratic demands between and within capital and social movements, means that 'the provision or regulation of the conditions of production is a highly contradictory process' (O'Connor 1998 p. 150).

The role of states in mediating capital and nature makes value an explicit object of political contestation. This contestation concerns what conceptions of value states codify and how valuation regimes operate in practice. Thus, contestation over value, understood from a Marxist perspective, occurs through other 'co-present' registers of value, such as scientific or neoclassical notions of value (Bigger & Robertson 2017 p. 69). Robertson and Wainwright (2013) consider the specific contradictions faced by states in market-based environmental policy. The context of the study is debates over the definition of value – whether market price, individual utility or ecosystem functions – in wetlands banking schemes in the United States. Different state agencies had competing positions on this question, with some favouring market devolution and others wishing to maintain decision-making based on scientific principles. The contest is interpreted in terms of the need for the state to both create new opportunities for accumulation and maintain its own capacity to regulate natural conditions for the reproduction of capitalism. Echoing O'Connor, they argue 'capitalist states must facilitate the measure of new values because they are necessarily involved in the regulation of capitalism's transformation of the natural environment' (Robertson & Wainwright 2013 p. 900). However, Robertson and Wainwright (2013 p. 899) conclude that in doing so, the state must 'thread a relatively fine needle: to ensure that the capitalist value form expands but prevent it from becoming the sole means of determining the identification of objects and the measurement of their qualities'. The reach, force, and priority of value determinations in carbon markets represent three dimensions of this tension, and it is the first of these to which this chapter now turns.

5.3 Contesting the 'Value' of Carbon

5.3.1 *The Reach of Value: Industrial Gas Offset Restrictions*

The relationship between the EU ETS and CDM – a contentious issue since the negotiation of the Linking Directive in 2004 – was again the subject of contestation in debates over the eligibility of industrial gas offset credits in 2010–11. At stake was the reach of carbon market value determinations in organising emissions reductions between installations in the EU ETS and projects in the CDM. Specifically, the contestation concerned whether the value determinations of carbon markets reached as far as industrial gas destruction projects primarily located in China and India by continuing to incorporate these within processes of carbon commodification.

The issue was placed on the agenda by campaigns that opposed the use of credits produced by destroying industrial gases, especially HFC-23 from the production of refrigerant gases and nitrous oxide (N_2O) from the production of adipic acid (as distinct from nitric acid production), from various segments of the environment movement. Some, such as the more climate justice-oriented Carbon Trade Watch and Friends of the Earth, used the issue of industrial gas offsets as part of a broader campaign to oppose carbon offsets or carbon markets in general (Bullock et al. 2009; Gilbertson & Reyes 2009). Others, such as Brussels-based carbon market research and advocacy organisation CDM Watch (now Carbon Market Watch) and large environmental organisation World Wide Fund for Nature (WWF), campaigned to ban industrial gas offsets to improve the overall effectiveness of carbon trading (Environmental Investigation Agency & CDM Watch 2010; Öko-Institut 2007).

CDM Watch adopted a techno-political strategy to effectively expose the questionable environmental integrity of industrial gas offsets on the CDM's own 'additionality' terms. Reports from experts in private consultancies commissioned by the group demonstrated that many of the emissions reductions from HFC-23 projects were non-additional. This was because the UN methodology used to calculate credit issuance encouraged increases in HCFC-22 production, another greenhouse gas and ozone depleting substance, entirely for the purposes of earning credits through the destruction of HFC-23, which is a by-product of the process (Schneider 2011). Similarly, many credits produced from destroying N_2O were also found to be non-additional because the relevant methodology had encouraged a shift in adipic acid production away from non-CDM plants that were voluntarily abating N_2O to CDM plants that could earn credits (Schneider et al. 2010). Industrial gas projects were also criticised for creating negative social and environmental outcomes at the local level (Bryant et al. 2015).

WWF focused on the threat posed by industrial gas offsets to the legitimacy of carbon markets more generally, arguing that 'the use of bad quality credits in the EU ETS is often used by opponents to the system as an argument against cap & trade in general and discredits this market-based instrument globally, making it harder to "sell" it in other regions of the world' (WWF Europe 2010). Reform was therefore needed to safeguard, in a post-political sense, the carbon market from the effects of further politicisation. The organisation argued that a ban on offset credits from 1 January 2013, with no possibility of banking into phase three, was necessary to boost carbon prices, reduce the overall EU ETS surplus and favour investment in higher quality CDM projects, such as renewable energy. Further, the industrial gas offset ban was pitched as a step towards additional bans of other controversial project types including efficient coal-fired power stations and large hydroelectric dams (WWF Europe 2010).

Corporate responses focused on delaying any ban for as long as possible and ensuring it was limited to the particular environmental additionality issues affecting industrial gas projects. The strategy sought to ensure that reforms were contained within the efficiency paradigm underpinning carbon markets and not the broader social, political or economic goals suggested by environment groups – a post-political strategy to restrict the scope of debate. Enel and EDF, the two companies with the largest direct financial stakes in industrial gas projects, both being project participants in eight such projects, were most concerned about the timing of the ban (UNEP DTU 2018a). French state-owned electricity company EDF directly highlighted the financial impact of a phase three ban, arguing it would 'obliterate the value of those commitments' it had made on the basis that 'such credits were free from regulatory eligibility risks' (EDF Group 2010). The Carbon Markets and Investors Association (now known as the Climate Markets and Investors Association), which represents financial actors, also raised more general concerns about the regulatory risk associated with banning certain types of offset credits, stating:

Using [qualitative restrictions] for e.g. political leverage, regulating the profitability of projects, controlling the price of carbon or other reasons than maintaining the integrity of the EU ETS, are, from a market perspective, regulatory measures, which will sap investors' confidence in the EU ETS, the CDM, and future climate change mechanisms. (Carbon Markets and Investors Association 2010)

These positions of capital are indicative of the tensions faced by state institutions regulating the EU ETS. States attempting to foster value relations by extending the scope of abstraction embedded within carbon commodities are faced with contradictory impulses arising from the politicisation created by their central role in the process. The politicisation of abstraction processes, such as those related to the eligibility of particular project types, then threatens the functioning of the carbon market from the perspective of capital. This tension is clearly illustrated by Italian electricity company Enel's representation on the issue, which oscillates between arguing for the maximum abstraction needed for the circulation of homogenous commodities and pragmatically acknowledging political limits. Enel stressed it was important that 'all compliance instruments have the same value of one tonne' and warned that qualitative restrictions would 'lead to market fragmentation, as different acceptance of CERs/ERUs under distinct jurisdictions will further undermine liquidity and require market participants to create differentiated contracts for trading CERs/ERUs' (Enel 2010a, 2010b). While nevertheless acknowledging political concerns, Enel sought to limit reasons for qualitative restrictions to the economic logic of carbon markets, arguing 'justified doubts over the environmental integrity of a project type should therefore be the only legitimate reason for excluding certain types of CER/ERU' in order to 'maintain utmost confidence in the EU ETS as [an] unbiased market mechanism' (Enel 2010a).

At the conclusion of the consultation period on 25 November 2010, the Commission released its draft proposal for a full ban on offset credits produced by destroying HFC-23 and N_2O from adipic acid projects from the earlier date of 1 January 2013. The preamble to the proposal stated the ban was necessary to address damage to 'public confidence in market-based mechanisms', especially in light of inaction from the CDM Executive Board (European Commission 2010a). Following the release of the Commission's proposal, corporate actors, such as the International Emissions Trading Association (IETA), a pro-carbon trading group comprised of financial and carbon-intensive companies, focused on having the date pushed back from 1 January 2013 to 1 May 2013 to extend the eligibility of industrial gas offsets to the entirety of phase two, the final surrender date of which was 30 April 2013 (IETA 2010). Freedom of information requests revealed intense lobbying of the Commission by Enel and umbrella industry group BusinessEurope (Corporate Europe Observatory 2011).

EU national states, which had to approve the Commission's Regulation through the EU Climate Change Committee, voted on 21 January 2011 in line with corporate demands to push the date back to 1 May 2013, led by the governments of Italy, the United Kingdom, Poland, and Germany (Chestney 2011; European Commission 2011b). The delayed ban opened the door for an estimated additional 30–40 million industrial gas credits to be surrendered, which was criticised by groups such as CDM Watch (CDM

Watch 2011; Krukowska 2011). This significantly ameliorated the financial impact on companies such as Enel, which was able to surrender close to 17 million CERs for 2012 compared with fewer than 4 million for 2011, 99.5 per cent of which were from HFC-23 or N_2O adipic acid projects (European Commission 2013b).

Despite the weakening of the proposal, the campaign against industrial gas offsets successfully achieved its goal of banning the use of the credits. However, the broader goal of achieving additional qualitative offset restrictions on other problematic project types was not realised. Indeed, the Commission actively sought to quell corporate concerns about this prospect by making it clear that it was not considering further project type restrictions (European Commission 2010b). Therefore, the Commission limited the reach of carbon market value determinations to the extent necessary to secure sufficient legitimacy of the scheme while minimising political economic disruption for capital.

5.3.2 The Force of Value: Managing Allowance Supply

Debates over proposals to manage the supply of allowances circulating within the EU ETS were more explicitly contests over increasing carbon prices. These debates occurred in two stages: a short-term proposal for 'backloading' allowances over 2012–13 and a long-term proposal for a 'Market Stability Reserve' over 2014–15. Backloading involved temporarily withholding the auctioning of allowances scheduled for the beginning of phase three and reintroducing those allowances through larger auctions at the end of the phase. The Market Stability Reserve was proposed as a mechanism to automatically adjust allowance auctions upwards and downwards in response to certain levels of allowance surpluses and/or prices. Both backloading and Market Stability Reserve proposals were therefore fundamentally concerned with managing the force of carbon market value determinations in organising fossil fuel use, as translated through movements in carbon prices. They are also archetypal techno-political fixes, being concerned not with big questions over emissions goals or the choice of policy mechanisms, but the timing of regular carbon market events: the auctioning of allowances.

Although backloading would not affect the overall quantity of allowances auctioned in phase three, the Commission expected the measure would boost carbon prices in the short term and buy time for more permanent reform (European Commission 2012a pp. 12–15). The Commission proposed to implement backloading by amending the EU ETS Auctioning Regulation.

5.3 Contesting the 'Value' of Carbon

However, there were questions over whether this path was legally justified, so the Commission also decided to propose an amendment to the EU ETS Directive to achieve 'full legal certainty' over its powers (European Commission 2012a p. 5). The specific proposal to amend Article 10 of the Directive, which governs auctions, was that 'the Commission shall, where appropriate, adapt the timetable for each period so as to ensure an orderly functioning of the market' (European Commission 2012b). Amending a Directive requires a full decision-making procedure involving the Parliament and Council, which triggered a protracted debate on the issue.

Several environmental organisations once again actively engaged in political debates over backloading to support a strong proposal that could also lead to further reform. Sandbag, a UK-based research and campaigning organisation focused on carbon markets that also engaged with the industrial gas offset debate, published a series of widely distributed reports with detailed calculations of the accumulating allowance surplus in the EU ETS, highlighting the legacy it would leave in cancelling out future emissions reductions (e.g. Morris 2012). WWF and Greenpeace also adopted a strategy of engaging with the technical details of the surplus problem, and promoting the backloading solution, by appointing a private consultancy to assess the causes and size of the surplus and offer options for reform (Hermann & Matthes 2012). WWF and Greenpeace used this expert opinion as a basis to demand 1.4 billion allowances be backloaded, equal to their report's projected 2020 surplus. They also saw backloading as a step towards further reform of the scheme, which both organisations affirmed their support for, through a permanent cancellation of 2.2 billion allowances as part of a plan to increase the 2020 emissions target from 20 per cent to 30 per cent (Greenpeace Europe 2012; WWF Europe 2012). A key exception was Friends of the Earth, which shunned engagement with the formal consultation process over backloading in an explicit rejection that a techno-political solution was possible, arguing 'no amount of fiddling with the ETS will make the system fit for the challenge of tackling the climate crisis' (Friends of the Earth Europe 2013b).

A general split emerged between polluting industries on the backloading proposal, with the electricity sector in support and carbon-intensive manufacturing, including the iron and steel, cement, and chemicals industries, in opposition. For the electricity industry, with the exception of Polish companies such as Tauron, the backloading measure was necessary to save the EU ETS and fend off the adoption of alternative policies at the national level. In their submission in support of the proposal, EURELECTRIC, which represents electricity companies at the European level, stated that the 'ETS today is at risk of being undermined and replaced by other policy instruments'

(EURELECTRIC 2012). Similarly, French electricity company GDF Suez (now ENGIE) warned 'the credibility of the EU ETS is now at stake with a carbon price so low that it does not represent a valuable price signal' (GDF Suez 2012). Conversely, manufacturers, organised under the umbrella of the Alliance of Energy Intensive Industries, opposed backloading because any 'artificial cost increase' would reduce the international competitiveness of European industry (Alliance of Energy Intensive Industries 2012).

In contrast, electricity, gas, and manufacturing industries were opposed to the Commission's proposed amendment to the EU ETS Directive to ensure the legality of the backloading regulation on the basis that it would lead to ongoing discretionary state intervention. Similar to the debate over industrial gas offsets, these corporate actors aimed to limit the politicisation of the surplus issue. Responses from the Alliance of Energy Intensive Industries and German electricity company E.ON to the proposed amendment illustrate that this is grounded in corporate ambivalence about the role of the state in the carbon market. E.ON supported backloading because it recognised that some form of state intervention was necessary to secure the operation of the market, arguing that the measure would 'be regarded as a positive sign of policy-makers' commitment to the ETS. In a politically-grounded market such as the EU ETS, this is crucially important since it allows market participants to take a long-term view'. However, E.ON also opposed the Commission's proposed amendment to the Directive because it viewed ongoing intervention as a threat to that goal, arguing 'frequent market interventions to mitigate the effect of preceding interventions would destroy the trust of market participants in the "orderly functioning" of the market' (E.ON 2012). The Alliance of Energy Intensive Industries articulated this concern more explicitly. In addition to their objections to increased costs, the industry group argued 'the proposal puts an end to the notion of the ETS as a market-based instrument. Trying to manipulate carbon prices through political intervention will now require a risk calculation based on the likelihood of further political intervention' (Alliance of Energy Intensive Industries 2012). The post-political strategies of E.ON and the Alliance of Energy Intensive Industries are indicative of another tension created by carbon markets for states, this time in relation to supporting accumulation rather than gaining legitimacy. Value cannot circulate through carbon commodities without state regulation. However, state measures to support carbon prices, such as backloading, simultaneously undermine the calculative practices that capital uses to profitably participate in carbon markets.

Following the consultation process, the Commission made a more detailed backloading regulation proposal specifying that the auctioning of 900 million

5.3 Contesting the 'Value' of Carbon

allowances would be delayed between 2013 and 2015 and instead auctioned in 2019 and 2020 (European Commission 2012d). The majority of national states supported the proposal. Poland and Germany were notable exceptions. Poland was strongly opposed to any change because it feared the proposal would reduce auction revenue and hurt growth in its brown coal-dependent economy (Nelson 2012). The German government was undecided, partly due to a split between the supportive Environment Minister from the main governing party, the Christian Democratic Union, and the oppositional Economy Minister from the junior coalition partner, the Free Democratic Party (ENDS Europe 2012).

The debate in the Parliament was heavily focused on the question of whether the proposed amendment to the Directive would lead to ongoing intervention in the market. Opposition came primarily from MEPs in the conservative European People's Party grouping, while social democrat, liberal and green groupings were mostly in favour (Wettestad & Jevnaker 2016 p. 46). On 16 April 2013, following a parliamentary debate where supporters focused on the need to save the EU ETS and opponents argued it went against the market principles of the scheme, the backloading proposal was voted down 334 to 315, with 63 abstentions (European Parliament 2013b, 2013c). The vote led to a crash in the spot price of allowances by 40 per cent to a then record low of €2.70 (Flynn 2013a). Following the negative vote, states in favour of the proposal pushed to have it revisited. Environment ministers from the United Kingdom, France, the Netherlands, Sweden, Germany, Denmark, Portugal, Finland, and Slovenia, under the banner of the Green Growth Group, called on the proposal to be agreed upon by July (ENDS Europe 2013). Indeed, on 3 July 2013, the Parliament supported the Commission's proposal 344 votes to 311, with 46 abstentions.

The key legislative difference between the negative and positive votes was that in the latter, amendments were introduced restricting the potential for additional market intervention by the Commission (European Parliament 2013d). Under the amended version that was supported, backloading could only occur if it would not disadvantage any sector, the conditions for intervention were changed from 'shall, where appropriate' to 'may, in exceptional circumstances' and 900 million tonnes was set as the maximum total level of backloading (European Parliament 2013a). In addition to this weakening of the proposed Regulation, the political debate over it delayed the start date for backloading. The formation of a new German government, a coalition between the Christian Democratic Union and the Social Democratic Party, after the federal election in September 2013, paved the way for Germany to vote in support of backloading, with only Poland remaining opposed

138 *Contesting Carbon*

(Council of the European Union 2013; European Commission 2014j; Flynn 2013b). But by the time the amended Regulation was approved by the Parliament, Council and EU Climate Change Committee in December 2013 and January 2014, the rapid allowance surplus build up at the beginning of phase three had already occurred.

Following agreement of backloading, debates over long-term structural reform of the EU ETS, which would produce the Market Stability Reserve, took centre stage. In 2012, the Commission had released a report on the state of the carbon market, which included six options to 'tackle the growing structural supply-demand imbalance' in the EU ETS (European Commission 2012c p. 7). Those options were: (1) increasing the EU emissions reduction target from 20 to 30 per cent, (2) permanently retiring allowances in phase three, (3) revising downwards the yearly reduction in allowance allocations, (4) expanding the scope of the EU ETS to new sectors, (5) new quantitative restrictions on international offset credits, and (6) 'discretionary price management mechanisms' (European Commission 2012c pp. 8–11). The last option triggered debates that led to the adoption of the Market Stability Reserve.

The framing of option six as a *discretionary* price mechanism invited further political debate over the appropriate role of politics and the state in regulating the force of carbon market value determinations. The report gave two possible models for such a mechanism: a carbon price floor setting a minimum price for the auctioning of carbon allowances and a 'price management reserve' that would reduce the supply of allowances when the price fell below a certain level. The Commission warned, however, that 'discretionary price-based mechanisms, such as a carbon price floor and a reserve, with an explicit carbon price objective, would alter the very nature of the current EU ETS being a quantity-based market instrument' (European Commission 2012c p. 10).

Contributions from electricity, manufacturing, and finance industries, overwhelmingly opposed discretionary price management in the formal consultation over this proposal due to risks of politicising carbon price levels (European Commission 2013e p. 6). Swedish energy company Vattenfall articulated this position in stating:

There is an obvious risk that adding a price management tool (e.g. price floor, price cap or central bank) could introduce new scope for political subjectivity and thereby harm the credibility of the EU ETS as a market instrument … Introducing regulated EUA prices carries a risk of adding another source of regulatory risk in the sense that also the EUA price perimeters become sensitive to repeated political interventions. (Vattenfall 2013 p. 4)

As argued by the multi-sector pro-carbon trading lobby the IETA, such decisions should be left to capital, because 'by steering policy discussions towards what the right price levels should be, we would diminish sharply what markets to best i.e. price discovery' (International Emissions Trading Association 2013 p. 16).

In contrast, many contributions gave support for a mechanism for adjusting the supply of allowances, not in response to price changes, as originally proposed by the Commission, but in response to changes in the volume of allowances in circulation. For capital, such a mechanism had the distinct advantage of replacing discretionary state power and political contestation with administrative routine in a post-political fashion. GDF Suez highlighted the desirability of clear rules administered at arms-length from politics in calling for a supply adjustment mechanism managed by 'an independent authority based on well-defined and predictable criteria, with sufficient notice time, to prevent gaming and market manipulation for political reasons' (GDF Suez 2013 p. 4). For the IETA, such a mechanism would both make the EU ETS more market-like and reduce the need for ongoing political contestation because it 'would allow a supply response in the carbon market as in any other market; it would also play a role in reducing the temptation to review policy objective in response to such shocks' (International Emissions Trading Association 2013 p. 17).

As with backloading, environmental NGOs adopted contrasting strategies and positions. From the beginning of consultation over structural reform, a number of grassroots organisations, such as Carbon Trade Watch, the Corner House, and the Transnational Institute criticised the options proposed by the Commission for not considering whether the scheme should be repealed (European Commission 2013d). In contrast, more mainstream groups such as CAN Europe and Greenpeace called for measures that would reduce the supply of allowances, but opposed discretionary price management because it would undermine the potential to further expand global carbon markets through links between the EU ETS and other schemes (Climate Action Network Europe 2013; Greenpeace Europe 2013a). These groups, together with Sandbag, Carbon Market Watch, and WWF, therefore embraced the market-based paradigm, supporting the Market Stability Reserve with the goal of making it as forceful as possible in its capacity to withdraw allowances from the market (Climate Action Network Europe and others 2014).

The purportedly apolitical nature of an automatic allowance supply adjustment mechanism made the legislative process for the adoption of the Market Stability Reserve much smoother than for backloading. Indeed, the specific details of the proposal had technocratic origins in a 'panel of experts' from electricity and manufacturing industries, financial actors, researchers and analysts, NGOs, and state bureaucracies convened by the Commission (European Commission 2013e p. 6). Debate after the Commission made its

140 *Contesting Carbon*

formal proposal for a Market Stability Reserve mostly focused on the start date and provisions for compensation. Western European governments and electricity companies generally favoured an earlier start date from around 2017. While most Central and Eastern European governments, and representatives of energy intensive manufacturing industries, were wary of any measure that would increase carbon prices, the former focused on pushing the start-date to 2021, while the latter focused on securing ongoing free allocation (Wettestad & Jevnaker 2016 pp. 50–7).

The final Market Stability Reserve, supported by Parliament and Council in July and September 2015 had a compromise start date of 2019 and safeguarded free allowance provisions for carbon-intensive manufacturing and poorer states. It was agreed that the Market Stability Reserve would initially be supplied with all backloaded allowances and any allowances unallocated by 2020. It was also agreed that each year, the Commission would publish the total number of allowances in circulation. If the number is more than 833 million, 12 per cent of this number were to be removed from planned auctions and placed in the Reserve. If the number is less than 400 million allowances in circulation, 100 million allowances were to be released from the Reserve (European Parliament and Council 2015).

Contestation over backloading and the Market Stability Reserve was structured by the double-edged nature of the state in regulating the force of value determinations. From the perspective of capital, the state is necessary for carbon market value determinations to have force, but problems arise when that force is politically determined. Thus, in both cases, capital sought a post-political outcome that would limit the discretionary power of states to directly shape carbon prices. NGOs were split between more radical, grassroots groups wanting to scrap the EU ETS that completely opposed the force of value in organising climate action, and more mainstream groups seeking to augment the force of carbon market value determinations by making this a political issue, albeit one to be solved through techno-political means. Once implemented, backloading did not substantially raise carbon prices, with average spot prices increasing from €6 per tonne in 2014 to €7.70 in 2015, the first year of the reform (Hatchwell 2016). The effects of the Market Stability Reserve remain to be seen.

5.3.3 *The Priority of Value: 2030 Climate and Energy Package*

Contestation over the 2030 climate and energy package, which sets the broad framework for EU climate and energy policy between 2020 and 2030, extended beyond reform of the carbon market to its relationship with other policies. The 2020 package for the prior decade adopted a 'triple target' approach with separate emissions, renewables and energy efficiency targets. The so-called 20-20-20 model involved targets of a 20 per cent reduction in emissions, a 20 per cent improvement in energy efficiency and a 20 per cent share of renewable energy by 2020, made up of binding national level targets. A central point of debate was whether this multi-pronged model should be extended, or be replaced, to a greater or lesser extent, by a single emissions reduction target to be met though the EU ETS. The substance of the debate was therefore the priority of carbon market value determinations, relative to other organising principles, in the EU's efforts to address climate change.

While the two previous cases were triggered in response to political pressure, the Commission initiated debate on the 2030 package as part of the periodic review of EU climate and energy policy. It released a Green Paper in March 2013 that acknowledged that the EU ETS had 'not succeeded in being a major driver towards long term low carbon investments' but nonetheless proposed a package that could prevent 'national and sectoral policies undermining the role of the ETS and [the] level playing field it was meant to create' (European Commission 2013a p. 4). To achieve its goals, the Commission proposed a 40 per cent emission reduction target by 2030, to be primarily achieved through the EU ETS. It also gave support for the continuation of the multiple instruments approach at the European level as an alternative to national level policies provided they met the test of policy 'coherence' (European Commission 2013a pp. 7–9). Different interpretations of policy coherence dominated the ensuing debate.

The electricity and carbon-intensive manufacturing sectors were once again at odds over the stringency of the headline emissions target but were largely united in opposition to renewable energy and energy efficiency targets. The arguments against such targets rested on the dominant market logic of economics, asserting that specific renewables and efficiency policies undermined the cost-efficient achievement of the emissions reduction target via the EU ETS. This position was articulated, for example, by E.ON, which argued that 'interference between the instruments EU ETS, [renewable energy] promotion schemes and [the] energy efficiency directive have resulted in conflicts and spoiled economic efficiency especially of the EU ETS. Consequently, climate change measures were unable to deliver the economically desired outcome (abate climate change at lowest costs)' (E.ON 2013b). The other main German electricity company RWE summed up this overall position in advancing a 'maxim of "one target, one instrument"'. In doing so, RWE translated E.ON's techno-political appeal to a post-political position in which the carbon price was the only necessary coordination mechanism, guided by the principle of 'as much of the market as possible, but as little state control as is necessary' (RWE 2013).

Environmental organisations took the opposite approach in arguing that a coherent policy framework required the inclusion of other measures. However, Friends of the Earth, Greenpeace, and WWF each adopted different strategies on the relationship between the carbon market and other policies. Friends of the Earth used support for alternative policies to challenge the market logic of the EU ETS. First, the organisation challenged the narrow focus on least cost emissions reductions, articulated by E.ON, by pointing towards other benefits such as health improvements and the creation of jobs from alternative policies. Second, it highlighted the importance of the very questions carbon markets are neutral on. In contrast to RWE and E.ON, Friends of the Earth argued that alternative policies were essential precisely because of the political considerations they facilitate, stating: 'If we don't give guidance on how emission cuts will be made – by putting in place a coherent set of three targets – the door will be left open for false solutions like nuclear power, the replacement of coal with natural gas and unsustainable bioenergy, or carbon capture and storage' (Friends of the Earth Europe 2013a). Greenpeace's emphasis was subtly different, not directly challenging the logic of carbon trading, but deprioritising the instrument in relation to other approaches. Greenpeace argued that a coherent climate and energy package would first look to maximise energy efficiency and second meet the resulting lower energy demand with policies encouraging the deployment of renewables. Only after the potential of efficiency and renewable energy policy had been exhausted should the 'remaining part of the required abatement … be driven by a well-functioning EU emissions trading scheme' (Greenpeace Europe 2013b). WWF's approach was different again, using techno-political arguments on the interaction between carbon markets, investment and innovation to stress the complementarities of other policies in achieving the cost efficient emissions reduction goal of carbon markets (WWF Europe 2013).

Overlaying the conflicting industry and environmental movement positions on the priority of the carbon market were conflicts between national states over how alternative policies aligned with their domestic goals. The strongest national state opposition to multiple targets came from heavily coal-dependent Central and Eastern countries in the Visegrad 4+ Group. They were led by Poland and included the Czech Republic, Slovakia, Hungary, Bulgaria, and Romania (Ministry of the Environment 2013). The United Kingdom also came out in opposition to renewables and efficiency targets, echoing polluting industry in arguing that such targets 'risk pre-judging the cost effective pathway to 2030 [greenhouse gas] outcomes' and 'interact in a complex and unhelpful manner with other measures, notably the EU ETS' (Department of Energy and Climate Change 2013). The position was clearly consistent with the UK government's support for shale gas and nuclear power, which would be disadvantaged by renewable energy and energy efficiency policy (Department of Energy and Climate Change 2011).

Conversely, many other governments were in favour of a renewables target, including Germany, France, Denmark, Italy, Austria, Belgium, Ireland, and Portugal. Environment and energy ministers from these countries adopted a common position in the lead up to the Commission's proposal on the climate and energy package, arguing that a renewables target would enhance competitiveness, jobs and growth in Europe in the context of increasing global demand for renewable energy technologies (Mitterlehner et al. 2013). Many of the same ministers, from the governments of Belgium, Denmark, Germany, Greece, Ireland, Luxembourg, and Portugal, made a similar case for an energy efficiency target (Wathelet et al. 2014). However, support for multiple targets from these countries only extended as far as the EU level, rather than the national level targets of the 2020 package. For example, the governments of France and Germany maintained that states should have sovereignty and flexibility over their energy mix (Presidency of the Republic of France 2014). Therefore, national governments with different positions on the priority of value relations versus alternative criteria in climate policy were each conditioned by common imperatives to retain the capacity to actively shape responses to climate change.

The Commission's initial formal proposal, released on 22 January 2014, reflected the weight of arguments against the multiple target approach in heavily prioritising a single target and the role of the EU ETS in meeting it. In the proposal, the increase in the 2030 emissions reduction target to 40 per cent, from 20 per cent by 2020, was not matched by an equivalent increase in the renewable energy target, which would only rise from 20 per cent to 27 per cent and not be binding at the national level, as it had been in the previous climate and energy package (European Commission 2014a p. 6). The impact assessment released alongside the proposal made it clear that the carbon market was the reason the Commission did not consider higher renewable energy options, as such options 'would result in continuing increases of the surplus of allowances in the EU ETS up to 2030 and would therefore seriously undermine the future relevance of the ETS in providing the right incentives for low-carbon investment' (European Commission 2014f p. 47). Instead, the 27 per cent renewables target was informed by its modelling on the bare minimum required to achieve the 40 per cent emissions target, to ensure no

144 *Contesting Carbon*

greater obligations beyond what was cost efficient – an example of the 'performativity' of economic theory. Six months later, the Commission proposed to increase the energy efficiency target by slightly more than the renewables target but still less than the emissions target, to 30 per cent for the EU as a whole, from 20 per cent in the 2020 package (European Commission 2014d).

The residualisation of the renewables target and the absence of national level targets in the Commission's proposals brought the UK government on board (Flynn 2014). Similarly, the Visegrad countries maintained that there was 'no need' for other targets, but described the Commission's proposed targets as 'a step in the right direction' (Visegrad Group 2014a, 2014b). The final package agreed to on 23–24 October 2014 by the European Council composed of the heads of each member state, accepted the Commission's proposal for a 40 per cent emissions target and a 27 per cent renewables target but reduced the efficiency target to 27 per cent. In the process, the EU ETS was explicitly affirmed as the primary emissions reduction instrument, with the intention of extending the market to new sectors (General Secretariat of the Council 2014). Thus, the 2030 climate and energy package saw a consolidation of the EU ETS, which prioritised the value determinations of the carbon market over targeted support for renewable energy and energy efficiency.

The prioritisation of the carbon market in the 2030 package created divergent directions for EU climate policy. It created the impetus for further reform of the EU ETS in the post-2020, phase four period, strengthening earlier reforms. Parliament and Council agreed to further increase both the linear reduction factor reducing yearly allowance allocation levels and the rate at which allowances are placed into the Market Stability Reserve. However, the provisions for special treatment for certain actors encouraged by the carbon market framework were continued. Consequently, 'transitional' free allocation for manufacturing industries deemed to be exposed to international competitive pressures began to look increasingly permanent (European Parliament 2018). This real, but once again uneven, reform came at a significant cost to the suite of policies needed to act in a climate-changing capitalism. Reforms to the EU ETS sharpen the value determinations of carbon markets by creating conditions that are more conducive to the emergence of carbon as capital. As outlined in Chapter 4, the capitalisation of carbon risks entrenching the most profitable forms of carbon appropriation. These potentially negative outcomes would be mitigated by policies mandating renewable energy development or energy efficiency standards regardless of whether this constitutes the most profitable organisation of nature. Such policies can redirect or replace carbon market value determinations with concerns such as employment numbers and conditions, air and water

Conclusion 145

quality for health, and democratic control over energy. Alternative policies do continue to exist, and their outcomes are also a matter of contestation, but their position has been weakened within a marketised policy framework that is increasingly dominated by the carbon market.

Conclusion

The three cases in this chapter demonstrate that the EU ETS has indeed been actively constituted by a 'politics of market design' that has developed beyond questions of support for or opposition to carbon markets. For environment groups, this techno-political shift can be assessed in terms of immediate and longer-term policy outcomes. On both levels, success has been real, varied and limited. In the immediate term, industrial gas offsets were banned and allowance auctions were back-loaded. Campaigns that used these issues to delegitimise the carbon market helped create political pressure that delivered these outcomes. However, over the course of the policy processes in the offset restriction and backloading debates, the potential effectiveness of each measure was eroded due to delays in and the weakening of final outcomes compared with the original proposals. In the longer term, both were agreed to in ways that limited the capacity for future reform of the same kind. Yet, some other reform has since taken place in both areas, most notably the Market Stability Reserve, but the start date of 2019, two full decades since debate on the EU ETS first began, signals a disjuncture between the slow pace of reform achieved through a politics of market design and the rapidly changing climate.

The residualisation of renewables and energy efficiency targets in the EU's 2030 package represented a serious setback for action on climate change. The need for such policies is acknowledged by MacKenzie (2009b p. 174), who states that 'the problem of combating climate change is much too far-reaching and complex to be solved by a single class of instruments such as emissions markets'. While environmental groups stridently opposed the 2030 outcome, there are continuities between it and the industrial gas and allowance supply cases. As a result of the depressed carbon market, in all three cases, the politics of market design became focused on the need to reform the EU ETS in order to save it. Arguments of this nature used to achieve reform in the first two cases were effectively deployed by capital to consolidate the EU ETS at the expense of alternative policies in the third case. In making the argument, capital was systematically advantaged by the economic logic of carbon markets.

A key thread running through all the cases has been the tensions created for states by the use of carbon markets as a means to regulate the production of climate change. This is not a question of more or less state. An extensive state apparatus underpins the value determinations of carbon markets. But the democratic, capitalist, and bureaucratic dimensions of states were faced with tensions between securing public legitimacy, supporting accumulation and maintaining the capacity to regulate natural conditions according to their particular goals. Between these competing imperatives, the institutionalisation of the market-based approach pushed outcomes towards securing a greater role for carbon market value determinations in climate policy. This is the crux of the third major contradiction of carbon markets in a climate-changing capitalism identified in this book: the institutionalisation of carbon markets privileges political actors and interventions that mobilise the singular logic of carbon pricing, undermining the portfolio of climate policies required to slow climate change. The marketisation of climate policy in the EU has thus shaped climate politics by encouraging sharp political contestation over carbon market reform while disadvantaging policy alternatives outside the market paradigm.

This conclusion lends support to arguments that post-political forms of governance, such as carbon markets, narrow political pathways. However, there are aspects of carbon market politics that do not entirely align with Swyngedouw's (2010 p. 225) contention that 'the post-political disavows … antagonisms by displacing conflict and disagreement on to the terrain of consensually manageable problems, expert knowledge and interest intermediation'. While post-political *strategies* were clearly evident, particularly among fossil fuel industries, this did not translate to the creation of wholly post-political *conditions*. Capital's engagement with carbon markets is largely defensive in character. Rather than representing a positive embrace of technocratic solutions, the general consensus of polluting capital over the continuation of the carbon market is a real political tactic shaped by concrete material interests. The post-political frame also risks glossing over the contradictions faced by state institutions in managing marketised forms of governance and thus failing to appreciate any political fragility in existing arrangements that can be exposed and targeted politically. Lastly, the interventions by groups that used formal engagement to denounce the carbon market illustrates ongoing room for dissent even within the policy process, supported by radical climate activism outside of it (Chatterton et al. 2013; Wainwright & Mann 2013). This indicates an important role for movements to use the space that still remains – contrary to techno-political and post-political pronouncements – to posit radical democratic alternatives that do not devolve decision-making over responses to climate change to carbon markets. The Conclusion surveys some of these alternatives in light of the analysis in this book.

Conclusion

The EU ETS was displaced from its position as the world's largest carbon market in December 2017 when the Chinese government announced details of its long-awaited national carbon trading scheme (National Development and Reform Commission 2017). The Chinese carbon market, upon commencement, covered approximately 3 Gt CO_2 per year, compared to the approximately 1.8 Gt CO_2 per year covered in the EU ETS (Jotzo et al. 2018 p. 265). China's position as the world's largest emitter of greenhouse gases, and the centrality of its commitments to the outcomes of the Paris Agreement, means that this scheme will ensure that carbon markets remain central to global climate policy, beyond the EU and the UN.

There are important differences between the Chinese carbon market and the EU ETS. The Chinese government is adopting a gradual approach to the roll-out of its carbon market. Initially, the market is limited to electricity generation, although the size of the sector and its carbon-intensity means that this represents about 8 per cent of global greenhouse gas emissions (Jotzo et al. 2018 p. 265). Financial practices are also limited to the trading of spot allowances by polluting enterprises on a national exchange, in order to limit price volatility and speculation (Reuters 2017). Lastly, the early years of the scheme are focused on building the necessary market infrastructure by building emissions data verification and reporting processes and simulating allocation, trading and compliance systems. The Chinese government has stated that it intends have a fully operational market after 2020, with an expanded sectoral coverage and more market participants and financial products, including links to domestic or international offsetting schemes (Jotzo et al. 2018; National Development and Reform Commission 2017).

These early design elements indicate the contradictions of carbon markets in a climate-changing capitalism, identified in this book in relation to the EU ETS and its links with the Kyoto mechanisms, are amplified in case of the

147

Chinese carbon market. The first contradiction, that carbon markets use formally equal market transactions to address a substantively unequal climate problem, is especially stark given the high level of state ownership of fossil fuel assets in China. The Chinese electricity sector is far more concentrated and centralised than Europe's, meaning its carbon market is even further away from idealised economic models. In 2014, coal fuelled 67 per cent of installed capacity in China, which included over 60 large-scale power stations of greater than 1,000MW in size. 94 per cent of the total installed coal capacity was either wholly (61 per cent) or majority (33 per cent) state-owned (Hervé-Mignucci et al. 2015 p. 26).

The next contradiction, where the economic viability of carbon markets requires ongoing fossil fuel use, is given a new inflection by the relative weakness of private finance in the climate space in China. Trading restrictions in the national carbon market follow the lead of the pilot schemes established at city and province level from 2013. These schemes operated through mostly state-owned exchanges, and were characterised by low trading volumes and little participation of private finance, which has limited experience and interest in climate finance in China (Lo 2016 pp. 61–77). Without opportunities for financial capital to benefit, the impetus for states to institute well-functioning carbon markets, from the perspective of dominant political economic accounts, is missing. The reluctance of the Chinese state to regulate against its own fossil fuel interests through the carbon market is evident in the method of allocation, which provides free allowances that increase with the output levels of installation, and thus does not place an absolute cap on emissions (Gan 2018).

The final contradiction, between the singular logic of carbon pricing and the need for a pluralistic policy framework, is manifesting in pressures to subordinate other climate and energy policies to the carbon market. China has a range of policies in place to encourage investment in renewable energy, the expansion of electric vehicles and public transport, and increased energy efficiency, but important government research centres have begun prioritising carbon pricing in their policy recommendations (Liu et al. 2016). Carbon pricing is also creating new pressures for energy liberalisation, to enable generators and grid operators to better respond to the carbon price signal by increasing coal efficiency levels or switching to gas (Slater 2017; Timperley 2018). Thus, the institutionalisation of market-based policy is encouraging techno-political reforms where the Chinese state builds the market infrastructure necessary to improve the operation of the carbon market while potentially reducing its capacity to comprehensively plan for decarbonisation.

This book therefore offers an approach that can inform further research as market solutions to climate change continue on their bumpy road through the Paris Agreement, China and elsewhere (see Lederer 2017). Placing carbon markets, or any other climate policy, within a climate-changing capitalism connects causes of, and responses to, climate change in a critical way. From this perspective, capitalism produces climate change as a socio-ecological, economic, and political crisis that is shaping the future of capitalism. The market-based approach makes state-instituted commodification of nature a key mediator in the co-production of capitalism and climate change. This is because carbon commodities sit between accumulation by appropriation in fossil fuel industries, which drives climate change, and accumulation by capitalisation in financial markets, which drives its marketisation. There is also scope to apply notions of appropriation, commodification and capitalisation, developed from work in Marxist ecology, as a typology of capitalist relations with, and within, nature, to study contradictions in other versions of 'selling nature to save it' (McAfee 1999).

The contradictions of carbon markets in a climate-changing capitalism revealed in the preceding chapters represent disjunctures between the climate change problem and the carbon market solution. A relatively small number of companies in state and private hands control a large proportion of greenhouse gas emissions through their ownership of large-scale polluting infrastructure. However, carbon markets risk inducing transitions that favour relatively marginal climate actions, entrench the most profitable forms of fossil fuel use, and disadvantage alternative, necessary, policy solutions. The course of climate-changing capitalism is shaped by a range of actors, institutions, and relations beyond the combustion of fossil fuels in electricity and manufacturing sectors in contemporary Europe, and beyond the impact of the EU ETS and its links with the Kyoto mechanisms. To draw attention to the contradictions of carbon markets is not to deny this broader context but to 'insist that responses to environmental crises are more likely to be successful to the extent that this crisis is accurately assessed' (Smith 2008 p. 247).

The limitations of carbon markets have promoted consideration of alternatives, including degrowth, *buen vivir,* and democratic mechanisms for allocating emissions rights (Felli 2018; McAfee 2015; Stuart et al. 2017). Recent orientations by activists in climate movements have much to offer these discussions because they have adopted strategies that respond to more accurate assessments of the capitalist production of climate change. Non-violent direct actions aimed at gas mines, oil pipelines, or coal-fired power stations, dubbed 'Blockadia', seek to confront climate change in places that, due to the spatially concentrated, networked aspects of fossil fuel infrastructure, can either prevent, or reduce, large amounts of emissions. By seeking to effect a withdrawal of carbon-intensive lending and investment, divestment campaigns challenge the legitimacy of corporations, in which control over fossil fuels has become so socially centralised, that just a handful wield political economic power to guarantee climate chaos (Klein 2014). These mobilisations have made steps towards addressing climate change is ways that are attuned to the uneven socio-spatial organisation of emissions, and provide principles for governments in formulating alternative climate policies.

The concentration and centralisation of emissions revealed in the EU ETS makes planning a transition away from fossil fuels using a suite of renewable energy, energy efficiency, and other climate policies both necessary and feasible. It is necessary to discriminate between actors according to their contribution to the climate problem by creating strict timetables to replace the most polluting coal-fired power stations and other large-sale sources of pollution with clean alternatives, implemented by directly targeting the small number of publicly and privately owned corporations that own them. This is likely to represent a much more efficacious path to a post-carbon economy because, if adequately enforced, it guarantees required transformations in carbon-intensive energy systems, which requires not only investment in carbon-free technologies, but the rapid phase out of fossil fuels. While the political barriers to such an approach are significant, its regulatory feasibility is aided by the relatively small number of ultimate owners and polluting installations that need to be administered. Further, extensive state control over emissions places governments in a particularly strong position to immediately address, rather than marketise, their own significant direct contribution to climate change.

Any approach that directly targets the largest corporate and state polluters would face obstacles including enhanced corporate strategies to evade accountability, and state institutions that, after decades of marketisation in all areas of public policy, are disinclined to make necessary climate investments. Yet, twenty years of carbon markets has neither negated corporate opposition to effective climate action, nor quelled political demands for the state to lead the necessary post-carbon transformation. While the EU ETS has delivered some emissions reductions, financial opportunities, and policy reforms, it has also demonstrated that market solutions tend to limit the potential for democratic decision-making over pathways to a safe climate by elevating dominant logics and interests. In contrast, planning for decarbonisation through more targeted and multi-pronged forms of regulation would place the terms of climate policy on a more democratic, and climate-friendly, footing.

References

Abrell, J., Ndoye, A., & Zachmann, G. (2011). *Assessing the impact of the EU ETS using firm level data* (Document de Travail), Bureau d'economie theorique et appliquee. Retrieved from www.beta-umr7522.fr/productions/publications/2011/2011-15.pdf

Alberici, S., Boeve, S., van Breevoort, P., & Deng, Y. (2014). *Subsidies and costs of EU energy: final report,* Ecofys/European Commission. Retrieved from https://ec.europa.eu/energy/sites/ener/files/documents/ECOFYS%202014%20Subsidies%20and%20costs%20of%20EU%20energy_11_Nov.pdf. Last accessed: 11 November 2014.

Alcock, F. (2008). Conflicts and coalitions within and across the ENGO community. *Global Environmental Politics,* **8**(4), 66–91.

Alliance of Energy Intensive Industries. (2012). *Position of the alliance of energy intensive industries on the Commission proposal to back-load (set-aside) EU ETS allowances.* Retrieved from http://ec.europa.eu/clima/consultations/docs/0017/organisations/unicobre_2_en.pdf

Altvater, E. (2006). The social and natural environment of fossil capitalism. In L. Panitch & C. Leys, eds., *Socialist Register 2007,* London: The Merlin Press, pp. 37–59.

Anderson, B., & Maria, C. D. (2011). Abatement and allocation in the pilot phase of the EU ETS. *Environmental and Resource Economics,* **48**(1), 83–103.

Andreucci, D., García-Lamarca, M., Wedekind, J., & Swyngedouw, E. (2017). "Value Grabbing": a political ecology of rent. *Capitalism Nature Socialism,* **28**(3), 28–47.

Apeldoorn, B. V. (2000). Transnational class agency and European governance: the case of the European Round Table of Industrialists. *New Political Economy,* **5**(2), 157–181.

ArcelorMittal. (2010). *Annual Report 2009: Management Report,* Luxembourg: ArcelorMittal.

ArcelorMittal. (2011). *Annual Report 2010,* Luxembourg: ArcelorMittal.

ArcelorMittal. (2013). *Annual Report 2012,* Luxembourg: ArcelorMittal.

ArcelorMittal. (2015). *Annual Report 2014,* Luxembourg: ArcelorMittal.

Bachram, H. (2004). Climate fraud and carbon colonialism: the new trade in greenhouse gases. *Capitalism Nature Socialism,* **15**, 5–20.

Bailey, I. (2007). Neoliberalism, climate governance and the scalar politics of EU emissions trading. *Area,* **39**(4), 431–442.

References

Bailey, I. (2010). The EU emissions trading scheme. *Wiley Interdisciplinary Reviews: Climate Change*, **1**(1), 144–153.

Bailey, I., & Maresh, S. (2009). Scales and networks of neoliberal climate governance: the regulatory and territorial logics of European Union emissions trading. *Transactions of the Institute of British Geographers*, **34**(4), 445–461.

Bailey, I., & Rupp, S. (2004). Politics, industry and the regulation of industrial greenhouse-gas emissions in the UK and Germany. *European Environment*, **14**(4), 235–250.

Bailey, I., & Wilson, G. A. (2009). Theorising transitional pathways in response to climate change: technocentrism, ecocentrism, and the carbon economy. *Environment and Planning A*, **41**(10), 2324–2341.

Bakker, K. (2003). *An Uncooperative Commodity: Privatizing Water in England and Wales*, Oxford: Oxford University Press.

Bakker, K. (2005). Neoliberalizing nature? Market environmentalism in water supply in England and Wales. *Annals of the Association of American Geographers*, **95**(3), 542–565.

Baumert, K. A., Herzog, T., & Pershing, J. (2005). *Navigating the Numbers: Greenhouse Gas Data and International Climate Policy*, USA: World Resources Institute.

BDI – Bundesverband der Deutschen Industrie. (2001). *Position paper on green paper on greenhouse gas emissions trading within the European Union*. Retrieved from http://ec.europa.eu/environment/archives/docum/0087_en.htm

Benton, T. (1989). Marxism and natural limits: an ecological critique and reconstruction. *New Left Review*, (178), 51–86.

Benton, T. (1992). Ecology, socialism and the mastery of nature: a reply to Reiner Grundmann. *New Left Review*, (194), 55–74.

Betsill, M. (2002). Environmental NGOs meet the sovereign state: the Kyoto Protocol negotiations on global climate change. *Colorado Journal of International Environmental Law and Policy*, **13**, 49–64.

Betsill, M., & Hoffmann, M. J. (2011). The contours of "cap and trade": the evolution of emissions trading systems for greenhouse gases. *Review of Policy Research*, **28**(1), 83–106.

Bieler, A. (2015). "Sic vos non vobis" (for you, but not yours): the struggle for public water in Italy. *Monthly Review*, **67**(5), 35–50.

Bieler, A., & Morton, A. D. (eds.). (2001). *Social Forces in the Making of New Europe*, Basingstoke: Palgrave Macmillan.

Bieler, A., & Morton, A. D. (2018). *Global Capitalism, Global War, Global Crisis*, Cambridge: Cambridge University Press.

Bigger, P. (2017). Hybridity, possibility: Degrees of marketization in tradeable permit systems. *Environment and Planning A*, Online early. doi:10.1177/0308518X17737786

Bigger, P., & Robertson, M. (2017). Value is simple. Valuation is complex. *Capitalism Nature Socialism*, **28**(1), 68–77.

Blok, A. (2011). Clash of the eco-sciences: carbon marketization, environmental NGOs and performativity as politics. *Economy and Society*, **40**(3), 451–476.

Bloomberg New Energy Finance. (2012, January 11). Global carbon market expands 10% in 2011. Retrieved 15 June 2016, from http://about.newenergyfinance.com/about/press-releases/global-carbon-market-expands-10-in-2011/

Bloomberg New Energy Finance. (2014, January 8). Value of the world's carbon markets to rise again in 2014. Retrieved 10 November 2014, from http://about.newenergyfinance.com/about/press-releases/value-of-the-worlds-carbon-markets-to-rise-again-in-2014/

References

BNP Paribas Corporate and Investment Banking. (2014). Developing the green economy. Retrieved 18 September 2014, from http://cib.bnpparibas.com/Why_BNP_Paribas/Acting-Responsibly/Developping-the-Green-Economy/page.aspx/171

Böhm, S., & Dabhi, S. (eds.). (2009). *Upsetting the Offset: The Political Economy of Carbon Markets*, London: MayFlyBooks.

Böhm, S., & Dabhi, S. (2011). Fault lines in climate policy: what role for carbon markets? *Climate Policy*, **11**(6), 1389–1392.

Böhm, S., Misoczky, M. C., & Moog, S. (2012). Greening capitalism? A Marxist critique of carbon markets. *Organization Studies*, **33**(11), 1617–1638.

Böhringer, C. (2014). Two decades of European climate policy: a critical appraisal. *Review of Environmental Economics and Policy*, **8**(1), 1–17.

Bokhoven, T., Ahmels, P., Blacklock, P., et al. (2001). *European Climate Change Programme (ECCP) ensuring its effectiveness – update statement of the clean industry groups, environmental NGOs and academic experts.* Retrieved from www.caneurope.org/resources/archive/eu-climate-policy-before-2007/824-2001-mar-eccp-ensuring-its-effectiveness

Bond, P. (2012). Emissions trading, new enclosures and eco-social contestation. *Antipode*, **44**(3), 684–701.

Bonefeld, W. (Ed.). (2001). *The Politics of Europe*, Basingstoke: Palgrave Macmillan.

Bontrup, H., & Marquardt, R. (2015). *Die Zukunft der großen Energieversorger*, Hannover/Lüdinghausen: Greenpeace Germany. Retrieved from www.greenpeace.de/sites/www.greenpeace.de/files/publications/zukunft-energieversorgung-studie-20150309.pdf

Bortolotti, B., & Faccio, M. (2009). Government control of privatized firms. *The Review of Financial Studies*, **22**(8), 2907–2939.

Boyd, E., Boykoff, M., & Newell, P. (2011). The "new" carbon economy: what's new? *Antipode*, **43**(3), 601–611.

Boyd, E., Hultman, N., Timmons Roberts, J., et al. (2009). Reforming the CDM for sustainable development: lessons learned and policy futures. *Environmental Science & Policy*, **12**(7), 820–831.

Boyd, E., & Schipper, E. L. (2002). The Marrakech Accord – at the crossroad to ratification: Seventh Conference of the Parties to the United Nations Framework Convention on Climate Change. *The Journal of Environment & Development*, **11**(2), 184–190.

Bracking, S. (2015a). Performativity in the Green Economy: how far does climate finance create a fictive economy? *Third World Quarterly*, **36**(12), 2337–2357.

Bracking, S. (2015b). The anti-politics of climate finance: the creation and performativity of the Green Climate Fund. *Antipode*, **47**(2), 281–302.

Braun, M. (2009). The evolution of emissions trading in the European Union – the role of policy networks, knowledge and policy entrepreneurs. *Accounting, Organizations and Society*, **34**(3–4), 469–487.

Brenner, N. (1998). Between fixity and motion: accumulation, territorial organization and the historical geography of spatial scales. *Environment and Planning D*, **16**, 459–482.

Bridge, G. (2011). Resource geographies 1: making carbon economies, old and new. *Progress in Human Geography*, **35**(6), 820–834.

Bridge, G., Bouzarovski, S., Bradshaw, M., & Eyre, N. (2013). Geographies of energy transition: space, place and the low-carbon economy. *Energy Policy*, **53**, 331–340.

Bryan, D., & Rafferty, M. (2006). *Capitalism with Derivatives*, Hampshire: Palgrave Macmillan.

Bryan, D., & Rafferty, M. (2013). Fundamental value: a category in transformation. *Economy and Society*, **42**(1), 130–153.

Bryan, D., Rafferty, M., & Jefferis, C. (2015). Risk and value: finance, labor, and production. *South Atlantic Quarterly*, **114**(2), 307–329.

Bryant, G. (2016). Creating a level playing field? The concentration and centralisation of emissions in the European Union Emissions Trading System. *Energy Policy*, **99**, 308–318.

Bryant, G., Dabhi, S., & Böhm, S. (2015). 'Fixing' the climate crisis: capital, states and carbon offsetting in India. *Environment and Planning A*, **47**(10), 2047–2063.

Buckley, P. (2017). *State of the EU Emissions Trading System 2017. Asking Questions of the Numbers: Leaders and Laggards*, Sandbag.

Bullock, S., Childs, M., & Picken, T. (2009). *A Dangerous Distraction. Why Offsetting is Failing the Climate and People: The Evidence*, Friends of the Earth England, Wales and Northern Ireland. Retrieved from www.foe.co.uk/resource/briefing_notes/dangerous_distraction.pdf

Bumpus, A. G. (2011). The matter of carbon: understanding the materiality of tCO2e in carbon offsets. *Antipode*, **43**(3), 612–638.

Bumpus, A. G., & Liverman, D. M. (2008). Accumulation by decarbonization and the governance of carbon offsets. *Economic Geography*, **84**, 127–155.

Bureau van Dijk. (2014). Orbis database. Retrieved 16 July 2014, from https://orbis.bvdinfo.com

Bureau van Dijk. (2017). Orbis database. Retrieved 8 September 2017, from https://orbis.bvdinfo.com

Burkett, P. (1999). *Marx and Nature*, Basingstoke: Palgrave Macmillan.

Burtraw, D., Evans, D. A., Krupnick, A., Palmer, K., & Toth, R. (2005). Economics of pollution trading for SO2 and NOX. *Annual Review of Environment and Resources*, **30**(1), 253–289.

Büscher, B. (2012). Nature on the move: the value and circulation of liquid nature and the emergence of fictitious conservation. *New Proposals: Journal of Marxism and Interdisciplinary Inquiry*, **6**(1–2), 20–36.

Callon, M. (2009). Civilizing markets: carbon trading between in vitro and in vivo experiments. *Accounting, Organizations and Society*, **34**, 535–548.

Camco. (2009, March 2). Why structuring is important for CDM development. Retrieved 6 November 2014, from www.camcocleanenergy.com/blog/why-structuring-is-important-for-cdm-development

Carbon Markets and Investors Association. (2010). Comitology process on EU-ETS offset standards. Retrieved from http://ec.europa.eu/clima/consultations/docs/0004/registered/cmia_en.pdf

Carney, M. (2015, September). *Breaking the tragedy of the horizon – climate change and financial stability*, Speech by Mr Mark Carney, Governor of the Bank of England and Chairman of the Financial Stability Board, at Lloyd's of London, London. Retrieved from www.bis.org/review/r151009a.pdf

Cartel, M., Boxenbaum, E., Aggeri, F., & Caneill, J.-Y. (2017). Policymaking as collective bricolage: the role of the electricity sector in the making of the European carbon market: Corporate Engagement in Politics and Governance. In C. Garsten & A. Sörbom, eds., *Power, Policy and Profit: Corporate Engagement in Politics and Governance*, Edward Elgar Publishing.

Carton, W. (2017). Dancing to the rhythms of the fossil fuel landscape: landscape inertia and the temporal limits to market-based climate policy. *Antipode*, **49**(1), 43–61.

Castree, N. (1995). The nature of produced nature: materiality and knowledge construction in Marxism. *Antipode*, **21**, 12–48.

Castree, N. (2003). Commodifying what nature? *Progress in Human Geography*, **27**(3), 273–297.

Castree, N. (2008a). Neoliberalising nature: processes, effects, and evaluations. *Environment and Planning A*, **40**(1), 153–173.

Castree, N. (2008b). Neoliberalising nature: the logics of deregulation and reregulation. *Environment and Planning A*, **40**(1), 131–152.

Castree, N. (2014). The Anthropocene and geography I: the back story. *Geography Compass*, **8**(7), 436–449.

Castree, N., & Christophers, B. (2015). Banking spatially on the future: capital switching, infrastructure, and the ecological fix. *Annals of the Association of American Geographers*, **105**(2), 378–386.

CDC Climat. (2009). The EU ETS as a cash cow. *Tendances Carbone: Monthly Bulletin on the European Carbon Market* (35).

CDM Watch. (2011). *Climate campaigners hail European ban on industrial gas offsets as an historic victory for environmental integrity*. Retrieved from http://carbonmarketwatch.org/wp-content/uploads/2011/01/110121-EU-Member-States-endorse-ban-on-industrial-gas-offsets.pdf

CE Delft, & Öko-Institut. (2015). *Ex-post Investigation of Cost Pass-Through in the EU ETS: An Analysis for Six Sectors*, Luxembourg: European Commission.

CEFIC. (2001). *CEFIC position on greenhouse gas emissions trading*. Retrieved from http://ec.europa.eu/environment/archives/docum/pdf/0087_business_associations1.pdf

Chancel, L., & Piketty, T. (2015). *Carbon and Inequality: From Kyoto to Paris*, Paris School of Economics.

Chatterton, P., Featherstone, D., & Routledge, P. (2013). Articulating climate justice in Copenhagen: antagonism, the commons, and solidarity. *Antipode*, **45**(3), 602–620.

Chemelot. (2014). Companies: OCI Nitrogen. Retrieved 18 September 2014, from www.chemelot.nl/default.aspx?id=3&template=bedrijf.htm&bid=70&taal=en

Chestney, N. (2009a, March 26). Poll-table-EU carbon emissions, price forecasts to 2020. *Reuters News*. Retrieved from http://uk.reuters.com/article/2009/02/18/carbon-emissions-idUKLG61152420090218

Chestney, N. (2009b, May 29). Concerns mount over EU, U.S. carbon markets link. *Reuters*. Retrieved from http://uk.reuters.com/article/2009/05/29/btscenes-us-carbon-market-linkage-idUKTRE54S2O320090529

Chestney, N. (2010, January 7). Frustrated carbon traders try other commodities. *Reuters*, London. Retrieved from www.reuters.com/article/2010/01/07/us-carbon-market-idUSTRE6062SR20100107

Chestney, N. (2011, January 19). Update 3-EU likely to delay 2013 carbon offset ban-sources. *Reuters*. Retrieved from www.reuters.com/article/2011/01/19/eu-carbon-hfc-idINNLDE70H16M20110119

Chevallier, J. (2012). *Econometric Analysis of Carbon Markets*, Dordrecht: Springer Netherlands.

Christiansen, A. C., & Wettestad, J. (2003). The EU as a frontrunner on greenhouse gas emissions trading: how did it happen and will the EU succeed? *Climate Policy*, **3**(1), 3–18.

Christophers, B. (2012). Anaemic geographies of financialisation. *New Political Economy*, **17**(3), 271–291.

Christophers, B. (2013). *Banking Across Boundaries: Placing Finance in Capitalism*, West Sussex: Wiley-Blackwell.

Christophers, B. (2016a). For real: land as capital and commodity. *Transactions of the Institute of British Geographers*, **41**(2), 134–148.

Christophers, B. (2016b). Risking value theory in the political economy of finance and nature. *Progress in Human Geography*, 0309132516679268.

Clark, B., & York, R. (2005). Carbon metabolism: global capitalism, climate change, and the biospheric rift. *Theory and Society*, **34**, 391–428.

Climate Action Network Europe. (2002). *No credible climate policy without strong rules*. Retrieved from www.climnet.org/resources/archive/doc_download/1207-2002-sep-29cane-ep-no-credible-climate-policy-without-strong-rules

Climate Action Network Europe. (2004). *The Directive linking the EU greenhouse gas emissions trading scheme with the Kyoto project mechanisms: NGO briefing on negotiations with Council for a first reading agreement*. Retrieved from www.caneurope.org/resources/archive/press-releases/1000-mar-2004-ngo-briefing-the-directive-linking-the-eu-ghg-emissions-trading-scheme-with-the-kp/file

Climate Action Network Europe. (2013). *CAN Europe's contribution to the European Commission's public consultation on options to strengthen the EU Emissions Trading System*. Retrieved from https://ec.europa.eu/clima/sites/clima/files/docs/0017/organisations/can_en.pdf

Climate Action Network Europe, WWF Europe, Carbon Market Watch, Greenpeace Europe, & Sandbag. (2014). *CAN Europe's Position on the Market Stability Reserve*. Retrieved from www.caneurope.org/docman/emissions-trading-scheme/2486-can-europe-s-position-on-the-market-stability-reserve

Climate Experts. (2009). *Clean Development Mechanism project design document for "Yingpeng HFC23 decomposition project."* Retrieved from https://cdm.unfccc.int/filestorage/F/5/0/F50UYQ6A971HCGETO3NSPJZ2VK4LWB/CDM_PDD_YINGPENG_v1.5_Apr%2020%202009_clean%20text._1947?t=YzF8bmNvc2s3fDBhIcIP2oFP8mXrg2xPUNce

CME Group. (2016). Monthly Energy Review. Retrieved 17 March 2016, from www.cmegroup.com/trading/energy/monthly-energy-review.html

Coase, R. E. (1960). The problem of social cost. *The Journal of Law and Economics*, **3**, 1–44.

Cohen, A., & Bakker, K. (2014). The Eco-Scalar Fix: Rescaling Environmental Governance and the Politics of Ecological Boundaries in Alberta, Canada. *Environment and Planning D: Society and Space*, **32**(1), 128–146.

Collard, R.-C., & Dempsey, J. (2013). Life for sale? The politics of lively commodities. *Environment and Planning A*, **45**(11), 2682–2699.

Collard, R.-C., & Dempsey, J. (2017). Capitalist natures in five orientations. *Capitalism Nature Socialism*, **28**(1), 78–97.

Cooper, M. H. (2015). Measure for measure? Commensuration, commodification, and metrology in emissions markets and beyond. *Environment and Planning A*, **47**(9), 1787–1804.

Cormier, A., & Bellassen, V. (2013). The risks of CDM projects: how did only 30% of expected credits come through? *Energy Policy*, **54**, 173–183.

Corporate Europe Observatory. (2011). *Laughing all the way to the (carbon offset) bank: collusion between DG Enterprise and business lobbyists*, Corporate Europe Observatory. Retrieved from http://corporateeurope.org/sites/default/files/sites/default/files/files/article/cdm_ban_delay_final.pdf

Council of the European Union. (2013). *Press release 3285th Council meeting: agriculture and fisheries*. Retrieved from www.consilium.europa.eu/ueDocs/cms_Data/docs/pressData/en/agricult/140120.pdf

Cox, P., Simpson, H., & Turner, S. (2010). *The Post-Trade Infrastructure for Carbon Emissions Trading: A Report Prepared for the City of London Corporation*, London: City of London Economic Development/Bourse Consult.

Dallos, G. (2014). *Locked in the Past: Why Europe's Big Energy Companies Fear Change*, Hamburg: Greenpeace Germany.

Damro, C., & Luaces Méndez, P. (2003). Emissions trading at Kyoto: from EU resistance to union innovation. *Environmental Politics*, **12**, 71–94.

de Bruyn, S., Schep, E., & Cherif, S. (2016). *Calculation of additional profits of sectors and firms from the EUETS* (16.7H44.18), CD Delft.

Delarue, E., Voorspools, K., & D'haeseleer, W. (2008). Fuel switching in the electricity sector under the EU ETS: review and prospective. *Journal of Energy Engineering*, **134**(2), 40–46.

Demeritt, D. (2001a). Scientific forest conservation and the statistical picturing of nature's limits in the Progressive-era United States. *Environment and Planning D: Society and Space*, **19**(4), 431–459.

Demeritt, D. (2001b). The construction of global warming and the politics of science. *Annals of the Association of American Geographers*, **91**, 307–337.

Dempsey, J. (2015). Fixing biodiversity loss. *Environment and Planning A*, **47**(12), 2555–2572.

Dempsey, J., & Suarez, D. C. (2016). Arrested development? The promises and paradoxes of "Selling Nature to Save It." *Annals of the American Association of Geographers*, **106**(3), 653–671.

Department for Environment, Food, and Rural Affairs. (2003). *Commentary on preliminary 1st year results and 2002 transaction log*. Retrieved from http://webarchive.nationalarchives.gov.uk/20130123162956/http:/www.defra.gov.uk/environment/climatechange/trading/pdf/ets-commentary-yr1.pdf

Department of Energy and Climate Change. (2011). *2010 to 2015 government policy: energy industry and infrastructure licensing and regulation*, Government of the United Kingdom. Retrieved from www.gov.uk/government/publications/2010-to-2015-government-policy-energy-industry-and-infrastructure-licensing-and-regulation/2010-to-2015-government-policy-energy-industry-and-infrastructure-licensing-and-regulation

Department of Energy and Climate Change. (2013). *A 2030 framework for climate energy policies: UK Government response to Commission green paper COM (2013) 169 final 1*, Government of the United Kingdom. Retrieved from http://ec.europa.eu/energy/consultations/20130702_green_paper_2030_en.htm

Descheneau, P. (2012). The currencies of carbon: carbon money and its social meaning. *Environmental Politics*, **21**(4), 604–620.

Descheneau, P., & Paterson, M. (2011). Between desire and routine: assembling environment and finance in carbon markets. *Antipode*, **43**, 662–681.

Domanico, F. (2007). Concentration in the European electricity industry: the internal market as solution? *Energy Policy*, **35**(10), 5064–5076.

Drax Group. (2014). Our history | Drax. Retrieved 13 March 2014, from www.drax.com/about-us/our-history/

Ecofys. (2009). *Methodology for the free allocation of emission allowances in the EU ETS post 2012: sector report for the refinery industry*, European Commission. Retrieved from www.ecofys.com/files/files/091102_refineries.pdf

Economist Intelligence Unit. (2002, October 3). EU industry: emissions trading causing controversy. *Economist Intelligence Unit – ViewsWire*, p. 94.

Ecorys. (2008). *Study on the competitiveness of the European steel sector*, European Commission. Retrieved from http://ec.europa.eu/enterprise/sectors/metals-minerals/files/final_report_steel_en.pdf

Ecorys, Öko-Institut, Cambridge Econometrics, & TNO. (2013). *Carbon Leakage Evidence Project: Factsheets for Selected Sectors*, Rotterdam: Ecorys.

EcoSecurities. (2011). *Clean Development Mechanism project design document for "Tianfu coalmine methane project."* Retrieved from http://cdm.unfccc.int/filestorage/K/C/1/KC1PLX0GUDRBJVT2FE4OH5IQY3M9Z7/Tianfu%20revised%20PDD_v6_clean%2020110511.pdf?t=eFR8bnIzbXlifDBTjsDPG_BTbd4w4kjr_amg

Edenhofer, O., Pichs-Madruga, R., Sokona, Y., et al. (2014). Technical summary. In O. Edenhofer, R. Pichs-Madruga, Y. Sokona, et al., eds., *Climate Change 2014: Mitigation of Climate Change. Contribution of Working Group III to the Fifth Assessment Report of the Intergovernmental Panel on Climate Change*, Cambridge and New York: Cambridge University Press.

EDF Group. (2010). *EDF Group position on principles related to "restrictions of carbon credits."* Retrieved from http://ec.europa.eu/clima/consultations/docs/0004/registered/edf_group_en.pdf

Egenhofer, C., Alessi, M., Georgiev, A., & Fujiwara, N. (2011). *The EU Emissions Trading System and Climate Policy Towards 2050: Real Incentives to Reduce Emissions and Drive Innovation?*, Brussels: Centre for European Policy Studies (CEPS).

Ekers, M., & Prudham, S. (2015). Towards the socio-ecological fix. *Environment and Planning A*, **47**(12), 2438–2445.

Ekers, M., & Prudham, S. (2017). The metabolism of socioecological fixes: capital switching, spatial fixes, and the production of nature. *Annals of the American Association of Geographers*, **107**(6), 1370–1388.

Ekers, M., & Prudham, S. (2018). The socioecological fix: fixed capital, metabolism, and hegemony. *Annals of the American Association of Geographers*, **108**(1), 17–34.

Ellerman, A. D., & Buchner, B. K. (2007). The European Union Emissions Trading Scheme: origins, allocation, and early results. *Review of Environmental Economics and Policy*, **1**(1), 66–87.

Ellerman, A. D., Convery, F. J., & De Perthuis, C. (2010). *Pricing Carbon: The European Union Emissions Trading Scheme*, Cambridge: Cambridge University Press.

Ellerman, A. D., & Joskow, P. L. (2008). *The European Union's Emissions Trading System in Perspective*, Pew Center on Global Climate Change.

Ellerman, A. D., Marcantonini, C., & Zaklan, A. (2016). The European Union Emissions Trading System: ten years and counting. *Review of Environmental Economics and Policy*, **10**(1), 89–107.

Ellerman, A. D., & Montero, J.-P. (1998). The declining trend in sulfur dioxide emissions: implications for allowance prices. *Journal of Environmental Economics and Management*, **36**(1), 26–45.

Elsworth, R., Worthington, B., & Buick, M. (2011). *Der Klimagoldesel: who are the winners of the EU ETS in Germany?*, Sandbag. Retrieved from https://sandbag.org.uk/site_media/pdfs/reports/Die_Klimagoldesel_8thNov_ENGLISH_FIN.pdf

ENDS Europe. (2012, November 30). *CO2 market intervention plan suffers new delay*. ENDS Europe. Retrieved from www.endseurope.com/30136

References 159

ENDS Europe. (2013, May 7). *Nine ministers call for backloading deal by July.* ENDS Europe. Retrieved from www.endseurope.com/31680

Enel. (2010a). *A view on CDM qualitative restrictions.* Retrieved from http://ec.europa.eu/clima/consultations/docs/0004/registered/enel_3_en.pdf

Enel. (2010b). *Enel-Endesa position on CDM qualitative restrictions.* Retrieved from http://ec.europa.eu/clima/consultations/docs/0004/registered/enel_1_en.pdf

Enel. (2014). *Report on corporate governance and ownership structure for year 2013.* Retrieved from http://www.enel.com/en-GB/doc/report2013/corporate_governance_report_for_year_2013.pdf

Energie Agentur NRW. (2010). CO2 emissions per capita in NRW and Germany. Retrieved 27 April 2015, from www.energieagentur.nrw.de/infografik/grafik.asp?RubrikID=3152

Environmental Investigation Agency, & CDM Watch. (2010). *HFC-23 offsets in the context of the EU Emissions Trading Scheme.* Retrieved from www.eia-international.org/files/reports199-1.pdf

E.ON. (2011). *Centrale Emile Huchet.* Retrieved from www.eon.fr/content/dam/eon-fr/fr/downloads/Brochures/Entreprise_Sites/Fiche_Emile%20Huchet_V2011_V2.pdf

E.ON. (2012). *E.ON position on review of the auction time profile for the EU Emissions Trading System.* Retrieved from http://ec.europa.eu/clima/consultations/docs/0016/organisation/eon_en.pdf

E.ON. (2013a). Connah's Quay. Retrieved 8 May 2015, from www.eon-uk.com/584.aspx

E.ON. (2013b). *E.ON answer to consultative communication of the commission green paper "a 2030 framework for climate and energy policies" as of 27th March 2013.* Retrieved from http://ec.europa.eu/energy/consultations/20130702_green_paper_2030_en.htm

E.ON. (2014a). E.ON Global Commodities. Retrieved 2 October 2014, from www.eon.com/content/eon-com/en/about-us/structure/company-finder/e-dot-on-global-commodities.html

E.ON. (2014b). Power & carbon. Retrieved 2 October 2014, from www.eon.com/en/business-areas/trading/overview/power-and-carbon.html

E.ON. (2015a). *E.ON facts & figures.* Retrieved from www.eon.com/content/dam/eon-com/ueber-uns/publications/EON_Facts_and_Figures_2015.pdf

E.ON. (2015b). E.ON history 1923–99. Retrieved 21 March 2015, from www.eon.com/en/about-us/profile/history/1923-99.html

E.ON. (2015c). Ironbridge. Retrieved 7 May 2015, from www.eon-uk.com/578.aspx

E.ON. (2015d). Owned generation. Retrieved 21 May 2015, from www.eon.com/en/business-areas/power-generation/energy-mix/owned-generation.html

E.ON. (2015e). Schkopau power plant. Retrieved 7 May 2015, from www.eon.com/en/about-us/structure/asset-finder/schkopau.html

E.ON. (2015f). Scholven power plant. Retrieved 21 March 2015, from www.eon.com/content/eon-com/en/about-us/structure/asset-finder/scholven.html

Ervine, K. (2013a). Carbon markets, debt and uneven development. *Third World Quarterly*, **34**(4), 653–670.

Ervine, K. (2013b). Diminishing returns: carbon market crisis and the future of market-dependent climate change finance. *New Political Economy*, **19**(5), 723–747.

Ervine, K. (2017). How low can it go? Analysing the political economy of carbon market design and low carbon prices. *New Political Economy*, **0**(0), 1–21.

EURELECTRIC. (2000). *Union of the electricity industry – EURELECTRIC position paper on the Commission's green paper on greenhouse gas emissions trading*

160 References

within the EU (COM 87/2000). Retrieved from http://ec.europa.eu/environment/archives/docum/pdf/0087_business_associations2.pdf

EURELECTRIC. (2012). *Consultation on the review of the auction time profile for the EU Emissions Trading System: EURELECTRIC response*. Retrieved from http://ec.europa.eu/clima/consultations/docs/0016/organisation/eurelectric_en.pdf

EUROFER. (2001). *EUROFER view on emissions trading – comments to the green paper COM(2000)87*. Retrieved from http://ec.europa.eu/environment/archives/docum/pdf/0087_business_associations2.pdf

European Commission. (2000a). *Green paper on greenhouse gas emissions trading within the European Union*, COM(2000) 87 final.

European Commission. (2000b). *Mandate – working group 1 of the European Climate Change Programme: "flexible mechanisms."* Retrieved from http://ec.europa.eu/clima/policies/eccp/first/docs/wg1_mandate_en.pdf

European Commission. (2001a). *Chairman's summary record of stakeholder consultation meeting (with industry and environmental NGOs) 4 September 2001*. Retrieved from http://ec.europa.eu/clima/policies/ets/docs/record_of_stakeholder_consultation_meeting_en.pdf

European Commission. (2001b). *Final report: ECCP working group 1 "flexible mechanisms."* Retrieved from http://ec.europa.eu/clima/policies/eccp/first/docs/final_report_en.pdf

European Commission. (2001c). *Green paper on greenhouse gas emissions trading within the European Union: summary of submissions*. Retrieved from http://ec.europa.eu/environment/archives/docum/pdf/0087_summary.pdf

European Commission. (2003). Proposal for a Directive of the European Parliament and of the Council amending the Directive establishing a scheme for greenhouse gas emission allowance trading within the Community, in respect of the Kyoto Protocol's project mechanisms, SEC(2003) 785.

European Commission. (2005). *Special rights in privatised companies in the enlarged Union – a decade full of developments* (Commission Staff Working Document).

European Commission. (2008). Commission decision concerning the unilateral inclusion of additional greenhouse gases and activities by the Netherlands in the Community emissions trading scheme pursuant to Article 24 of Directive 2003/87/EC of the European Parliament and of the Council, C(2008) 7867.

European Commission. (2009). Commission decision instructing the Central Administrator of the Community Independent Transaction Log to enter corrections to the National Allocation Plan table of The Netherlands into the Community Independent Transaction Log, C(2009).

European Commission. (2010a). *Draft Commission Regulation of determining, pursuant to Directive 2003/87/EC of the European Parliament and of the Council, certain restrictions applicable to the use of international credits from projects involving industrial gases*. Retrieved from http://ec.europa.eu/clima/news/docs/2010112502_proposal_restrictions_final_en.pdf

European Commission. (2010b). Questions & answers on emissions trading: use restrictions for certain industrial gas credits as of 2013 (memo/10/615). Retrieved from http://europa.eu/rapid/press-release_MEMO-10-615_en.htm

European Commission. (2010c). *Refining the supply of petroleum products in the EU* (Commission Staff Working Document, SEC(2010) 1398 final). Retrieved from http://eur-lex.europa.eu/legal-content/EN/TXT/PDF/?uri=CELEX:52010SC1398&from=EN

European Commission. (2011a). *Energy roadmap 2050* (No. COM (2011) 855). Retrieved from http://eur-lex.europa.eu/legal-content/EN/TXT/PDF/?uri=CELEX: 52011DC0885&from=EN

European Commission. (2011b). Regulation on determining, pursuant to Directive 2003/87/EC of the European Parliament and of the Council, certain restrictions applicable to the use of international credits from projects involving industrial gases, 550/2011.

European Commission. (2012a). *Proportionate Impact Assessment accompanying the document Commission Regulation (EU) No …/.. of XXX amending Regulation (EU) No 1031/2010 in particular to determine the volumes of greenhouse gas emission allowances to be auctioned in2013–2020* (Commission Staff Working Document).

European Commission. (2012b). *Proposal for a Decision of the European Parliament and of the Council amending Directive 2003/87/EC clarifying provisions on the timing of auctions of greenhouse gas allowances* (COM(2012) 416).

European Commission. (2012c). *The state of the European Carbon Market 2012 (Report from the Commission to the European Parliament and the Council)*, Brussels: European Commission.

European Commission. (2012d, November 12). Commission submits draft amendment to back-load 900 million allowances to the years 2019 and 2020. Retrieved 4 December 2014, from http://ec.europa.eu/clima/news/articles/news_2012111203_en.htm

European Commission. (2013a). *A 2030 framework for climate and energy policies* (Green paper).

European Commission. (2013b). *CERs and ERUs surrendered under the EU ETS.* Retrieved from http://ec.europa.eu/clima/policies/ets/registry/docs/compliance_2012_ic_en.xls

European Commission. (2013c). Commission Regulation establishing a Union Registry pursuant to Directive 2003/87/EC of the European Parliament and of the Council, Decisions No 280/2004/EC and No 406/2009/EC of the European Parliament and of the Council and repealing Commission Regulations (EU) No 920/2010 and No 1193/2011 Text with EEA relevance, 389/2013.

European Commission. (2013d). Consultation on structural options to strengthen the EU Emissions Trading System [Text]. Retrieved 9 February 2018, from https://ec.europa.eu/clima/consultations/articles/0017_en

European Commission. (2013e). *Options for structural measures to strengthen the EU Emissions Trading System: Main outcomes of the public consultation.*

European Commission. (2013f, July 17). State aid: Commission decides on two German support schemes for energy-intensive industries. Retrieved 22 October 2014, from http://europa.eu/rapid/press-release_IP-13-704_en.htm

European Commission. (2014a). *A policy framework for climate and energy in the period from 2020 to 2030* (Communication From The Commission To The European Parliament, The Council, The European Economic And Social Committee And The Committee Of The Regions). Retrieved from http://eur-lex.europa.eu/legal-content/EN/TXT/PDF/?uri=CELEX:52014DC0015&from=EN

European Commission. (2014b). *Classification of installations in the EUTL Registry based on the NACE 4 statistical classification.* Retrieved from http://ec.europa.eu/clima/policies/ets/cap/leakage/docs/installation_nace_rev2_matching_en.xls

European Commission. (2014c). Commission Regulation amending Regulation (EU) No 601/2012 as regards global warming potentials for non-CO2 greenhouse gases, 206/2014.

162 *References*

European Commission. (2014d). *Energy efficiency and its contribution to energy security and the 2030 framework for climate and energy policy* (Communication From The Commission To The European Parliament And The Council). Retrieved from http://ec.europa.eu/energy/efficiency/events/doc/2014_eec_communication_adopted.pdf

European Commission. (2014e). European Union Transaction Log. Retrieved 16 July 2014, from http://ec.europa.eu/environment/ets/

European Commission. (2014f). Impact Assessment Accompanying the document Communication from the Commission to the European Parliament, the Council, the European Economic and Social Committee and the Committee of the Regions: A policy framework for climate and energy in the period from 2020 up to 2030 (Commission Staff Working Document). Retrieved from http://eur-lex.europa.eu/legal-content/EN/TXT/PDF/?uri=CELEX:52014SC0015&from=EN

European Commission. (2014g). Impact assessment accompanying the document Proposal for a Decision of the European Parliament and of the Council concerning the establishment and operation of a market stability reserve for the Union greenhouse gas emission trading scheme and amending Directive 2003/87/EC (Commission Staff Working Document, SWD(2014) 17 final).

European Commission. (2014h). *List of stationary installations in the Union Registry as of 27.02.2014.* Retrieved from http://ec.europa.eu/clima/policies/ets/registry/documentation_en.htm

European Commission. (2014i). *Outcome of the October 2014 European Council.* Retrieved from http://ec.europa.eu/clima/policies/2030/docs/2030_euco_conclusions_en.pdf

European Commission. (2014j, January 8). EU Climate Change Committee agrees back-loading. Retrieved 4 December 2014, from http://ec.europa.eu/clima/news/articles/news_2014010801_en.htm

European Commission. (2014k, April 3). Union Registry. Retrieved 6 March 2014, from http://ec.europa.eu/clima/policies/ets/registry/documentation_en.htm

European Commission. (2015a). *EU ETS Handbook.*

European Commission. (2015b). *Impact Assessment Accompanying the document Proposal for a Directive of the European Parliament and of the Council amending Directive 2003/87/EC to enhance cost-effective emission reductions and lowcarbon investments (No. SWD(2015) 135 final)*, Brussels: European Commission.

European Commission. (2015c, March 26). National allocation plans. Retrieved 16 April 2015, from http://ec.europa.eu/clima/policies/ets/pre2013/nap/documentation_en.htm

European Commission. (2016). *The EU Emissions Trading System (EU ETS).* Retrieved from http://ec.europa.eu/clima/publications/docs/factsheet_ets_en.pdf

European Commission. (2017). European Union Transaction Log. Retrieved 8 September 2017, from http://ec.europa.eu/environment/ets/

European Commodity Clearing. (2014). Operations. Retrieved 18 September 2014, from www.ecc.de/ecc-en/operations

European Energy Exchange. (2012). EU emission allowances | secondary market. Retrieved 16 June 2015, from www.eex.com/en/market-data/emission-allowances/spot-market/european-emission-allowances#!/2012/02/28

European Environment Agency. (2012, November 29). EUA future prices 2005–2011 [Figure]. Retrieved 8 January 2014, from www.eea.europa.eu/data-and-maps/figures/eua-future-prices-200520132011

European Environment Agency. (2014a). *Annual European Union greenhouse gas inventory 1990–2012 and inventory report 2014: executive summary*, Copenhagen: European Environment Agency. Retrieved from www.eea.europa.eu/publications/european-union-greenhouse-gas-inventory-2014

European Environment Agency. (2014b). *EU ETS data viewer: User manual and background note*. Retrieved from www.eea.europa.eu/data-and-maps/data/european-union-emissions-trading-scheme-eu-ets-data-from-citl-6/eu-ets-data-viewer-manual/eu-ets-data-viewer-manual/at_download/file

European Environment Agency. (2015a, March 19). EEA greenhouse gas – data viewer. Retrieved 17 April 2015, from www.eea.europa.eu/publications/data-and-maps/data/data-viewers/greenhouse-gases-viewer

European Environment Agency. (2015b, October 9). EU Emissions Trading System (ETS) data viewer [Page]. Retrieved 18 March 2016, from www.eea.europa.eu/data-and-maps/data/data-viewers/emissions-trading-viewer

European Environment Agency. (2016). *Trends and projections in the EU ETS in 2016: The EU Emissions Trading System in numbers* (No. 24/2016), Luxembourg.

European Parliament. (2013a). Amendment adopted by the European Parliament on 3 July 2013 on the proposal for a decision of the European Parliament and of the Council amending Directive 2003/87/EC clarifying provisions on the timing of auctions of greenhouse gas allowances, COM(2012)0416 – C7-0203/2012 – 2012/0202(COD).

European Parliament. (2013b, April 15). Debates – Monday, 15 April 2013 – Strasbourg: revised edition. Retrieved 4 December 2014, from www.europarl.europa.eu/sides/getDoc.do?type=CRE&reference=20130415&secondRef=TOC&language=EN

European Parliament. (2013c, April 16). 2012/0202(COD) – 16/04/2013 decision by Parliament, 1st reading/single reading. Retrieved 4 December 2014, from www.europarl.europa.eu/oeil/popups/summary.do?id=1260015&t=e&l=en

European Parliament. (2013d, July 3). 2012/0202(COD) – 03/07/2013 text adopted by Parliament, partial vote at 1st reading/single reading. Retrieved 4 December 2014, from www.europarl.europa.eu/oeil/popups/summary.do?id=1283730&t=e&l=en

European Parliament. (2018, June 2). Climate: MEPs pass law to cut CO2 emissions and fund low-carbon innovation. Retrieved 12 February 2018, from www.europarl.europa.eu/news/en/press-room/20180202IPR97023/climate-meps-pass-law-to-cut-co2-emissions-and-fund-low-carbon-innovation

European Parliament and Council. (2003). Directive establishing a scheme for greenhouse gas emission allowance trading within the Community and amending Council Directive 96/61/EC, 2003/87/EC.

European Parliament and Council. (2004). Directive amending Directive 2003/87/EC establishing a scheme for greenhouse gas emission allowance trading within the Community, in respect of the Kyoto Protocol's project mechanisms, 2004/101/EC.

European Parliament and Council. (2008). Directive concerning integrated pollution prevention and control, 2008/1/EC.

European Parliament and Council. (2009). DIRECTIVE 2009/29/EC OF THE EUROPEAN PARLIAMENT AND OF THE COUNCIL of 23 April 2009 amending Directive 2003/87/EC so as to improve and extend the greenhouse gas emission allowance trading scheme of the Community.

European Parliament and Council. (2014). Consolidated version of Directive 2003/87/EC of the European Parliament and of the Council establishing a

164 *References*

scheme for greenhouse gas emission allowance trading within the Community, 2003/87/EC.

European Parliament and Council. (2015). DECISION (EU) 2015/1814 OF THE EUROPEAN PARLIAMENT AND OF THE COUNCIL of 6 October 2015 concerning the establishment and operation of a market stability reserve for the Union greenhouse gas emission trading scheme and amending Directive 2003/87/EC, 2015/1814.

European Report. (2002, March 6). Steel – EUROFER slams emission trading rights directive. *European Report*.

European Round Table of Industrialists. (2001). *Response to the European Commission green paper on greenhouse gas emissions trading within the European Union*. Retrieved from http://ec.europa.eu/environment/archives/docum/pdf/0087_business_associations1.pdf

European Union. (2012a). Consolidated version of the Treaty on European Union, C 326.

European Union. (2012b). Consolidated version of the Treaty on the functioning of the European Union, C 326.

Eurostat. (2015). Electricity generated from renewable sources. Retrieved 15 May 2015, from http://ec.europa.eu/eurostat/tgm/table.do?tab=table&init=1&language=en&pcode=tsdcc330&plugin=1

Eurostat. (2017). Electricity production, consumption and market overview. Retrieved 2 March 2018, from http://ec.europa.eu/eurostat/statistics-explained/index.php/Electricity_production,_consumption_and_market_overview

Federal Ministry for Economy Affairs and Energy. (2012). *Hintergrundpapier zur sog. Strompreiskompensation*, Government of Germany. Retrieved from www.bmwi.de/BMWi/Redaktion/PDF/S-T/strompreiskompensation-hintergrundpapier, property=pdf,bereich=bmwi2012,sprache=de,rwb=true.pdf

Federici, S. (2014). *Caliban and the Witch: Women, the Body and Primitive Accumulation*, Second, Brooklyn, NY: Autonomedia.

Felli, R. (2014). On climate rent. *Historical Materialism*, **22**(3–4), 251–280.

Felli, R. (2015). Environment, not planning: the neoliberal depoliticisation of environmental policy by means of emissions trading. *Environmental Politics*, **24**(5), 641–660.

Felli, R. (2018). Beyond the critique of carbon markets: The real utopia of a democratic Climate Protection Agency. *Geoforum*. doi:10.1016/j.geoforum.2018.02.031

Fine, B. (2013). Financialization from a Marxist perspective. *International Journal of Political Economy*, **42**(4, Winter), 47–66.

Flåm, K. (2009). Restricting the import of 'emission credits' in the EU: a power struggle between states and institutions. *International Environmental Agreements: Politics, Law and Economics*, **9**, 23–38.

Flynn, V. (2013a, April). Major blow for ETS as MEPs reject backloading plan. *ENDS Europe*. Retrieved from www.endseurope.com/article/31402/major-blow-for-ets-as-meps-reject-backloading-plan

Flynn, V. (2013b, November 6). German coalition deal on 40% EU CO2 goal. *ENDS Europe*. Retrieved from www.endseurope.com/33742/

Flynn, V. (2014, March 3). Fault lines emerge in ministers' 2030 debate. *ENDS Europe*. Retrieved from www.endseurope.com/35014/

Frame, D. J. (2011). The problems of markets: science, norms and the commodification of carbon. *The Geographical Journal*, **177**(2), 138–148.

Fraser, N. (2014a). Behind Marx's hidden abode. *New Left Review*, (86), 55–72.

Fraser, N. (2014b). Can society be commodities all the way down? Post-Polanyian reflections on capitalist crisis. *Economy and Society*, **43**(4), 541–558.

Friends of the Earth Europe. (2013a). *Submission on the European Commission's green paper on a 2030 framework for climate and energy policies*. Retrieved from http://ec.europa.eu/energy/consultations/20130702_green_paper_2030_en.htm

Friends of the Earth Europe. (2013b, February 19). Dangerous over-reliance on failing EU carbon trading scheme. Retrieved 5 December 2014, from www.foeeurope.org/Dangerous-over-reliance-failing-EUETS-190213

Gan, N. (2018, January 3). Will China's carbon scheme work without an emissions cap? *South China Morning Post*. Retrieved from www.scmp.com/news/china/policies-politics/article/2125896/big-black-hole-chinas-carbon-market-ambitions

GDF Suez. (2012). *Consultation on review of the auction time profile for the EU Emissions Trading System (ETS): GDF SUEZ answer*. Retrieved from http://ec.europa.eu/clima/consultations/docs/0016/organisation/gdf_en.pdf

GDF Suez. (2013). *GDF SUEZ answer to the public consultation on ETS structural measures*.

GDF Suez. (2014). *By-laws of GDF Suez*. Retrieved from https://www.gdfsuez.com/wp-content/uploads/2015/05/engie-bylaws-april-28-2015.pdf

General Secretariat of the Council. (2014). *European Council (23 and 24 October 2014) – conclusions* (EUCO 169/14 CO EUR 13 CONCL 5), Brussels: European Council. Retrieved from www.consilium.europa.eu/uedocs/cms_data/docs/pressdata/en/ec/145397.pdf

German Emissions Trading Authority. (2015). *German auctioning of emission allowances periodical report: annual report 2014*, Berlin: Federal Environment Agency. Retrieved from http://ec.europa.eu/clima/policies/ets/cap/auctioning/docs/ger_report_2014_en.pdf

Ghosh, S., & Sahu, S. K. (eds.). (2011). *The Indian Clean Development Mechanism: Subsidizing and Legitimizing Corporate Pollution, An Overview of CDM in India with Case Studies from Various Sectors*, Kolkata: DISHA.

Gilbertson, T., & Reyes, O. (2009). *Carbon Trading: How It Works and Why It Fails* (Critical currents no. 7), Uppsala, Sweden: Dag Hammarskjöld Foundation.

Global Carbon. (2010). *Joint Implementation project design document for "installation of CCGT-400 at Shaturskaya TPP, OGK-4, Moscow area, Russia."* Retrieved from http://ji.unfccc.int/UserManagement/FileStorage/KW4VQ6IJ2U RMGN0TB8L975PECOF1HS

Gore, T. (2015). *Extreme Carbon Inequality*, Oxfam.

Greenpeace Europe. (2012). *Contribution of Greenpeace European Unit, vzw-asbl, to the European Commission consultation regarding the review of the EU ETS auction profile*. Retrieved from http://ec.europa.eu/clima/consultations/docs/0016/organisation/greenpeace_en.pdf

Greenpeace Europe. (2013a). *Contribution of Greenpeace European Unit to the European Commission consultation on structural options to strengthen the EU Emissions Trading System*. Retrieved from https://ec.europa.eu/clima/sites/clima/files/docs/0017/organisations/greenpeace_en.pdf

Greenpeace Europe. (2013b). *Submission to the European Commission public consultation on a 2030 framework for climate and energy policies*. Retrieved from http://ec.europa.eu/energy/consultations/20130702_green_paper_2030_en.htm

Gronwald, M., & Hintermann, B. (eds.). (2015). *Emissions Trading as a Policy Instrument: Evaluation and Prospects*, Cambridge, MA: MIT Press.

Grubb, M., Vrolijk, C., & Brack, D. (1999). *The Kyoto Protocol: a guide and assessment*, London: Earthscan.

Harvey, D. (1995). Globalization in question. *Rethinking Marxism*, **8**(4), 1–17.

Harvey, D. (1996). *Justice, Nature and the Geography of Difference*, Cambridge, MA: Blackwell.

Harvey, D. (2001a). Globalization and the spatial fix. *Geographische Revue*, **2**, 23–30.

Harvey, D. (2001b). *Spaces of Capital: Towards a Critical Geography*, New York: Routledge.

Harvey, D. (2003a). *The New Imperialism*, Oxford: Oxford University Press.

Harvey, D. (2003b). The "new" imperialism: accumulation by dispossession. In L. Panitch & C. Leys, eds., *Socialist Register 2004*, London: The Merlin Press, pp. 63–87.

Harvey, D. (2006). *The Limits to Capital*, London: Verso.

Hatchwell, P. (2016, January 12). EU carbon price rebounds in 2015. *ENDS Europe*. Retrieved from www.endseurope.com/article/44934/eu-carbon-price-rebounds-in-2015

Hay, C. (1994). Environmental security and state legitimacy. *Capitalism Nature Socialism*, **5**, 83–97.

Heede, R. (2013). Tracing anthropogenic carbon dioxide and methane emissions to fossil fuel and cement producers, 1854–2010. *Climatic Change*, 1–13.

Hermann, H., & Matthes, F. (2012). *Strengthening the European Union Emissions Trading Scheme and Raising Climate Ambition: Facts, Measures and Implications*, Öko-Institut for WWF and Greenpeace.

Hervé-Mignucci, M., Wang, X., Nelson, D., & Varadarajan, U. (2015). *Slowing the Growth of Coal Power in China: The Role of Finance in State-Owned Enterprises*, Climate Policy Institute.

Heynen, N., McCarthy, J., Prudham, S., & Robbins, P. (2007). False promises. In N. Heynen, J. McCarthy, S. Prudham, & P. Robbins, eds., *Neoliberal Environments: False Promises and Unnatural Consequences*, London; New York: Routledge, pp. 1–21.

Heynen, N., & Robbins, P. (2005). The neoliberalization of nature: Governance, privatization, enclosure and valuation. *Capitalism Nature Socialism*, **16**(1), 5–8.

High-Level Commission on Carbon Prices. (2017). *Of the High-Level Commission on Carbon Prices*, Washington, DC: The World Bank.

Hoffman, N., & Twining, J. (2009). *Profiting from the Low-Carbon Economy*, McKinsey & Company. Retrieved 12 March 2018, from www.mckinsey.com/industries/financial-services/our-insights/profiting-from-the-low-carbon-economy

Hsiang, S., Kopp, R., Jina, A., et al. (2017). Estimating economic damage from climate change in the United States. *Science*, **356**(6345), 1362–1369.

Huber, M. (2009). Energizing historical materialism: fossil fuels, space and the capitalist mode of production. *Geoforum*, **40**(1), 105–115.

Huber, M. (2017). Value, nature, and labor: a defense of Marx. *Capitalism Nature Socialism*, **28**(1), 39–52.

Huber, M. (2018). Resource geographies I: valuing nature (or not). *Progress in Human Geography*, **42**(1), 148–159.

Huber, M. T., & McCarthy, J. (2017). Beyond the subterranean energy regime? Fuel, land use and the production of space. *Transactions of the Institute of British Geographers*, **42**(4), 655–668.

IETA. (2010, December 14). Statement on EU proposal on qualitative restrictions on offset use in EU ETS. Retrieved 8 December 2014, from www.ieta.org/index.php?

References

option=com_content&view=article&id=219:statement-on-eu-proposal-on-qualitative-restrictions-on-offset-use-in-eu-ets&catid=20:press-releases&Itemid=88

Intercontinental Exchange. (2009). *List of permitted cover and haircut rates: extension to include emissions allowances.* Retrieved from www.theice.com/publicdocs/clear_europe/circulars/C09070.pdf

Intercontinental Exchange. (2015). *Prohibited list of EUAs, CERs and ERUs.* Retrieved from www.theice.com/publicdocs/futures/Prohibited_List_of_EUAs_CERs_ERUs.xls

Intercontinental Exchange. (2016). ICE Clear Europe: Risk Management. Retrieved 11 March 2016, from www.theice.com/clear-europe/risk-management#margins-europe

Intercontinental Exchange. (2017). Emissions Futures and Options. Retrieved 24 March 2017, from www.theice.com/emissions

Intergovernmental Panel on Climate Change. (2014). *Climate Change 2014: Synthesis Report. Contribution of Working Groups I, II and III to the Fifth Assessment Report of the Intergovernmental Panel on Climate Change*, Geneva: IPCC.

International Emissions Trading Association. (2013). *Response to consultation on structural options to strengthen the EU Emissions Trading System.*

International Emissions Trading Association. (2015, October 20). 20 Business Groups Call on Governments to include Markets in 2015 Climate Agreement. Retrieved 6 March 2018, from www.ieta.org/page-18192/3766347

International Energy Agency. (2015). *Energy and Climate Change*, Paris: OECD/IEA.

International Swaps and Derivatives Association. (2015). *SwapsInfo 2014 Year in Review.* Retrieved from www2.isda.org/images/file_exts/fileext_pdf.png

Jessop, B. (2006). Spatial fixes, temporal fixes and spatio-temporal fixes. In N. Castree & D. Gregory, eds., *David Harvey: A Critical Reader*, Malden, MA: Blackwell Publishing Ltd, pp. 142–166.

Johnson, L. (2013). Catastrophe bonds and financial risk: securing capital and rule through contingency. *Geoforum*, **45**, 30–40.

Johnson, L. (2015). Catastrophic fixes: cyclical devaluation and accumulation through climate change impacts. *Environment and Planning A*, **47**(12), 2503–2521.

Jotzo, F. (2005). Developing countries and the future of the Kyoto Protocol. *Global Change, Peace & Security*, **17**(1), 77–86.

Jotzo, F., Karplus, V., Grubb, M., et al. (2018). China's emissions trading takes steps towards big ambitions. *Nature Climate Change*, **8**(4), 265–267.

Kama, K. (2014). On the borders of the market: EU emissions trading, energy security, and the technopolitics of 'carbon leakage.' *Geoforum*, **51**, 202–212.

Kanter, J. (2007, July 6). In London's financial world, carbon trading is the new big thing. *The New York Times*. Retrieved from www.nytimes.com/2007/07/06/business/worldbusiness/06carbon.html

Kay, K. (2017). A hostile takeover of nature? Placing value in conservation finance. *Antipode*, Online early. doi:10.1111/anti.12335

Kay, K., & Kenney-Lazar, M. (2017). Value in capitalist natures: an emerging framework. *Dialogues in Human Geography*, **7**(3), 295–309.

Klein, N. (2014). *This Changes Everything: Capitalism vs the Climate*, New York: Simon & Schuster.

References

Knox-Hayes, J. (2013). The spatial and temporal dynamics of value in financialization: analysis of the infrastructure of carbon markets. *Geoforum*, **50**(0), 117–128.

Knox-Hayes, J. (2016). *The Cultures of Markets: The Political Economy of Climate Governance*, Oxford: Oxford University Press. Retrieved from www.oxfordscholarship.com/10.1093/acprof:oso/9780198718451.001.0001/acprof-9780198718451

Koch, N., Fuss, S., Grosjean, G., & Edenhofer, O. (2014). Causes of the EU ETS price drop: recession, CDM, renewable policies or a bit of everything? – new evidence. *Energy Policy*, **73**, 676–685.

Koch, N., Grosjean, G., Fuss, S., & Edenhofer, O. (2016). Politics matters: Regulatory events as catalysts for price formation under cap-and-trade. *Journal of Environmental Economics and Management*, **78**, 121–139.

Krukowska, E. (2011, January 22). EU delays ban on imported CO2 credits by four months. *Bloomberg*. Retrieved from www.bloomberg.com/news/2011-01-21/eu-delays-ban-on-imported-co2-credits-by-four-months-update2-.html

Kuch, D. (2015). *The Rise and Fall of Carbon Emissions Trading*, London: Palgrave Macmillan UK. Retrieved from http://link.springer.com/10.1057/9781137490384

Labban, M. (2010). Oil in parallax: scarcity, markets, and the financialization of accumulation. *Geoforum*, **41**(4), 541–552.

Labban, M. (2014). Against value: accumulation in the oil industry and the biopolitics of labour under finance. *Antipode*, **46**(2), 477–496.

Lane, R. (2012). The promiscuous history of market efficiency: the development of early emissions trading systems. *Environmental Politics*, **21**(4), 583–603.

Lane, R., & Stephan, B. (2015). Zombie markets or zombie analyses? Revivifying the politics of carbon markets. In B. Stephan & R. Lane, eds., *The Politics of Carbon Markets*, London: Routledge, pp. 1–23.

Le Quéré, C., Moriarty, R., Andrew, R., & Peters, G. (2014). *Global carbon budget 2014*, Global Carbon Project. Retrieved from www.globalcarbonproject.org/carbonbudget/14/files/GCP_budget_2014_lowres_v1.02.pdf

Lederer, M. (2017). Carbon trading: who gets what, when, and how? *Global Environmental Politics*, **17**(3), 134–140.

Levy, D., & Egan, D. (1998). Capital contests: national and transnational channels of corporate influence on the climate change negotiations. *Politics and Society*, **26**, 337–362.

Levy, D., & Egan, D. (2003). A neo-Gramscian approach to corporate political strategy: conflict and accommodation in the climate change negotiations. *Journal of Management Studies*, **40**(4), 803–829.

Leyshon, A., & Thrift, N. (2007). The capitalization of almost everything the future of finance and capitalism. *Theory, Culture & Society*, **24**(7–8), 97–115.

Liu, Q., Tian, C., & Zheng, X. (2016). *Climate and Energy Policy Solutions for China: Quantitative Analysis and Policy Recommendations for the 13th Five Year Plan*, National Center for Climate Change Strategy and International Cooperation.

Lo, A. (2016). *Carbon Trading in China*, London: Palgrave Macmillan UK. Retrieved from http://link.springer.com/10.1057/9781137529008

Lobell, D. B., Burke, M. B., Tebaldi, C., et al. (2008). Prioritizing climate change adaptation needs for food security in 2030. *Science*, **319**(5863), 607–610.

Loftus, A., & March, H. (2015). Financialising nature? *Geoforum*, **60**, 172–175.

Lohmann, L. (2005). Marketing and making carbon dumps: commodification, calculation and counterfactuals in climate change mitigation. *Science as Culture*, **14**(3), 203–235.

References

Lohmann, L. (2006). *Carbon Trading: A Critical Conversation on Climate Change, Privatization and Power*, Sweden: Dag Hammarskjöld Foundation.

Lohmann, L. (2009). Toward a different debate in environmental accounting: the cases of carbon and cost-benefit. *Accounting, Organizations and Society*, **34**, 499–534.

Lohmann, L. (2010). Uncertainty markets and carbon markets: variations on Polanyian themes. *New Political Economy*, **15**(2), 225–254.

Lohmann, L. (2011a). Financialization, commodification and carbon: the contradictions of neoliberal climate policy. In L. Panitch, G. Albo, & V. Chibber, eds., *Socialist Register 2012*, Vol. 48, London: The Merlin Press.

Lohmann, L. (2011b). The endless algebra of climate markets. *Capitalism Nature Socialism*, **22**(4), 93–116.

Lövbrand, E., & Stripple, J. (2011). Making climate change governable: accounting for carbon as sinks, credits and personal budgets. *Critical Policy Studies*, **5**(2), 187–200.

Lövbrand, E., & Stripple, J. (2012). Disrupting the public–private distinction: excavating the government of carbon markets post-Copenhagen. *Environment and Planning C: Government and Policy*, **30**(4), 658–674.

Lovell, H. (2013). Climate change, markets and standards: the case of financial accounting. *Economy and Society*, 1–25.

Lovell, H., Bebbington, J., Larrinaga, C., & Aguiar, T. R. S. de. (2013). Putting carbon markets into practice: a case study of financial accounting in Europe. *Environment and Planning C: Government and Policy*, **31**(4), 741–757.

Lovell, H., & Liverman, D. (2010). Understanding carbon offset technologies. *New Political Economy*, **15**(2), 255–273.

Lovell, H., & MacKenzie, D. (2011). Accounting for carbon: the role of accounting professional organisations in governing climate change. *Antipode*, **43**(3), 704–730.

MacKenzie, D. (2009a). Making things the same: gases, emission rights and the politics of carbon markets. *Accounting, Organizations and Society*, **34**(3–4), 440–455.

MacKenzie, D. (2009b). *Material Markets: How Economic Agents are Constructed*, Oxford: Oxford University Press.

Malm, A. (2013). The origins of fossil capital: from water to steam in the British cotton industry. *Historical Materialism*, **21**(1), 15–68.

Malm, A. (2016). *Fossil Capital: The Rise of Steam Power and the Roots of Global Warming*, London: Verso.

Malm, A., & Hornborg, A. (2014). The geology of mankind? A critique of the Anthropocene narrative. *The Anthropocene Review*, **1**(1), 62–69.

Mann, G. (2010). Value after Lehman. *Historical Materialism*, **18**(4), 172–188.

Mann, G., & Wainwright, J. (2018). *Climate Leviathan: A Political Theory of our Planetary Future*, London: Verso.

Mansfield, B. (2004). Neoliberalism in the oceans: "rationalisation," property rights, and the commons question. *Geoforum*, **35**, 313–326.

Mansfield, B. (2008). Introduction: property and the remaking of nature–society relations. In B. Mansfield, ed., *Privatization: Property and the Remaking of Nature–Society Relations*, Malden, MA: Blackwell, pp. 1–13.

Markussen, P., & Svendsen, G. T. (2005). Industry lobbying and the political economy of GHG trade in the European Union. *Energy Policy*, **33**(2), 245–255.

Martin, R., Muûls, M., & Wagner, U. J. (2016). The impact of the European Union Emissions Trading Scheme on regulated firms: what is the evidence after ten years? *Review of Environmental Economics and Policy*, **10**(1), 129–148.

Marx, K. (1976). *Capital Volume I*, London: Penguin Books/New Left Review.
Marx, K. (1991). *Capital Volume III*, London: Penguin Books/New Left Review.
Matthews, K., & Paterson, M. (2005). Boom or bust? The economic engine behind the drive for climate change policy. *Global Change, Peace & Security*, **17**, 59–75.
McAfee, K. (1999). Selling nature to save it? Biodiversity and green developmentalism. *Environment and Planning D: Society and Space*, **17**(2), 133–154.
McAfee, K. (2003). Neoliberalism on the molecular scale: economic and genetic reductionism in biotechnology battles. *Geoforum*, **34**(2), 203–219.
McAfee, K. (2015). Green economy and carbon markets for conservation and development: a critical view. *International Environmental Agreements: Politics, Law and Economics*, **16**(3), 333–353.
McCarthy, J. (2004). Privatizing conditions of production: trade agreements as neoliberal environmental governance. *Geoforum*, **35**(3), 327–341.
McCarthy, J. (2013). We have never been "post-political." *Capitalism Nature Socialism*, **24**(1), 19–25.
McCarthy, J. (2015). A socioecological fix to capitalist crisis and climate change? The possibilities and limits of renewable energy. *Environment and Planning A*, **47**(12), 2485–2502.
McCarthy, J., & Prudham, S. (2004). Neoliberal nature and the nature of neoliberalism. *Geoforum*, **35**(3), 275–283.
McGlade, C., & Ekins, P. (2015). The geographical distribution of fossil fuels unused when limiting global warming to 2°C. *Nature*, **517**(7533), 187–190.
McKinsey & Company. (2014). *Beyond the storm – value growth in the EU power sector*.
Meckling, J. (2011). *Carbon Coalitions: Business, Climate Politics and the Rise of Emissions Trading*, Cambridge, MA: MIT Press.
Meckling, J., Sterner, T., & Wagner, G. (2017). Policy sequencing toward decarbonization. *Nature Energy*, **2**(12), 918.
Methmann, C. (2013). The sky is the limit: global warming as global governmentality. *European Journal of International Relations*, **19**(1), 69–91.
Mies, M. (1986). *Patriarchy and Accumulation on a World Scale: Women and the International Division of Labour*, London: Zed Books.
Milieu, Danish National Environmental Research Institute, & Center for Clean Air Policy. (2004). *Comparison of the EU and US approaches towards acidification, eutrophication and ground level ozone*, European Commission. Retrieved from http://ec.europa.eu/environment/archives/cafe/activities/pdf/case_study1.pdf
Millward, R. (2008). *Private and Public Enterprise in Europe: Energy, Telecommunications and Transport 1830–1990*, Cambridge: Cambridge University Press.
Ministry of the Environment. (2013). *Communication from the Commission – green paper – a 2030 framework for climate and energy policies: responses by the Government of Poland within public consultations*, Government of Poland. Retrieved from http://ec.europa.eu/energy/consultations/20130702_green_paper_2030_en.htm
Mitchell, T. (2009). Carbon democracy. *Economy and Society*, **38**(3), 399–432.
Mitterlehner, R., Wathelet, M., Lidegaard, M., et al. (2013, December 23). Call for a renewable energy target in EU's 2030 climate and energy framework. Retrieved from www.greenpeace.org/eu-unit/Global/eu-unit/reports-briefings/2013/8%20Countries%20Renewable%20letter.pdf
Moore, J. W. (2015). *Capitalism in the Web of Life: Ecology and the Accumulation of Capital*, London: Verso.

Moore, J. W. (Ed.). (2016). *Anthropocene or Capitalocene? Nature, History, and the Crisis of Capitalism*, Oakland: PM Press.

Moore, J. W. (2017). The Capitalocene, Part I: on the nature and origins of our ecological crisis. *The Journal of Peasant Studies*, 44(3), 594–630.

Moore, J. W. (2018). The Capitalocene Part II: accumulation by appropriation and the centrality of unpaid work/energy. *The Journal of Peasant Studies*, 45(2), 237–279.

Morris, D. (2012). *Losing the lead? Europe's flagging carbon market*, Sandbag. Retrieved from https://sandbag.org.uk/site_media/pdfs/reports/losing_the_lead.pdf

Morris, D. (2014). *Slaying the dragon: vanquish the surplus and rescue the ETS*, Sandbag.

National Development and Reform Commission. (2017, December 18). Program for the establishment of a national carbon emissions trading market (power generation industry). Retrieved from https://chinaenergyportal.org/national-carbon-emissions-trading-market-establishment-program-power-generation-industry/

NEFCO. (2010, September 16). KfW Bankengruppe, NEFCO, Banco Santander and Eolia Renovables conclude carbon finance transaction in Mexico. Retrieved 12 November 2011, from www.nefco.org/news/kfw_bankengruppe_nefco_banco_santander_and_eolia_renovables_conclude_carbon_finance_transaction

Nelson, A. (2012, December 11). EU dismisses Polish warnings over carbon market fix. *EurActiv*. Retrieved from www.euractiv.com/climate-environment/eu-denies-polish-claim-backloads-news-516565

Neuhoff, K., Schopp, A., Boyd, R., Stelmakh, K., & Vasa, A. (2012). *Banking of Surplus Emissions Allowances: Does the Volume Matter?*, Berlin: German Institute for Economic Research.

Newell, P. (2000). *Climate for Change: Non-state Actors and the Global Politics of Greenhouse*, Cambridge: Cambridge University Press.

Newell, P. (2008). The marketization of global environmental governance. In J. Park, K. Conca, & M. Finger, eds., *The Crisis of Global Environmental Governance: Towards a New Political Economy of Sustainability*, London: Routledge, pp. 77–95.

Newell, P. (2012). The political economy of carbon markets: the CDM and other stories. *Climate Policy*, 12(1), 135–139.

Newell, P. (2014). Dialogue of the deaf? The CDM's legitimation crisis. In B. Stephan & R. Lane, eds., *The Politics of Carbon Markets*, London: Routledge, pp. 212–236.

Newell, P., & Paterson, M. (1998). A climate for business: global warming, the state and capital. *Review of International Political Economy*, 5, 679–703.

Newell, P., & Paterson, M. (2009). The politics of the carbon economy. In M. Boykoff, ed., *The Politics of Climate Change: A Survey*, London: Routledge, pp. 80–99.

Newell, P., & Paterson, M. (2010). *Climate Capitalism: Global Warming and the Transformation of the Global Economy*, Cambridge: Cambridge University Press.

Nordhaus, W. D. (2017). Revisiting the social cost of carbon. *Proceedings of the National Academy of Sciences*, 114(7), 1518–1523.

Nye, M., & Owens, S. (2008). Creating the UK emission trading scheme: motives and symbolic politics. *European Environment*, 18(1), 1–15.

Oberthür, S., & Ott, H. (1999). *The Kyoto Protocol: International Climate Policy for the 21st Century*, Berlin: Springer Verlag.

O'Connor, J. (1973). *The Fiscal Crisis of the State*, New York: St. Martin's Press.

O'Connor, J. (1998). *Natural Causes: Essays in Ecological Marxism*, New York: The Guilford Press.

Öko-Institut. (2007). *WWF background note to the report "Is the CDM fulfilling its environmental objectives? An evaluation of the CDM and options for improvement,"* WWF. Retrieved from http://d2ouvy59p0dg6k.cloudfront.net/downloads/cdm_report_wwf_background_paper.pdf

Osborne, T. (2015). Tradeoffs in carbon commodification: a political ecology of common property forest governance. *Geoforum*, **67**(Supplement C), 64–77.

Osborne, T., & Shapiro-Garza, E. (2018). Embedding carbon markets: complicating commodification of ecosystem services in Mexico's forests. *Annals of the American Association of Geographers*, **108**(1), 88–105.

Padis, G. M. (2011). Carbon credits as collateral. *Journal of Technology Law & Policy*, **16**, 343.

Parenti, C. (2012). *Tropic of Chaos: Climate Change and the New Geography of Violence*, New York: Nation books.

Parenti, C. (2015). The 2013 ANTIPODE AAG Lecture The environment making state: territory, nature, and value. *Antipode*, **47**(4), 829–848.

Patel, R., & Moore, J. W. (2017). *A History of the World in Seven Cheap Things: A Guide to Capitalism, Nature and the Future of the Planet*, Oakland: University of California Press.

Paterson, M. (1996). *Global Warming and Global Politics*, London: Routledge.

Paterson, M. (2010). Legitimation and accumulation in climate change governance. *New Political Economy*, **15**, 345–368.

Paterson, M. (2012). Who and what are carbon markets for? Politics and the development of climate policy. *Climate Policy*, **12**(1), 82–97.

Paterson, M. (2014). Governing mobilities, mobilising carbon. *Mobilities*, **9**(4), 570–584.

Paterson, M., & Stripple, J. (2012). Virtuous carbon. *Environmental Politics*, **21**(4), 563–582.

Paulsson, E. (2009). A review of the CDM literature: from fine-tuning to critical scrutiny? *International Environmental Agreements: Politics, Law and Economics*, **9**, 63–80.

Pearse, R. (2016). The coal question that emissions trading has not answered. *Energy Policy*, **99**, 319–328.

Pearse, R. (2017a). Gender and climate change: Gender and climate change. *Wiley Interdisciplinary Reviews: Climate Change*, **8**(2), e451.

Pearse, R. (2017b). *Pricing Carbon in Australia: Contestation, the State and Market Failure*, Abingdon, Oxon: Routledge.

Pearse, R., & Böhm, S. (2014). Ten reasons why carbon markets will not bring about radical emissions reduction. *Carbon Management*, **5**(4), 325–337.

Pell, E. H. (2014, January 9). ICE loses carbon trading market share to EEX in 2013. *Environmental Finance*. Retrieved from www.environmental-finance.com/content/news/ice-loses-carbon-trading-market-share-to-eex-in-2013.html

PGE Group. (2015). Oddział Elektrownia Bełchatów. Retrieved 24 March 2015, from www.elbelchatow.pgegiek.pl/

Philp, L. (2013). *Stranded costs from the demise of the Clean Development Mechanism*, CO2 Spain. Retrieved from www.co2spain.com/strandedcosts.php

References

Pigou, A. C. (1932). *The economics of welfare*, Fourth edition, London: Macmillan and Co. Limited.

Point Carbon. (2011). ICE maintains zero collateral value for carbon units. *Carbon Market Europe*, **10**(23).

Point Carbon. (2013, June 4). *JP Morgan sells EcoSecurities to Mercuria: sources*. Point Carbon. Retrieved from www.pointcarbon.com/news/1.2401344

Polanyi, K. (1944). *The Great Transformation*, New York: Farrar & Rinehart.

Presidency of the Republic of France. (2014, February 19). Décisions du Conseil des ministres franco-allemand. Retrieved 16 December 2014, from www.elysee .fr/communiques-de-presse/article/decisions-du-conseil-des-ministres-franco-allemand-frde/

Prudham, S. (2003). Taming trees: capital, science, and nature in Pacific Slope tree improvement. *Annals of the Association of American Geographers*, **93**(3), 636–656.

Prudham, S. (2007). The fictions of autonomous invention: accumulation by dispossession, commodification and life patents in Canada. *Antipode*, **39**(3), 406–429.

Prudham, S. (2009). Commodification. In N. Castree, D. Demeritt, D. Liverman, & B. Rhoads, eds., *A Companion to Environmental Geography*, West Sussex: Wiley-Blackwell.

Reuters. (2017, November 15). China's top climate official rules out carbon futures, tax: media. *Reuters*. Retrieved from https://uk.reuters.com/article/us-china-climatechange/chinas-top-climate-official-rules-out-carbon-futures-tax-media-idUKKBN1DF03V

Reyes, O. (2011). Zombie carbon and sectoral market mechanisms. *Capitalism Nature Socialism*, **22**(4), 117–135.

Robbins, P., & Luginbuhl, A. (2005). The last enclosure: resisting privatization of wildlife in the Western United States. *Capitalism Nature Socialism*, **16**(1), 45–61.

Robertson, M. M. (2000). No net loss: wetland restoration and the incomplete capitalization of nature. *Antipode*, **32**(4), 463–493.

Robertson, M. M. (2004). The neoliberalization of ecosystem services: wetland mitigation banking and problems in environmental governance. *Geoforum*, **35**, 361–373.

Robertson, M. M. (2006). The nature that capital can see: science, state, and market in the commodification of ecosystem services. *Environment and Planning D: Society and Space*, **24**, 367–387.

Robertson, M. M. (2007). Discovering price in all the wrong places: the work of commodity definition and price under neoliberal environmental policy. *Antipode*, **39**(3), 500–526.

Robertson, M. M. (2012). Measurement and alienation: making a world of ecosystem services. *Transactions of the Institute of British Geographers*, **37**(3), 386–401.

Robertson, M. M., & Wainwright, J. D. (2013). The value of nature to the state. *Annals of the Association of American Geographers*, **103**(4), 890–905.

Rosewarne, S. (2010). Meeting the challenge of climate change: the poverty of the dominant economic narrative and market solutions as subterfuge. *Journal of Australian Political Economy*, **66**, 17–50.

Rosewarne, S., Goodman, J., & Pearse, R. (2014). *Climate Action Upsurge: The Ethnography of Climate Movement Politics*, New York: Routledge.

Royal Dutch Shell. (2012). Focus: improving energy efficiency at Pernis refinery. Retrieved 27 April 2015, from http://reports.shell.com/sustainability-report/2012/ourapproach/climatechange/focuspernisrefinery.html

Russo, E., & Odeska, M. (2009, September). *E.ON Carbon Sourcing experience to tackle climate change in Russia*, Presented at the Association of European

174 *References*

Businesses conference on "Kyoto Protocol Implementation", Moscow. Retrieved from www.aebrus.ru/upload/iblock/20b/20bc7fb3fbcd6bd9edcabd1ab dacc0a5.pdf

RWE. (2013). *Response to the green paper "a 2030 framework for climate and energy policies."* Retrieved from http://ec.europa.eu/energy/consultations/20130702_green_paper_2030_en.htm

RWE. (2014a). Facts & figures. Retrieved from www.rwe.com/web/cms/mediablob/en/108808/data/114404/54/rwe/investor-relations/presentations-videos/Facts-Figures-2014.pdf

RWE. (2014b). Niederaussem power plant. Retrieved 23 September 2014, from www.rwe.com/web/cms/en/60132/rwe-power-ag/locations/lignite/niederaussem-power-plant/

RWE and E.ON. (2001). *Summary of the opinion on the EU green paper on the trading of greenhouse gas emission.* Retrieved from http://ec.europa.eu/environment/archives/docum/0087_en.htm

RWE Innogy. (2014). Heidelberg cogeneration plant. Retrieved 23 September 2014, from www.rwe.com/web/cms/en/66030/rwe-innogy/technologies/heidelberg-cogeneration-plant/

RWE Supply & Trading. (2014). Short facts about RWE Supply & Trading. Retrieved 1 October 2014, from www.rwe.com/web/cms/en/111356/rwe-supply-trading/about-rwe-supply-trading/

Salleh, A. (2009). Ecological debt: Embodied debt. In A. Salleh, ed., *Eco-Sufficiency and Global Justice: Women Write Political Ecology*, London: Pluto Press.

Salleh, A. (2017). *Ecofeminism as Politics: Nature. Marx and the Postmodern*, Second edition, London: Zed Books.

Schmalensee, R., Joskow, P. L., Ellerman, A. D., Montero, J. P., & Bailey, E. M. (1998). An interim evaluation of sulfur dioxide emissions trading. *Journal of Economic Perspectives*, **12**(3), 53–68.

Schneider, L. (2009). Assessing the additionality of CDM projects: practical experiences and lessons learned. *Climate Policy*, **9**(3), 242–254.

Schneider, L. (2011). Perverse incentives under the CDM: an evaluation of HFC-23 destruction projects. *Climate Policy*, **11**(2), 851–864.

Schneider, L., Lazarus, M., & Kollmuss, A. (2010). *Industrial N2O Projects under the CDM: Adipic acid – A Case of Carbon Leakage?*, Somerville, MA: Stockholm Environment Institute.

Shell Global. (2008). Cutting deeper into the barrel. Retrieved 27 April 2015, from www.shell.com/global/products-services/solutions-for-businesses/globalsolutions/about-global-solutions/key-projects/pernis.html

Shell Global. (2015). Products. Retrieved 27 April 2015, from www.shell.com/global/products-services/solutions-for-businesses/shipping-trading/environmental-trading-solutions/products.html

Shell Netherlands. (2015). The refinery. Retrieved 27 April 2015, from www.shell.nl/nld/aboutshell/shell-businesses/pernis/welkom-shell-pernis/raffinaderij.html

Skjærseth, J. B., & Wettestad, J. (2008). *EU emissions Trading: Initiation, Decision-Making and Implementation*, Hampshire: Ashgate Publishing Ltd.

Skjærseth, J. B., & Wettestad, J. (2009). The origin, evolution and consequences of the EU Emissions Trading System. *Global Environmental Politics*, **9**(2), 101–122.

Slater, H. (2017, December 29). China's carbon market needs ambition. Retrieved 16 April 2018, from www.chinadialogue.net/article/show/single/en/10330-China-s-carbon-market-needs-ambition

References

Smith, K. (2007). *The Carbon Neutral Myth: Offset Indulgences for the Climate Sins*, Amsterdam: Carbon Trade Watch and Transnational Institute.

Smith, N. (2006). Nature as accumulation strategy. In L. Panitch & C. Leys, eds., *Socialist Register 2007*, London: The Merlin Press, pp. 19–41.

Smith, N. (2008). *Uneven Development: Nature, Capital, and the Production of Space*, Third edition, London: Verso.

St Martin, K. (2005). Disrupting enclosure in New England fisheries. *Capitalism Nature Socialism*, **16**(1), 63–80.

Stavins, R. N. (1998). What can we learn from the grand policy experiment? Lessons from SO2 allowance trading. *The Journal of Economic Perspectives*, **12**(3), 69–88.

Steffen, W., Crutzen, P. J., & McNeill, J. R. (2007). The anthropocene: are humans now overwhelming the great forces of nature. *AMBIO: A Journal of the Human Environment*, **36**(8), 614–621.

Steitz, C. (2014, March 4). RWE warns of frugal future after historic net loss. *Reuters*. Retrieved from http://uk.reuters.com/article/2014/03/04/uk-rwe-results-idUKBREA230YD20140304

Stephan, B. (2012). Bringing discourse to the market: the commodification of avoided deforestation. *Environmental Politics*, **21**(4), 621–639.

Stephan, B., & Lane, R. (eds.). (2015). *The Politics of Carbon Markets*, London: Routledge.

Stephan, B., & Paterson, M. (2012). The politics of carbon markets: an introduction. *Environmental Politics*, **21**(4), 545–562.

Stern, N. (2007). *The Economics of Climate Change: The Stern Review*, Cambridge: Cambridge University Press.

Stocker, T., Qin, D., Plattner, G., & Alexander, L. (2013). Technical summary. In T. Stocker, D. Qin, G. Plattner, & S. Tignor, eds., *Climate Change 2013: The Physical Science Basis. Contribution of Working Group I to the Fifth Assessment Report of the Intergovernmental Panel on Climate Change*, Cambridge: Cambridge University Press, pp. 33–115.

Storbeck, O. (2018, March 11). Eon deal with RWE set to transform German energy sector. *Financial Times*. Retrieved from www.ft.com/content/9ea7b254-2549-11e8-b27e-cc62a39d57a0

Straw, W., & Platt, R. (2013). *Up in smoke: How the EU's faltering climate policy is undermining the City of London*, Institute for Public Policy Research. Retrieved from www.ippr.org/publication/55/11509/up-in-smoke-how-the-eus-faltering-climate-policy-is-undermining-the-city-of-london

Stuart, D., Gunderson, R., & Petersen, B. (2017). Climate change and the Polanyian counter-movement: carbon markets or degrowth? *New Political Economy*, **0**(0), 1–14.

Sullivan, S. (2013). After the green rush? Biodiversity offsets, uranium power and the 'calculus of casualties' in greening growth. *Human Geography*, **6**(1).

Swyngedouw, E. (1999). Modernity and hybridity: nature, Regeneracionismo, and the production of the Spanish waterscape, 1890–1930. *Annals of the Association of American Geographers*, **89**(3), 443–465.

Swyngedouw, E. (2005). Dispossessing H2O: the contested terrain of water privatization. *Capitalism Nature Socialism*, **16**(1), 81–98.

Swyngedouw, E. (2010). Apocalypse forever? Post-political populism and the spectre of climate change. *Theory, Culture & Society*, **27**(2–3), 213–232.

Szabo, M. (2010, August 6). JP Morgan, Gunvor trade 1st 2020 EU carbon futures. *Reuters*, London. Retrieved from www.reuters.com/article/2010/08/06/carbon-2020-trade-idUSLDE6750YG20100806

Szabo, M. (2012, January 7). CER buyers seek contract rejigs, exits as prices collapse. *Point Carbon*.

Taylor, M. R., Rubin, E. S., & Hounshell, D. A. (2005). Regulation as the mother of innovation: the case of SO2 control. *Law & Policy*, **27**, 348.

Tietenberg, T. H. (2006). *Emissions Trading: Principles and Practice*, Washington, DC: Resources for the Future.

Timperley, J. (2018, January 29). Q&A: How will China's new carbon trading scheme work? Retrieved 16 April 2018, from www.carbonbrief.org/qa-how-will-chinas-new-carbon-trading-scheme-work

Tol, R. S. J. (2018). Policy brief – leaving an Emissions Trading Scheme: implications for the United Kingdom and the European Union. *Review of Environmental Economics and Policy*, **12**(1), 183–189.

Uhrig-Homburg, M., & Wagner, M. (2008). Derivative instruments in the EU Emissions Trading Scheme – an early market perspective. *Energy & Environment*, **19**(5), 635–655.

UNEP. (2018). About Montreal Protocol | OzonAction. Retrieved 28 March 2018, from http://web.unep.org/ozonaction/who-we-are/about-montreal-protocol

UNEP DTU. (2018a, March 1). CDM Pipeline. Retrieved 28 March 2018, from www.cdmpipeline.org/publications/CDMPipeline.xlsm

UNEP DTU. (2018b, March 1). JI Pipeline. Retrieved 12 March 2018, from www.cdmpipeline.org/publications/JiPipeline.xlsx

Uniper SE. (2018). Shareholder Structure. Retrieved 29 January 2018, from https://ir.uniper.energy/websites/uniper/English/1400/shareholder-structure.html

Unipro. (2018). Shaturskaya GRES. Retrieved 29 January 2018, from www.unipro.energy/en/about/structure/shaturskaya/

United Nations Framework Convention on Climate Change. (1992).

United Nations Framework Convention on Climate Change. (1995). Global Warming Potentials. Retrieved 7 May 2015, from http://unfccc.int/ghg_data/items/3825.php

United Nations Framework Convention on Climate Change. (1997). The Kyoto Protocol.

United Nations Framework Convention on Climate Change. (2001). The Marrakech Accords.

United Nations Framework Convention on Climate Change. (2014a). Clean Development Mechanism. Retrieved 28 September 2014, from https://cdm.unfccc.int/

United Nations Framework Convention on Climate Change. (2014b). Joint Implementation. Retrieved 28 September 2014, from http://ji.unfccc.int/index.html

United Nations Framework Convention on Climate Change. (2014c). Yingpeng HFC23 decomposition project. Retrieved 30 September 2014, from https://cdm.unfccc.int/Projects/DB/DNV-CUK1215776483.62/view

United Nations Framework Convention on Climate Change. (2015). The Paris Agreement.

Vattenfall. (2013). *Vattenfall's response to the European Commission's consultation on options for a structural reform to strengthen the EU Emissions Trading Scheme (EU ETS)*.

References

Vestreng, V., Myhre, G., Fagerli, H., Reis, S., & Tarrasón, L. (2007). Twenty-five years of continuous sulphur dioxide emission reduction in Europe. *Atmospheric Chemistry and Physics*, **7**(13), 3663–3681.

Victor, D. G., & House, J. C. (2006). BP's emissions trading system. *Energy Policy*, **34**(15), 2100–2112.

VIK - Verband der Industriellen Energie- und Kraftwirtschaft. (2001). *VIK-Position: Primat der Kostensenkung im internationalen Umweltschutz*. Retrieved from http://ec.europa.eu/environment/archives/docum/0087_en.htm

Visegrad Group. (2014a). *Joint statement of the informal meeting of ministers and representatives responsible for climate policy of the Visegrad Group Countries, Bulgaria and Romania*. Retrieved from www.mos.gov.pl/g2/big/2014_02/1f2fcbe4313eb55fe0b1c3c4a759b855.pdf

Visegrad Group. (2014b). *The Visegrad Group Countries, Romania and Bulgaria Joint Paper on the EU climate and energy framework 2020–2030*. Retrieved from www.mos.gov.pl/g2/big/2014_05/1ee07c384a09ab47f346d05eac59e11b.pdf

Vlachou, A. (2014). The European Union's Emissions Trading System. *Cambridge Journal of Economics*, **38**(1), 127–152.

Vlachou, A., & Konstantinidis, C. (2010). Climate change: the political economy of Kyoto flexible mechanisms. *Review of Radical Political Economics*, **42**(1), 32–49.

Vlachou, A., & Pantelias, G. (2017). The EU's Emissions Trading System, Part 2: a political economy critique. *Capitalism Nature Socialism*, **28**(3), 108–127.

Voß, J.-P. (2007). Innovation processes in governance: the development of 'emissions trading' as a new policy instrument. *Science and Public Policy*, **34**(5), 329–343.

Wainwright, J., & Mann, G. (2013). Climate Leviathan. *Antipode*, **45**(1), 1–22.

Walhain, S. (2006, January 20). The currency carbon, hard as the Euro. *Carbon Market Europe*.

Walker, R. (2017). Value and nature: rethinking capitalist exploitation and expansion. *Capitalism Nature Socialism*, **28**(1), 53–61.

Wathelet, M., Petersen, R. H., Gabriel, S., et al. (2014, June 17). Call for a proposal on a binding energy efficiency target for 2030 in light of the forthcoming EED review in July 2014. Retrieved from www.eceee.org/all-news/news/news_2014/2014-06-19/letter-to-Barroso

Werksman, J. (1998). The Clean Development Mechanism: unwrapping the 'Kyoto surprise.' *Review of European Community & International Environmental Law*, **7**(2), 147–158.

Wettestad, J. (2005). The Making of the 2003 EU Emissions Trading Directive: an ultra-quick process due to entrepreneurial proficiency? *Global Environmental Politics*, **5**(1), 1–23.

Wettestad, J. (2009). EU energy-intensive industries and emission trading: losers becoming winners? *Environmental Policy and Governance*, **19**(5), 309–320.

Wettestad, J., & Jevnaker, T. (2016). *Rescuing EU Emissions Trading*, London: Palgrave Macmillan UK.

Wigley, T. M. L. (2011). Coal to gas: the influence of methane leakage. *Climatic Change*, **108**(3), 601–608.

World Bank. (2006). *State and Trends of the Carbon Market 2006*, Washington, DC: World Bank.

World Bank. (2008). *State and Trends of the Carbon Market 2008*, Washington, DC: World Bank.

World Bank. (2010). *State and Trends of the Carbon Market 2010*, Washington, DC: World Bank.

World Bank. (2012). *State and Trends of the Carbon Market 2012*, Washington, DC: World Bank.

World Bank. (2014). *State and Trends of Carbon Pricing 2014*, Washington, DC: World Bank.

World Bank. (2015). *State and Trends of Carbon Pricing 2015*, Washington, DC: World Bank.

World Bank. (2016). *State and Trends of Carbon Pricing 2016*, Washington, DC: World Bank.

World Bank. (2017). *State and Trends of Carbon Pricing 2017*, Washington, DC: World Bank.

WWF Europe. (2010). *WWF response to the European Commission public consultation on a measure to introduce further quality restrictions on the use of credits from industrial gas projects.* Retrieved from http://ec.europa.eu/clima/consultations/docs/0004/registered/wwf_en.pdf

WWF Europe. (2012). *WWF response to the European Commission public consultation on review of the auction time profile for the EU Emissions Trading System.* Retrieved from http://ec.europa.eu/clima/consultations/docs/0016/organisation/wwf_en.pdf

WWF Europe. (2013). *Response to the European Commission public consultation on a 2030 climate and energy package.* Retrieved from http://ec.europa.eu/energy/consultations/20130702_green_paper_2030_en.htm

York, R. (2012). Asymmetric effects of economic growth and decline on CO2 emissions. *Nature Climate Change*, **2**(11), 762–764.

Zhu, B., & Chevallier, J. (2017). *Pricing and Forecasting Carbon Markets*, Cham, Switzerland: Springer International Publishing.

Index

abstraction, 25, 53–8, 60, 64–5, 84, 89–90, 92, 94, 96, 99, 108, 110, 113, 119–20, 132–3
   functional, 54, 56–7, 64, 67–8, 89, 92
   process, 56, 58, 64, 70, 89
   scalar, 56, 58, 64, 89
   spatial, 54, 56, 59, 64, 68–9, 89, 92
   temporal, 56, 64, 70, 85
accumulation, 3, 11–13, 16, 18, 26–7, 30–1, 42–3, 80–2, 95, 97–9, 108–14, 116–22, 129–30, 136, 146, 149
additionality, 74, 85, 91, 93, 95, 131–2
Alliance of Energy Intensive Industries, 136
appropriation, 3, 15–16, 18–19, 26–9, 32, 36, 41–4, 52–6, 60, 65, 71–3, 83–4, 86, 95–7, 99, 110, 113, 116, 118–19, 121–2, 129, 144, 149
   accumulation by, 3, 16, 99, 119
ArcelorMittal, 35, 87, 101–3

backloading, 124, 134–40, 145
Blockadia, 149
BP, 6, 46–7, 64, 76

capitalisation, 3, 16, 18, 32, 97, 99, 113–14, 118–19, 121, 129, 144
   accumulation by, 3, 16, 27, 43, 99, 112, 119, 149
carbon allowance, 2–3, 6–7, 15, 44, 54–5, 60, 64–5, 68–73, 83–4, 86, 88–9, 96, 100, 102–3, 110, 115–19, 121, 124–6, 134, 137–9, 144, 147
   allocation, 11, 13, 47, 49, 60, 62, 78, 86, 100–1, 103, 111, 114, 116, 124, 126, 128, 138, 140, 144
   auctioning, 48, 51, 61, 103, 134, 137, 145
   cap, 6–7, 55, 75–6, 78–9, 86, 111, 119, 125–6, 128
   European Union Allowance (EUA), 6, 65, 113
   surplus, 11, 15, 65, 67, 70, 87, 100–2, 105, 118, 135, 138, 143
   trading, 55, 61–2, 65, 100, 105
carbon credits, 2, 5–7, 9, 13–14, 16, 21, 61–2, 73, 77–8, 85–6, 88–90, 92, 94–5, 100, 103, 111, 117–18, 120, 131–3, 138
   Certified Emission Reduction (CER), 5, 7–8, 12, 84

   Emission Reduction Unit (ERU), 5, 7–8, 84
   qualitative limits, 7, 78–9, 123, 126, 132–4
   quantitative limits, 7, 78–9, 126, 138
   trading, 87–9, 96–7, 100–1, 104–5, 107–8
carbon instruments, 100
   futures, 99–100, 105, 107, 115, 118
   options, 99–100, 109, 115
   spot, 99–100, 107, 115–16, 137, 140
carbon leakage, 103, 126
carbon market as accumulation strategy, 11–13, 16, 97–9, 108–10, 119–22
Carbon Markets and Investors Association, 132
carbon price history, 8, 104–5, 107
carbon taxation, 8–9, 21, 45–6, 48, 50, 55, 107
Castree, Noel, 52–54
CDM Watch, 131, 133, 139
CEFIC, 50–1
China, 1, 76, 90–5, 131, 147–9
   Chinese carbon market, 17, 147–8
Clean Development Mechanism (CDM), 5–8, 13, 16, 73
   design of, 74, 82–6
   development of, 74, 77–8
Climate Action Network, 48, 50, 75, 79, 139
climate and energy package, 124, 127, 140, 142–4
climate change
   as an economic crisis, 16, 98
   as a political crisis, 16, 123
   as a socio-ecological crisis, 15, 43, 73, 96
climate-changing capitalism, 3, 15–19, 25–6, 28, 30–2, 36, 41, 43, 73, 95, 97, 99, 122–3, 144, 146–7, 149
Coase, Ronald, 19, 21–4
collateral, 16, 99, 114, 116–18
commodification, 3, 13, 15–16, 18, 27, 31–2, 42–4, 52–6, 68, 72–4, 83–4, 89, 92–3, 95, 97–9, 108–12, 118–21, 130–1, 149
   abstraction, 53, 56
   individuation, 53, 55
   privatisation, 53, 55

179

180 *Index*

concentration and centralisation of emissions, 32, 36–7, 39, 41, 102, 150
condition of production, 30–1, 97
contestation, 14–16, 18, 30–1, 44, 78, 82, 123–4, 126–31, 139, 145–6
contradictions of carbon markets, 3, 17–18, 43, 97, 99, 121, 123, 146–7, 149
Council of the European Union, 44–5, 50, 75, 78, 125–6, 135, 138, 140, 144
credit, 16, 99, 112, 114–18, 131

depoliticisation, 14–15, 124, 129
derivative, 11, 107
divestment, 109, 149
double internality, 26
  capitalism-in-climate, 26, 29, 31
  climate-in-capitalism, 26, 30–1

ecosystem services, 13, 52–4
EDF, 47, 63, 132
efficiency, 4–5, 9–10, 20–3, 25, 44, 46, 50–1, 71, 132, 141–4
  least cost, 9, 21, 24–5, 46, 52, 122, 141–2
electricity, 4, 6, 10, 28, 36–7, 47, 51, 56, 58, 60, 70–1, 75, 87–8, 91, 95–6, 102–4, 110, 115, 126, 132–3, 135–6, 138–9, 141, 147–9
Enel, 35, 40, 61, 87, 132–4
energy efficiency, 10, 17, 25, 48, 52, 141–5, 148, 150
E.ON, 16, 33, 35, 50, 52, 61, 63–4, 74, 80, 86–97, 136, 141–2
EURELECTRIC, 47, 51, 135
EUROFER, 50–1
European Climate Exchange, 104–5, 117
European Commission, 8, 14, 44, 46, 48, 50–1, 58, 78–9, 89, 96, 103, 125–6, 133–4, 136–41, 143–4
European Council, 125, 144
European Energy Exchange (EEX), 63–4, 68
European Parliament, 44, 46, 48–50, 125–6, 135, 137–8, 140, 144
European Union Emissions Trading System (EU ETS)
  design of, 6–7, 44, 50
  development of, 6, 44–7
  reform, 2, 9, 14–16, 123–6, 128, 150
European Union Emissions Trading System (EU ETS) Directive, 44, 48–9, 54–9, 78, 125, 135–7
exploitation, 27, 29, 65, 81, 86
externality, 9, 19–21

Federici, 27
feminism, 27
finance, 3, 11–12, 16, 63, 85, 97, 99, 107–9, 111–12, 119, 122, 138, 148–9
financial institutions, 1, 12, 62–3, 68, 98, 100, 105, 107–9, 113, 121, 132, 139
financialisation, 108, 112, 116
fossil fuels, 3, 12, 16–18, 26–9, 31–2, 37, 71, 109, 116, 118–19, 122, 149–50

France, 29, 35, 39–40, 61, 64, 88, 90–1, 93, 137, 143
Friends of the Earth, 48, 131, 135, 142
fuel switching, 10

GDF Suez, 33, 35, 40, 50, 61, 63–4, 87, 136, 139
Germany, 29, 60, 65, 68, 71, 78, 86, 88, 92–3, 103, 133, 137, 143
global warming potential, 55, 57, 68
Greenpeace, 79, 135, 139, 142

Harvey, David, 23–5, 74, 80–3, 85–6

industrial gas destruction, 92–4, 131, 133–4
installations
  public ownership, 39, 83
  size, 15, 36–7, 39, 67, 83
  ultimate owners, 33, 35–6, 39, 150
International Emissions Trading Association, 48, 133, 138–9

Joint Implementation (JI), 5–8, 16, 73, 86
  design of, 74, 82–5
  development of, 74, 76–8

Kyoto mechanisms, 7–8, 12, 16, 21, 42–3, 49, 72–4, 77–8, 80, 83–4, 89, 96–7, 124, 147, 149
Kyoto Protocol, 1, 5–7, 9, 45, 48, 57, 73–4, 76–8, 83–4, 92–3

labour, 25–9, 31–2, 37, 80–1, 110–13, 119–20, 122
legitimation, 11, 98, 130
level playing field, 44–5, 50–1, 141
Linking Directive, 74, 77–9, 84, 131
Lohmann, Larry, 108–9

MacKenzie, Donald, 14, 124, 127–8, 145
manufacturing, 6, 28–9, 36, 47, 50, 56, 58, 75, 100–2, 126, 135–6, 138–41, 144, 149
market failure, 9, 15, 18–19, 20, 22
Market Stability Reserve, 124, 140, 144
marketisation, 2, 4, 11, 15, 20, 23, 52, 123, 144, 146, 149–50
Marrakech Accords, 77, 85
Marxism, 11, 15, 19, 25–6, 31, 80, 85, 98, 108, 110–13, 127, 130, 149
Mies, Maria, 27
Moore, Jason W., 26–7, 30, 113

national allocation plan, 61, 79, 125
nature
  abstract social, 113, 119
  capitalist relations with and within, 3, 16, 18, 25, 28, 31, 42, 53, 97, 124, 149
  ideology of, 19, 23–5
  production of, 25–6, 28, 30–1, 82
Newell, Peter, 11–12, 109, 129

Index

O'Connor, James, 30–2, 97, 130
offset project, 1, 7, 9, 11–12, 14, 16, 73, 76, 86, 88–9, 97, 99–100, 116

Paris Agreement, 1–2, 147, 149
Paterson, Matthew, 11–13, 68, 77, 109
Pigou, Arthur Cecil, 19–24
planning, 150
Poland, 35, 37, 39–40, 59, 60, 68, 87–8, 126, 133, 137, 142
policy
    alternatives, 108, 124, 128, 148–50
    market-based, 1–6, 8, 12, 17, 21, 23–4, 30, 45–6, 82, 108–9, 122, 124, 128, 130, 132–3, 136, 139, 146, 148–9
politics of market design, 14, 124, 127, 145
post-politics, 16, 124, 127–8
post-structuralism, 9, 13, 127

renewable energy, 3, 17, 25, 28, 37, 48, 62, 70–1, 79, 96, 132, 141–4, 148, 150
rent, 16, 99, 109–11, 121
risk, 16, 51, 95, 99–100, 113–14, 117, 119–22, 126, 132, 135–6, 138, 142, 149
Robertson, Morgan, 53–4, 98, 111–12, 130
Russia, 90–2, 95
RWE, 16, 33, 35, 44, 52, 60–72, 87–9, 96, 141–2

Salleh, Ariel, 27, 29
Sandbag, 135, 139
Shell, 6, 46–7, 64, 69–70

Smith, Neil, 12, 23, 25–6, 30
socio-ecological fix, 82
spatial fix, 81–4, 86, 90
spatio-temporal fix, 16, 74, 86, 92–4, 97
state, the, 3, 11, 13, 15–16, 18, 21, 30–2, 81, 108, 116, 118, 120, 124, 129–30, 136, 140
Stern Review, 20
sulphur dioxide trading, 4, 8, 127
Swyngedouw, Erik, 15, 25–6, 124, 128–9, 146

techno-politics, 14–16, 124, 127
temporal fix, 85–6
ThyssenKrupp, 62, 87, 92, 101

uneven development, 26, 29, 80–1, 83
UNFCCC, 6, 74–6, 83–5
United Kingdom, 6, 12, 20, 29, 46–7, 57, 59–60, 68, 71, 76, 88, 92–3, 133, 137, 143–4
United States, 1, 4–6, 8, 29, 45, 74–7, 127, 130

value, 15–16, 18–19, 26–7, 29, 31, 80, 83, 85, 98–9, 109–13, 116–19, 121–2, 124, 127, 130–2, 134, 138, 140–1, 143–4, 146
    transaction value, 7, 105–6
Vattenfall, 63, 87, 138

windfall profits, 101–3, 105
world-ecology, 26, 30
World Wide Fund for Nature (WWF), 48, 79, 131–2, 135, 139, 142

Printed in the United States
By Bookmasters